IDIOT'S GUIDES.
AS EASY AS IT GETS!

Cognitive Behavioral Therapy

by Dr. Jayme Albin and Eileen Bailey

ALPHA

A member of Penguin Group (USA) Inc.

ALPHA BOOKS

Published by Penguin Group (USA) Inc.

Penguin Group (USA) Inc., 375 Hudson Street, New York, New York 10014, USA • Penguin Group (Canada), 90 Eglinton Avenue East, Suite 700, Toronto, Ontario M4P 2Y3, Canada (a division of Pearson Penguin Canada Inc.) • Penguin Books Ltd., 80 Strand, London WC2R 0RL, England • Penguin Ireland, 25 St. Stephen's Green, Dublin 2, Ireland (a division of Penguin Books Ltd.) • Penguin Group (Australia), 250 Camberwell Road, Camberwell, Victoria 3124, Australia (a division of Pearson Australia Group Pty. Ltd.) • Penguin Books India Pvt. Ltd., 11 Community Centre, Panchsheel Park, New Delhi—110 017, India • Penguin Group (NZ), 67 Apollo Drive, Rosedale, North Shore, Auckland 1311, New Zealand (a division of Pearson New Zealand Ltd.) • Penguin Books (South Africa) (Pty.) Ltd., 24 Sturdee Avenue, Rosebank, Johannesburg 2196, South Africa • Penguin Books Ltd., Registered Offices: 80 Strand, London WC2R 0RL, England

THE COMPLETE IDIOT'S GUIDE TO and Design are registered trademarks of Penguin Group (USA) Inc.

International Standard Book Number: 978-1-61564-615-9
Library of Congress Catalog Card Number: 2014904729

20 19   13 12 11 10 9 8

Interpretation of the printing code: The rightmost number of the first series of numbers is the year of the book's printing; the rightmost number of the second series of numbers is the number of the book's printing. For example, a printing code of 13-1 shows that the first printing occurred in 2013.

Printed in the United States of America

Note: This publication contains the opinions and ideas of its author. It is intended to provide helpful and informative material on the subject matter covered. It is sold with the understanding that the author and publisher are not engaged in rendering professional services in the book. If the reader requires personal assistance or advice, a competent professional should be consulted.

The author and publisher specifically disclaim any responsibility for any liability, loss, or risk, personal or otherwise, which is incurred as a consequence, directly or indirectly, of the use and application of any of the contents of this book.

Most Alpha books are available at special quantity discounts for bulk purchases for sales promotions, premiums, fundraising, or educational use. Special books, or book excerpts, can also be created to fit specific needs. For details, write: Special Markets, Alpha Books, 375 Hudson Street, New York, NY 10014.

Publisher: *Mike Sanders*
Executive Managing Editor: *Billy Fields*
Acquisitions Editor: *Brook Farling*
Development Editor: *Ann Barton*
Production Editor: *Jana M. Stefanciosa*

Cover Designer: *Laura Merriman*
Book Designer: *William Thomas*
Indexer: *Brad Herriman*
Layout: *Brian Massey*
Proofreader: *Jaime Julian Wagner*

This book is dedicated to my dear husband, Keith, for his patience and support in all of my pursuits. B and L.

—Jayme Albin

Dedicated to my daughter, Evelyn Bailey.
You bring sunshine into my life, every day.
I love you.

—Eileen Bailey

Contents

Part 4: CBT for Specific Conditions and Situations....................181

Appendixes

Introduction

Cognitive behavioral therapy (CBT) is different from traditional "talk" therapy. It is based on delving into your current thought processes rather than your past experiences. It requires your active participation in the process of getting better. You complete homework assignments to practice skills and techniques. When you work with a therapist, it is a collaborative effort, working together to set goals and prioritize issues.

CBT has been shown to be effective in treating a range of issues, including depression and anxiety. The methods described in this book help you look at your thoughts, not just as thoughts, but also as precursors to your emotions and behaviors. Once you understand your thought process, you have the choice to change it. You have the opportunity to look at situations, and life, differently. You have the choice to think in a more positive, healthy, and helpful way. CBT teaches you how.

You don't have to be "mentally ill" or have a disorder to benefit from CBT. The strategies used in CBT improve your life in many ways. They help you increase your self-esteem, overcome anger issues, and improve your relationships. You learn how to change your inner dialogue and get rid of old, outdated, negative views of yourself. You let go of perfectionist ideals and deal with the uncertainty of life. CBT teaches you how to be assertive and manage the inevitable stress in your life.

This book provides self-help exercises to get you on the road to feeling better. If you do choose to work with a therapist, this book is still helpful when used as a workbook. Together, you and your therapist go through sections that address your specific concerns. The exercises are easily used as homework assignments.

CBT is a skill-based therapy. You learn techniques for analyzing your thoughts and creating new beliefs and how to change your feelings and emotions by identifying the thoughts behind them. You learn how mindfulness, visualization, and relaxation fit into your overall feelings of well-being. As with all new skills, CBT takes practice and commitment. Once you learn these skills, you gain a healthier perspective of yourself, your life, and the world around you.

How This Book Is Organized

This book is designed as a self-help book. It gives explanations of CBT concepts and provides exercises to help you put those concepts into action. We understand you are not a medical professional and don't want to read a book full of medical jargon. For this reason, we tried to keep the focus of this book free of too much CBT terminology. When we introduce these words, we provide you with a general explanation of the term. There is a glossary at the end of the book should you need to look up any terms used in CBT.

To make this book easier to use, we have included many of the forms you need to complete the exercises in Appendix C. Some of these forms are used more than once. Make copies of the forms to give you enough to complete the exercises.

Part 1, Understanding CBT, covers the basics of CBT. It explains the theory behind CBT and the basic concepts you need to know to interpret your thoughts and feelings. It discusses the most common problematic thinking patterns and teaches you how to identify your thinking processes. We explain the difference between helpful and unhelpful emotions and how your thoughts relate to these emotions. Finally, we help you set goals for your getting better.

Part 2, CBT Techniques, covers the basic skills you will use throughout this book. You learn how to use the images in your mind to change your thoughts by changing the pictures. Making changes to your thinking can be scary, so we teach you different relaxation and meditation techniques to incorporate in your exercises. We explain another helpful technique, mindfulness, and give you exercises to help you learn how to be present in the moment. You learn how to talk to yourself in a positive way. Finally, you learn techniques for testing the strong beliefs you hold about yourself.

Part 3, CBT for Personal Growth, provides information and exercises for using CBT in your everyday life. We provide exercises to build self-acceptance and give you steps to improve your self-image. We discuss how perfectionism often leads to disappointment in life and give you specific ways you can create a more balanced view of yourself and your behavior. We focus on helping you improve your relationship by changing the way you think and communicate with your significant other. You learn how to stand up for yourself and deal with the daily stress of life.

Part 4, CBT for Specific Conditions and Situations, focuses on problems that often interfere with your ability to enjoy life. You complete thought analysis to identify patterns leading to depression and change your thoughts to feel better. CBT is also effective in treating anxiety and we give you a step-by-step approach to facing your fears and calming your worries. You learn techniques to tame your temper. We provide ways to say no to your addiction and deal with cravings. We also discuss obsessive-compulsive disorder and teach you how to see thoughts as simply thoughts, not premonitions of danger. Finally, we help you change how you feel about your body, giving you exercises to improve your body image.

Part 5, Moving Forward, discusses strategies for making CBT work, even after you completed the book. It examines common reasons CBT doesn't work and provides suggestions for overcoming them. We guide you in setting up a self-therapy session to maintain your new skills. Finally, we discuss finding and working with a therapist and what to expect during a typical CBT therapy session.

Extras

Pay attention to the sidebars throughout the book. They provide information and advice to help you make the most of your CBT.

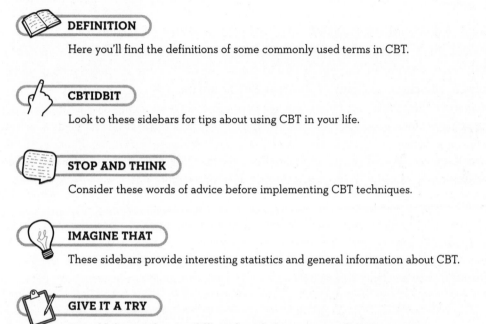

DEFINITION

Here you'll find the definitions of some commonly used terms in CBT.

CBTIDBIT

Look to these sidebars for tips about using CBT in your life.

STOP AND THINK

Consider these words of advice before implementing CBT techniques.

IMAGINE THAT

These sidebars provide interesting statistics and general information about CBT.

GIVE IT A TRY

Start thinking and acting differently with these suggested CBT exercises.

Acknowledgments

From Dr. Jayme Albin: I would like to acknowledge Eileen Bailey, my co-author, for all her hard work. I would also like to thank my clients from over the years, all of who have helped me grow personally and professionally.

From Eileen Bailey: This book would not have been possible without the help and support of my children, Evelyn and Soloman, who were forever understanding of the extra time I spent writing during this project. I would like to thank my "Fun and Fabulous 50 pluses" who are a constant inspiration of what women can accomplish; they listened when I needed to talk things through and were my cheerleaders when I needed encouragement. Thank you to my neighbor and friend, Sandie, for our weekly tea-time, during which I could view the information and exercises in the book through the eyes of a reader. To the numerous psychologists I spoke with when writing this book, your insights into the workings of CBT were invaluable. Many thanks to my co-author, Jayme, who shared her wealth of knowledge and expertise on cognitive behavioral therapy. As always, I would like to thank my agent, Marilyn Allen, and editor, Brook Farling, for the many hours they have spent bringing this book from concept to reality.

Trademarks

All terms mentioned in this book that are known to be or are suspected of being trademarks or service marks have been appropriately capitalized. Alpha Books and Penguin Group (USA) Inc. cannot attest to the accuracy of this information. Use of a term in this book should not be regarded as affecting the validity of any trademark or service mark.

Disclaimer

This book is meant as a self-help tool. It provides information and exercises to help you make improvements in your life. We discuss a number of medical conditions. This book is not meant to replace medical care.

The Basics of Cognitive Behavioral Therapy

Cognitive behavioral therapy (CBT) is based on the theory that your thoughts are responsible for your emotions and behaviors. When you pay attention to your thoughts and consciously change them to reflect a more positive and balanced way of looking the world, you can change your behaviors and feelings as well. This type of therapy began as a treatment for depression. Today, it is used not only to treat mental illness but also as a self-improvement tool.

This part explores the theory behind CBT. We discuss the benefits of this type of therapy and help you decide if CBT is right for you. We help you understand how your thoughts, feelings, and behaviors are related. We list common thinking errors and give you questions you can ask yourself to find a more balanced and positive perspective.

Understanding CBT

You may be wondering what, exactly, cognitive behavioral therapy is and whether it could help you. This chapter will answer those questions by explaining the basic premise behind CBT and examining the advantages and disadvantages of this type of therapy. Finally, we help you decide if this is the right therapy for you.

What Is CBT?

Cognitive behavioral therapy (CBT) is a type of psychotherapy that focuses on understanding how your thoughts, feelings, and behaviors are related. The process of CBT focuses on changing how you feel and behave by changing your way of thinking. You might believe external events of your life shape how you feel and act, but that is not true. It is your thoughts and your interpretation of events that drive your behaviors and feelings.

In This Chapter

- How thoughts, feelings, and behaviors are related
- The four steps of CBT
- Studying the effectiveness of CBT
- Determining if CBT is right for you

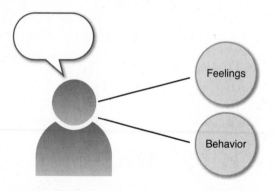

Your thoughts directly influence your feelings and behaviors.

Let's look at two scenarios. How are they different? Notice that when thoughts change, behaviors and feelings do as well.

Scenario 1: Imagine you have been looking for a job for several weeks. You've had a few interviews, but no job offers. You're beginning to think it is hopeless and you will never get a job. When you go on interviews you feel nervous before and during because you can't stop thinking about how you will mess up. You think about all of the negative ways your interviewer is judging you. You know you should keep looking, but all you can think about is how boring and upsetting it is. Instead of looking, you procrastinate by watching TV. You feel worthless.

It may be easy to blame your negative mood on the fact that you don't have a job, but not having a job isn't the problem. It is how you interpret and think about the situation and future situations that cause your mood and behavior.

Scenario 2: Now imagine you have been looking for a job for several weeks. You know that it takes weeks or months, sometimes longer to find a job. You know that it took some of your friends months to find one. You make a list of people you know who might be able to help you get a job. You ask them for specific contacts and tips to help improve your interviewing skills. You remind yourself that each interview is an opportunity to practice and another person who is now aware of your skills. When you go on interviews, you think about your skill sets and how they might benefit the organization. After each interview, you write down what went right and what went wrong and then brainstorm and practice strategies to improve. With each interview you become more confident. You remain hopeful and motivated.

In both situations you are jobless. The difference is your view of yourself, your view of others, and your expectations of the outcome. These different thought processes result in different behavior and emotional reactions. In the first description, you view the situation with negative beliefs and thoughts, leading to negative behavior (giving up the job search) and a negative mood (hopelessness and depression).

In the second approach, you focus on realistic outcomes and problem solving, which leads to effective behavior (continuing to look for a job) and a positive mood (hopefulness and motivation). The situation is a *trigger* to your thoughts, which leads to your behaviors and feelings.

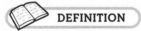 **DEFINITION**

> A **trigger** is an activation event. In CBT, we look at the beliefs and thoughts as they relate to a triggering event.

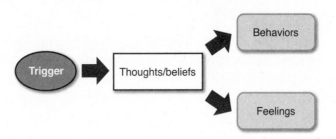

A situation or event triggers your thoughts and beliefs, which in turn shapes your behaviors and feelings.

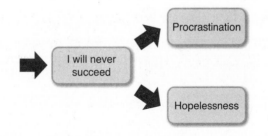

Perspective 1: While you might think your unsuccessful job search causes your feelings of hopelessness, it is your belief that you won't succeed that leads to procrastination and hopelessness.

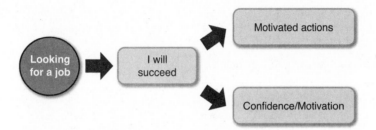

Perspective 2: Your interpretation of the job search, believing you will succeed, creates a more positive attitude and fosters continued motivation.

Your Turn: What Kind of Thinker Are You?

What kind of thinker are you? What is your immediate reaction to stressful events?

Think of something you worry about (or something you worried about in the past). Be specific. Write down your primary concerns. The following examples are concerns you might have based on the previous scenarios:

Perspective 1: I'm concerned I won't get a job before depleting all of my savings. I am concerned people will think I'm a loser. I am concerned that if I stay unemployed for longer than a six months I'll be pegged as "unhirable."

Perspective 2: I'm concerned I won't get a job before I have to dip into my savings. I'm concerned my former associates will think I made a mistake for quitting my last job before having a secure position. I'm concerned the longer I stay unemployed, the harder it will be to get a position.

Now look at your concerns and ask yourself: What is the worst possible outcome? What is the best possible outcome? What is the most realistic outcome?

Worst outcome: Never get a job

Best outcome: Get the job of my dreams that recovers my loss in savings

Realistic outcome: Get a job better than my last position with a reasonable salary

Which outcome does your list most closely resemble? The most realistic, the worst, or the best? This is likely how you automatically think about stressful scenarios.

GIVE IT A TRY

If your original concern doesn't resemble the most realistic outcome, go back and alter it to reflect the most realistic outcome. Then think about what behaviors and feelings might accompany this outcome.

When you are worried about something, it helps to see different possibilities. It also helps to see your concerns listed out in contrast to the most realistic outcomes. The next time you worry about something, list your concerns as the worst, best, and most realistic possible outcomes to help clarify your thinking.

The Theory Behind CBT

CBT examines the relationship between your thoughts and behaviors. CBT focuses on how you think about yourself, the world, and other people. It works on the premise that most emotional and behavioral reactions are learned and can therefore be unlearned and replaced with a new way of reacting. CBT aims to get you to a point where you can "do it yourself" and work out your own way of coping with problems. CBT is often described as guided self-help.

Some forms of psychotherapy focus on childhood experiences and how they influence your adult life. In contrast, CBT focuses on your current problems, creates goals for overcoming those problems, and gives you step-by-step tools to help change your perspective—thereby changing your behavior and mood.

CBT empowers you to be in control by giving you the choice between negative and positive thoughts. It provides you with a set of tools to make alternative choices. For example, instead of being emotionally overwhelmed, you can choose to be rational and create thoughts that are focused on coping and finding solutions. Rational thoughts are those based on facts and require the use of logical reasoning.

As you go through the CBT process in this book, try to consistently practice the exercises. In CBT, exercises are called *reality testing*. When you reality test, you assume your original negative thoughts are guesses as to what is happening or what might happen. Rather than seeing your original perspective as an accurate prediction, you test out other possibilities.

> **DEFINITION**
>
> **Reality testing** is when you look for facts to challenge your negative beliefs and predictions and then take action to test whether your beliefs are actually true.

A big part of CBT is learning to gather evidence that contradicts biases in your thinking. Some of this reality testing involves using behavior experiments to challenge your predictions and perspectives.

In keeping with the example about being unemployed, you assume in your negative thoughts "I will never get a job again, I will be unable to pay my rent and my family will be homeless." Reality testing asks you think about facts and then apply reasoning based on realistic values and outcomes. For example, you might think about how long it took you to get a job previously, how long it has taken others in your field and to find a new job in the current job market, and how much money you have in savings before you end up homeless.

CBT reality testing might have you challenge the assumption "I am not worthwhile" by asking you to pay attention to specific areas of life where you have succeeded. It might have you challenge your thoughts of being a "failure" by asking you to complete an experiment where you can readily see yourself as "successful." In the previous example, this could be securing at least one interview in the next week or successfully adding a new contact to your network.

CBT involves a specific set of steps:

1. Identify trigger events and conditions such as grief, anger, depression, or anxiety.

2. Raise awareness of your reactions to these triggers including thoughts, beliefs, emotions, and behaviors. Observe how you interpret the situations and events in your life.

3. Pinpoint negative and inaccurate thoughts and beliefs.

4. Identify your physical, emotional, and behavioral responses that come along with these negative and inaccurate thoughts.

5. Set behavior and emotional goals for how you want to react to these triggers.

6. Reality test the accuracy of your thinking by determining if it is based on fact or on inaccurate perceptions.

7. Create new thoughts and attitudes about stressful triggers.

8. Practice implementing these new attitudes, behaviors, and emotions. Learn to integrate them into your life as new habits.

> **CBTIDBIT**
>
> CBT is based on a lot of common sense that you already know and apply in other areas of your life. This book is about helping you sharpen these tools and apply them to stressful events.

There will be times, especially at the beginning, that you may feel uncomfortable or find the process painful. Changing long-standing beliefs about yourself, others, and the world around you is sometimes a difficult process. However, as you work through and practice each step, more helpful thinking and behavior will emerge. The exercises in this book will help you work through these steps.

Your Turn: Learning Your ABCs

The ABC chart is the staple of CBT. It is used to help you identify negative thought processes. Completing this worksheet builds your awareness of how you think and reveals patterns of negative and irrational thinking. In addition, it helps you see how your thoughts affect your behaviors and emotions. Use the ABC chart to help you stop seeing the trigger as the cause of your reactions and understand that it is your thoughts that cause your reaction.

A stands for Activating Event ("the trigger")

B stands for Belief or Thought

C stands for Consequence (behavioral and emotional)

Divide a paper into three columns. Label columns A, B, and C.

A: Activating Event	B: Belief or Thought	C: Consequence
I need to give a speech.	I am going to make a fool of myself. I will forget everything I want to say and everyone will think I'm stupid. I need to do well or else…	I feel anxious. My stomach hurts. I can't sleep. I can't focus.
I didn't get the promotion at work.	I deserved that promotion. I can't believe I was treated with such disrespect. My boss never liked me anyway. I work harder than anyone else. Hard work is what it's about; so this is just unfair.	I feel angry. I'm not going to try at work anymore. I'm going to tell my boss what I think of him.
I didn't get the job.	I need a job. The interviewer is judging me. I'll never get a job.	I feel sad. I'm never going to get a job. I should just quit.

 STOP AND THINK

If you are having a difficult time completing your chart, you might find it easier to work backward in the beginning. Start with the consequence—what you feel and your behavior—and then think about why you feel that way and what happened to bring on those thoughts.

This chart is one of the basic CBT tools, and one we'll return to often in this book, sometimes adding additional columns to help you understand and challenge your thoughts.

Understanding Themes

All feelings have related themes to the way you think. Here's a quick tip sheet to help you identify the thoughts that drive your feelings.

Anger/frustration: I perceive an obstacle threatening me in some way. The obstacle can be something from the past, present, or future.

Anxiety/nervousness: I perceive a threat that will harm me or challenge my security. The threat can be present or future.

Sadness/disappointment: I perceive something being taken from me. I won't be entirely satisfied as a result. The loss can be past, present, or anticipated in the future.

Excitement/happiness: I perceive receiving something that enhances my life situation. It can be past, present, or future anticipation.

Shame/embarrassment: I perceive that I am responsible for some wrongdoing toward others or myself.

Benefits of CBT

A number of research studies show CBT is as effective in treating disorders such as depression and anxiety as medication. Because CBT teaches skills that can be used even after treatment has ended, it is often more effective than medication. Some of the distinct advantages of this type of therapy include:

Short-term. When working with a therapist, the average number of sessions using CBT is 16. It is a closed-end treatment; unlike traditional therapy, it does not continue indefinitely.

Targeted. CBT teaches specific skills and corrects negative and problematic thinking processes. Once you understand how to use these skills, you "get better."

Structured. CBT includes specific tools, techniques, strategies, and steps.

Instructive. Whether you work with a therapist or use exercises in this book on your own, you learn to cope with stress and other problems in your life in a constructive way. You learn to counsel yourself.

Adaptive. CBT strategies are used in many different situations. You might have chosen to use CBT to overcome your fear of dogs or to manage your anger. However, once you learn to use the techniques, you can employ them in other areas of your everyday life.

Measurable. CBT works with specific goals—for example, overcoming your fear of flying—and has specific steps for reaching your goal. Because of this, you are able to see and measure your progress along the way.

IMAGINE THAT

CBT is one of the most extensively studied forms of psychotherapy with well over 300 published studies. A 2005 review of these studies showed it to be highly effective in treating depression, generalized anxiety disorder, panic disorder, social phobia, and post-traumatic stress disorder.

As you continue to use CBT and the techniques become habitual, you might notice improvement in all areas of your life. Your relationships become more fulfilling, your problem-solving skills at work improve, your self-esteem increases, and you feel a greater overall satisfaction with life.

Disadvantages of CBT

As with all treatments, CBT has its share of proponents and critics. Some critics worry that because CBT focuses so much on current problems, it doesn't adequately address underlying issues, such as childhood abuse, and help you resolve your feelings toward those. It is also an individual treatment; some family issues or interpersonal relationships causing problems in your life aren't necessarily addressed.

STOP AND THINK

Cognitive behavioral changes are lifestyle changes. It is a new way of looking at the world, yourself, and problem solving. CBT takes commitment. Just as your body needs a continuous exercise program to stay in shape, your mind needs continuous practice until thinking in a positive way becomes automatic.

There aren't many risks to using CBT. As discussed earlier in the chapter, you might feel uncomfortable or discouraged at first when facing long-held views of the world, your environment, and yourself. There may be times when you cry or feel angry or emotionally drained. You might feel anxiety or stress, such as when you are confronting fears. However, as you work through the exercises in this book, the discomfort should lessen. And, as you learn new coping skills, you can better deal with fears and negative thought patterns.

CBT takes commitment. With CBT, you need to complete exercises and train yourself to think in different ways. It takes time and energy to bring about positive change. CBT doesn't bring about instant results.

Your Turn: Is CBT Right for Me?

CBT works for many different conditions and situations, but that doesn't mean it is right for you. The following checklist covers some of the conditions and situations where CBT can help. Check all that apply to you.

❑ Anger problems

☑ Anxiety

❑ Body dysmorphic disorder

❑ Chronic fatigue

❑ Chronic pain

☑ Depression

❑ Eating disorders (e.g., anorexia, bulimia)

❑ Gambling

❑ Guilt and shame

❑ Hoarding

☑ Low self-esteem

☑ Obsessive-compulsive disorder

❑ Panic attacks

❑ Performance anxiety

❑ Personality disorder

❑ Post-traumatic stress disorder

❑ Sexual or relationship problems

☑ Sleep problems

☑ Social phobia

❑ Specific phobias (e.g., fear of flying or dogs)

☑ Spending money excessively

☑ Stress

❑ Substance abuse

☑ Worrying

You might have checked more than one area, as problems tend to overlap. Don't worry; most people have more than one problem. As you use CBT strategies, you will find secondary problems improve as well.

In addition to identifying specific problems, there are other considerations before beginning CBT. This type of therapy is solution-oriented, not talk-oriented. Even when you work with a therapist, there is less emphasis on talking about your week and more emphasis on learning and practicing how to process your triggers differently. However, some people find they want someone to listen. Consider the following and check those that apply to you:

CBT Readiness Quiz:

- ❑   1. I am ready to make positive change in my life.
- ☑   2. There are practical problems, such as sleep problems, anxiety, anger, or depression, that I would like to improve.
- ❑   3. I am willing to commit time each week to completing exercises.
- ❑   4. I have a support system of friends and family.
- ☑   5. I am able to work independently or I can use this book with my therapist.
- ☑   6. I don't want to keep dwelling on the past; I would like to solve problems in my present and future life.
- ❑   7. I need to deal with issues before focusing on specific areas to improve.
- ❑   8. I don't know what I want to improve; I just know I don't like my life.
- ❑   9. I don't know if I have the time to complete the exercises at this time in my life.
- ❑   10 I am alone and feel that this might stir up too much emotion.
- ❑   11. I feel I need the help of a therapist to work on the exercises and want someone who will listen to my problems.
- ☑   12. I have unresolved issues from my past I think should be addressed.

If you checked any of the items in numbers 1 through 6, you are ready to delve into CBT and make it work for you. If you checked more items in numbers 7 through 12, you may want to consider working with a CBT therapist and using this book as a tool.

The Least You Need to Know

- Your thoughts lead to feelings, which influence your actions.
- CBT empowers you to choose positive thinking over negative thinking patterns.
- Skills learned through CBT can be carried over to many aspects of your life.
- CBT is an effective strategy for dealing with many conditions and situations, such as depression, anxiety, anger, and relationships.

CHAPTER 2

Interpreting Your Thoughts and Feelings

Are your thoughts a result of your feelings? Or are your feelings a result of your thoughts? It is important to understand not only which causes which, but also how to separate your thoughts from your feelings. In Chapter 1, you learned how your thoughts cause feelings and behaviors. In this chapter, you'll learn how feelings sometimes lead to unhealthy thought patterns. The exercises will help you move from reasoning based on your feelings to reasoning based on your thoughts. We'll look at some common unhealthy thought patterns and provide strategies for beginning to look at situations in your life in a more helpful way.

In This Chapter

- How your thoughts influence your feelings
- Distinguishing between emotions and thoughts
- Becoming aware of unhealthy thought patterns
- Stopping to question and challenge your thoughts

Thoughts, Feelings, and Behaviors

Thoughts, feelings, and behaviors work together in a continuous cycle. First, you have a thought, which influences how you feel and behave. You then have thoughts about those feelings and actions, which influence how you think and behave. The cycle continues, repeating itself over and over. It can be positive or negative, depending on your thoughts.

Imagine you are at a party where you don't know anyone. As you make your way around the room, you spot a familiar face but cannot recall the person's name. You recognize her as someone who used to sit near you to at work, but you haven't seen her since she left the company a few years back. You start to feel nervous. You think, "I'm embarrassed that I don't remember her name. I should avoid her; I'm too nervous to chat with her." As you walk away, you validate your actions thinking, "We were never friends to begin with; why waste my time?" You feel a sense of relief.

You might believe you felt nervous because you couldn't remember your co-worker's name and that you walked away because you felt nervous. However, it was not the situation that caused your feelings, and it was not your feelings that caused you to walk away. It was your perception of the situation that caused you to walk away.

The thoughts might have come so quickly that you were unaware of them until you felt nervous, but they were present the entire time.

Maybe you were so focused on the feeling of nervousness that you did not notice your immediate thoughts. You may have thought the following:

- I should only approach people I know well.

- It's pretty pathetic that I can't remember her name.

- I should have kept in touch.

- People I don't know well are intimidating.

- She is very well-dressed and will judge me.

These thoughts created a feeling of anxiousness. It is that feeling you acted on—avoiding the person for the rest of the night so you wouldn't feel uncomfortable. This anxious feeling also influenced your thoughts for the remainder of the party. You became self-conscious and worried you were underdressed. You thought others would notice your discomfort and felt that you didn't belong at the party. These new thoughts brought about new feelings of despair. You left the party feeling like a failure.

In this example, you allowed your emotions to control your thoughts and therefore control your actions. Your reasoning and *self-talk* revolved around how you felt, not the facts of the situation. When you make a conscious decision to change your self-talk into a more positive view of the situation, you change how you respond.

📖 **DEFINITION**

Self-talk is running commentary in your mind. It is the voice in your head, your internal dialogue, that reflects and interprets the world around you. Self-talk can be positive or negative.

Using the ABC chart described in Chapter 1, the party scenario looks like this.

A: Activating Event	B: Belief or Thought	C: Consequences
I see someone who looks familiar.	I don't know her well enough to approach her. I am pathetic because I can't remember her name. Talking to people I don't know well is intimidating. She will judge me because she is well-dressed.	Embarrassment Nervousness Look away and avoid her
I feel uncomfortable and nervous. My hands are shaking. My heart is racing.	I can't handle feeling uncomfortable. My nervousness will show and she will judge me because I am anxious.	Nervousness Avoid her Leave party

From this table, you see that your original thoughts and feelings led to a new activating event and therefore a new set of feelings and behaviors. By stopping, examining your thoughts, and coming up with alternative beliefs, you change your perception of the situation and your behaviors.

Using your ABC chart, add two additional columns:

D: New Beliefs

E: New Consequences

Your new beliefs are ways of combating your immediate reaction. It takes practice to notice these thoughts, analyze them, and come up with a more helpful and healthy way of looking at the situation. The following table gives you examples of new, alternative thoughts and how your behaviors change once you look at the situation with a new perspective.

A: Activating Event	B: Belief or Thought	C: Consequences	D: New Beliefs	E: New Consequences
I see a well-dressed woman at a party. I know her but can't remember her name.	She will judge me. She will be upset that I don't know her name. It's my fault that I didn't keep in touch with her. I should only talk to people I know well. I can't handle feeling uncomfortable, it's a sign I should avoid her.	Nervousness Self-blame Avoid her Leave party	I don't need to know everyone well in order to say "hi." This is an opportunity to get to know her better. She is just as guilty of not keeping in touch. I'm dressed nicely, too. Her judgments are harmless.	Feeling more relaxed. A little nervous but not too uncomfortable. Approach her and catch up.
I feel uncomfortable. My hand is shaking My heart is racing a bit.	I can't handle feeling uncomfortable. Feeling uncomfortable is a sign I should avoid her. She will judge my nervousness.	Nervousness Self-blame Avoid her Leave party	I don't have to let my uncomfortable feelings run my life. I can take a few deep breaths and calm down.	Feeling more confident. She is probably nervous too. I can approach her.

Your Turn: New Beliefs

In Chapter 1, you began an ABC chart listing some of your worries. Use this chart and add columns D (New Beliefs) and E (New Consequences). Try to come up with new ways of looking at the situation and imagine how your behavior changes when you have this new perspective.

GIVE IT A TRY

Over the next week, keep track of when you feel stressed or upset. Complete the ABCDE chart, trying to come up with alternative or new beliefs and think about what new consequences could occur.

Completing this exercise helps open your mind to new beliefs, or at least the possibility of new beliefs. In the beginning, you might not believe all the new beliefs you write down. That's okay. Work on carrying out the new behaviors, even when you don't believe the beliefs behind them. As you do, you begin to accept the beliefs.

Separating Thoughts from Emotions

By now, you should understand that it is your thoughts that drive your emotions and by changing what you think, you can change your emotions. You can make a conscious decision to review your thoughts and agree or disagree with them. You can make a conscious decision to change them.

There might be times you find separating your thoughts from your emotions is difficult and confusing. It is often helpful to work backward. First, consider how you are feeling and then think about what happened, the triggering event or situation, to make you feel that way. Then focus on the thoughts. For example, "I'm feeling hurt and angry. Brian said he would call at 7 P.M. and he didn't call." You identified your feelings and the triggering event.

Now, you can consider the thoughts you had as a result of the triggering event. You may have thought, "I am not important to Brian." Try changing this thought to, "I know I am important to Brian. Something must have come up. I'm sure he'll call when he has a chance," or "I know I matter to Brian and although I'd like him to call I don't really need to talk to him right now." Immediately, your emotions change. You are no longer angry or hurt. Instead, you are calm and confident in your relationship.

Believing your new thoughts isn't always easy. You might think, "Maybe something came up… or maybe it didn't. Maybe he just doesn't care." When you find yourself reverting back to your negative thoughts, practice sitting with your new thought. Close your eyes. Silently repeat the new thought while resisting the old thought. Every time your mind returns to the old thought, repeat the new thought and resist dwelling on the old thought.

We often place the blame for our feelings on someone or something else. You might say, "Brian made me mad because he didn't call when he said he would." It is not Brian who made you mad; it is your perception—Brian doesn't care—that caused you to be hurt and angry. Learning to separate your thoughts and emotions gives you control of how you feel and react to a situation.

Mixing up emotions and thoughts leads to a cycle of negative thinking. Once you begin thinking, "I'm not important to Brian," you start thinking of events to justify this belief. You interpret past events through this lens, even if it isn't true. You think about last week when he brushed you off because he was on a business call. You think about the time last month when he didn't listen to your point of view. By the time Brian does call, you are sure the relationship is doomed because he simply doesn't care. Instead of separating your thoughts and emotions, you have allowed your emotions to drive your thoughts.

Another common example of a negative, emotion-driven thought process is avoidance. Typically, the more you avoid something, the more you fear it. Imagine you have a fear of flying. The more you avoid getting on a plane, the more your fear grows. You might believe that it is necessary for you to avoid flying because you can't manage the uncomfortable feeling that comes along when you fly. Using the ABC method, the following shows how negative thinking can lead to more negative thinking:

A: I have to get on an airplane.

B: It's uncomfortable to ___ ___ can't handle the discomfort of flying.

C: Avoid the flight. Rel___

Because avoiding the f___ ___ve thinking:

B: I always need to avo___

C: Embarrassment. T___ ___ain.

Now, imagine you m___ ___ving your emotions to control both your th___

Original B: It's unc___ ___ing.

Alternative B: I car___ ___mfortable on the airplane. I can do deep breat___

Original B: I alwa___

Alternative B: The more I fly the easier it wil___ ___y discomforts.

As you see, negative thinking usually causes more negative thinking. It becomes a cycle; you think a negative thought and feel and react in a negative way, which causes you to be in a bad mood, which causes more bad thoughts, which worsens your mood, which causes even more negative thoughts. The following section looks at some common negative thinking patterns and questions you can ask yourself to combat these thought processes.

Problematic Thinking Patterns

If you think something often enough, you believe it is true. If you think in the same way often enough, it becomes a habit, even if it is unhelpful thinking. We use *cognitive distortions* to convince us of something that isn't true or to justify our feelings and actions. For example, if you tell yourself that you fail every time you try something new because you are not the best, you justify not trying new things. This is seeing things in absolutes—one type of problematic thought patterns. There are a number of different types of *cognitive distortions*.

> **DEFINITION**
>
> **Cognitive distortions** are biased habits in the way you think. They cause overly rigid and negative thoughts. It's like wearing rose colored glasses and assuming everything is a shade of pink.

Catastrophizing

When you catastrophize, you magnify every problem and assume everything is going to end in a large, negative disaster. You believe your imagined outcome is a given, that the only way the situation ends will be terrible. You fail to take steps to prevent the problem; after all, it's already set in stone.

Examples:

- You have a fight with your boyfriend and assume you are going to break up.

- You make a small mistake at work and think you are going to get fired.

Questions to ask yourself:

- What evidence do I have to prove or disprove my conclusion?

- How likely is this to happen?

- What are other possible outcomes?

> **CBTIDBIT**
>
> Think about a small problem in your life, such as not finding a parking space at the mall. Consider this a "1." Now think about the worst possible situation that could happen in your life, for example losing your home in a fire. This is a "10." Whenever you encounter a problem, give it a rating somewhere in between these two scenarios based on how much it would disrupt your life. This helps you put situations in perspective.

Mind Reading

When you engage in mind reading, you guess what other people are thinking and assume it is true. You automatically assume others have a negative opinion of you and become angry, anxious, or depressed because of these assumptions. You act as though your ideas are correct without reality testing.

Examples:

- You see some people whispering and assuming they are talking about you. You tell them off, giving them a reason not to like you.

- You see someone on the street that you recently met and he ignores you. You assume he doesn't like you and doesn't want to talk to you. You stop trying to make friends.

Questions to ask yourself:

- What are some alternative explanations?

- How can I test my guess?

Fortune-Telling

Fortune-telling is a thought pattern in which you make predictions about the future, often with a negative outcome, and feel discouraged or behave based on a reality that hasn't yet happened and may never happen.

Examples:

- You want to ask a girl out and assume she will say no. You don't bother.

- Your boss calls you to "talk about the last project." You assume he is angry at you. You avoid the conversation.

Questions to ask yourself:

- What would happen if I take the risk and do it anyway?

- What else might happen?

- If the negative does happen, what steps can I take to deal with it?

IMAGINE THAT

Optimists use cognitive distortions to their benefit—they believe positive events occurred because of them and that any positive event is proof that more good things will happen. They see negative events as limited to specific situations and attribute problems to external events. They focus on where they have control and assume they can make things right in the future. For example, an optimist sees getting a promotion as proof of their hard work and expects more promotions will occur in the future. An optimist sees not getting a promotion as perhaps a limit of the company's resources. So they continue to work just as hard being hopeful that their promotion will come.

Black-and-White Thinking

When you think in terms of black and white, you categorize outcomes and assume things will either be good or bad. Your bad category is large and includes most outcomes and your good outcomes are limited.

Examples:

- Your daughter applies to 10 colleges but has her heart set on one in particular. You assume any school other than her first choice will be socially and scholastically awful for her.

- You try a new sport and when you are not the fastest, you think you are a failure. You stop playing so you never get better.

- Your friend does not invite you somewhere and you think he is not a good friend. You stop calling him.

Questions to ask yourself:

- Is there some middle ground I am ignoring?

- Am I imposing superhuman qualities on myself?

- What is the evidence for and against this thinking?

Overgeneralizing

When you overgeneralize, you assume that what happened once will always happen, and something that didn't happen will never happen. You see problems as never-ending and hopeless. You use the words "always" or "never" to describe specific situations. You ignore exceptions and focus on global results. You assume that because a situation ended poorly in the past, it will always end that way.

Examples:

- You think, "I always mess up."

- You think, "I can't trust anyone."

- You didn't get the promotion you wanted and now believe you will never get promoted. You stop working hard.

- You get blown off by a date and assume you will be alone forever. You stop going on dates.

Questions to ask yourself:

- Am I attributing too much importance to a one-time event? Can I focus on this as a specific incident?

- Are there parts that I can control in the future? Are there past events that I am ignoring?

- Do I need everything to go my way? Do I need everyone to like me?

STOP AND THINK

Success comes from investing in a situation even if it is not ideal. By assuming the ship that sailed without you was the only and best just leaves you stranded. Think about one time you did not get exactly what you wanted in life. Did you stop there and assume there were no other options? Or did you continue on and look for something equally good or better?

Personalization and Blame

Thought patterns of personalization and blame happen when you take responsibility for events out of your control or blame others for events in their control. You make things that have nothing to do with you about you.

Examples:

- The taxi driver goes down a street where there is a detour. You assume he is trying to take advantage of you rather than thinking he was not informed.

- You make plans with a friend and then have to cancel. He sounds disappointed. You assume he is mad at you rather than thinking he is just disappointed he cannot see you.

- Your husband forgets your anniversary. You think he has done it on purpose because you forget to celebrate his promotion rather than thinking, "We are both forgetful people, especially when it comes to these types of events."

Questions to ask yourself:

- What are the other factors that contributed to the situation?

- Which factors of a situation are your responsibility? Where do you have control?

- If someone else is angry or upset, are they upset with you or with the situation?

Ignoring the Positive

When you ignore the positive, you always look at the negative aspects of a situation. You discredit any positive information and turn it around to be negative. You filter information and use only the information that supports your negative view. You believe life is unfair.

Examples:

- A date blows you off; you assume he was the "one" and don't consider that he may not have been right for you.

- You don't get a job; you assume it was the perfect position and forget that maybe another job is a better fit.

- A co-worker asks if you want to go to lunch; you assume she asked only because no one else was around.

- A friend asks you for a favor; you think, "Now I know why we are really friends."

Questions to ask yourself:

- What are the positive elements to the situation?

- What information are you forgetting?

> **IMAGINE THAT**
>
> According to the American Psychological Association, people who see the glass as "half full" are healthier. They live longer, have lower rates of depression, don't catch colds as often, have a reduced risk of dying from cardiovascular disease, and rate their emotional well-being higher than those who have a negative view of life.

"Should" and "Must"

When you think in absolutes, you have strong beliefs and rules about how other people should act and become angry when they don't act in that way. You make demands on the behavior of others. You use "should" statements on yourself, "I should have done that," and feel guilty for what you did or didn't do.

Examples:

- You see someone at a party whom you don't know very well and avoid talking to him or her. You think, "I should only approach people I know well."

- A cashier is rude to you and you become angry because you were not treated with respect. You think, "People must treat me with respect."

- You are mad at yourself because you can't find your keys and you know you should have put them on the key hook. You think, "I should always be responsible."

- A friend cancels plans and you assume you're not important to him or her. You feel disappointed. You think, "People who care about me should honor their commitments."

Questions to ask yourself:

- Are there exceptions to your rules? What are the circumstances that cause the flexibility?

- What are reasons why others may live by other rules?

- Does this person have different beliefs or priority that compete with my ideas of how they should and must be have?

Emotional Reasoning

When you use emotional reasoning, you base conclusions about yourself, others, and the world around on your feelings. You assume that if you feel something, it must be true.

Examples:

- I see someone well-dressed at a party. I feel intimidated so I assume he or she is intimidating.

- I feel nervous about getting on airplane. I assume my nervousness is a sign of danger.

- I make a mistake at work. I feel embarrassment. I assume others are judging me and saying I am responsible.

Questions to ask yourself:

- What are the thoughts behind me feeling? Can I restructure them?

- Can I focus on the facts not the emotions?

CBTIDBIT

Distorted thinking easily causes you to categorize requests about your behavior or the behavior of others as demands rather than a statement of preference or desire. This causes unnecessary defensiveness and negative emotions. Over the next week, practice viewing all requests as statements of preference rather than impositions.

Labeling

When you engage in labeling, you label your own behavior and the behavior of others in a negative way, such as "I am so stupid" and "He is lazy."

Examples:

- Your brother-in-law is having a hard time finding a job; you think he is lazy and no good.

- You made a mistake at work; you believe you are loser.

Questions to ask yourself:

- How can I state this by focusing on specific actions without making personal attacks?

- What positive traits in myself and others can I focus on?

Your Turn: Notice Your Thoughts

Use the ABC worksheet introduced in Chapter 1. See if you can spot the distortion type for each thought or sets of thoughts. Don't worry about doing it right or wrong. The point is to begin to develop awareness of your biases in thinking and notice your habits.

Situation: I see someone at party I am slightly familiar with. I cannot recall her name. She is well dressed.

Thought: "I should only approach people whom I know well."
Distortion: "Should" statement. I'm applying an internal rule that limits my behavior.

Thought: "It's pretty pathetic of me that I can't recall her name. I should have kept better in touch."
Distortion: Personalization (self-blame) and labeling. I'm making it all my fault. I'm calling myself names that are not motivating.

Thought: "People I don't know well are intimidating."
Distortion: Emotional reasoning. I feel intimated and I am drawing conclusions from my feelings.

Thought: "She is very well-dressed and will judge me."
Distortion: Mind reading. I am assuming she will judge me harshly. I have no evidence of this. I can't get inside her head.

When you first start CBT and begin working on the exercises in the book, it may not be possible to sit down and work through your thoughts on paper. You also might not yet be able to catch your negative thought patterns and work through the process in your mind. Take time after the situation to write down what you thought and what you might have changed during the situation. Keep at it. With continued practice, you will begin to catch and change your thoughts immediately.

The Least You Need to Know

- Your thoughts influence your feelings and behaviors.
- Work backward to separate your thoughts from emotions. Think about how you are feeling, what happened, and then what you were thinking during the situation.
- There are many different problematic thinking processes. When you become aware of your thinking patterns, you can correct them to think in a more helpful way.
- Practice noticing your thoughts. Try to identify what thought patterns are at work. Ask yourself questions to counteract those thought patterns.

CHAPTER 3

Automatic Thoughts, Assumptions, and Core Beliefs

You interpret the world around you instantly, without any conscious effort. As you go through the day, thoughts pop into your mind, telling you how to feel and how to react. You probably don't even realize this is happening because it occurs in a split second. Suppose you are at a party and run into an old friend. You feel happy and excited to see someone you know. Thoughts about times you spent together occur so quickly, you might not pay attention to them fully. You probably focus more on how you are feeling. You assume that seeing your friend made you feel happy, however it is your interpretation, your thoughts about the fun times you had together, that caused you to feel happy.

Your First Reaction

Remember, it isn't the event itself, but how you interpret the event, that creates your emotions. The immediate thoughts you have, the ones that occur spontaneously and without your consent, are called *automatic thoughts*. They are not planned and you don't spend time thinking them through. Often, you don't even realize you had a thought. Your automatic thoughts are a reflection of how you see yourself, other people, and the world around you.

Automatic thoughts can be positive or negative, depending on how you view the situation. If you see someone you know but cannot recall her name, your automatic thoughts might be, "How do I know her? She looks so familiar but I can't remember her name. I can still say hi…" or "I can't think of that person's name. I am so stupid; I blow everything."

> **DEFINITION**
>
> **Automatic thoughts** are those thoughts that pop in your mind without consent. They are present with or without your awareness.

As you worked through the exercises in Chapter 2, you learned to separate your emotions from your immediate reaction—your automatic thoughts. You learned that these thoughts drive your emotions. Even though they happen in an instant, you can learn to listen to, label, and then dispute your automatic thoughts and therefore change how you see yourself, others, and the world around you.

Your Turn: Listening to Self-Talk

Close your eyes. Imagine a situation where you had a mildly negative reaction. Visualize the scenario in your mind. As you replay the scene, try to connect with the emotion and listen to what you are saying to yourself.

Jot down your thoughts.

This exercise helps you to develop the ability to connect to what you are telling yourself. As you continue to practice, you will be able to better tune in to your self-talk as a situation is unfolding rather than having to look back on it later.

> **STOP AND THINK**
>
> Metacognition refers to being aware of your thoughts. As you practice, you will learn to be more in tune with your automatic thoughts and become more metacognitive.

Negative Automatic Thoughts

Negative automatic thoughts are often a reflection of a poor self-image, a sour or vulnerable view of your environment, or a belief that a situation is going to turn out poorly. These types of thoughts usually lead to negative emotions such as anger, anxiety, sadness, or guilt.

Some examples of negative automatic thoughts:

- He isn't interested in me. I'm so ugly. I will always be lonely.

- I don't feel well. I must be sick. There is something wrong with me.

- I overslept. I'm so stupid. Now I'm going to get fired.

- Tom is in a bad mood today. It must be my fault.

- My boss criticizes me. He's so arrogant. I can't deal with him.

- This project is so hard. I'll never get it done. I can't do anything.

- This person is annoying me. All my relationships fail. This one will, too. I should just give up now.

- I know I'll make a fool of myself when explaining this project to my co-workers.

- My friend was going through a hard time and I didn't call her. I am a terrible friend; she probably won't ever talk to me again.

- That salesperson was rude. I must have upset her.

- My husband asked me to do the laundry. Why is he on my case?

- My mother is calling. I wonder what she wants from me now.

When left to run rampant, your negative automatic thoughts impact your mood, self-esteem, and overall feelings of happiness. It is easier and more believable for you to think negatively about yourself than to think positively. These thoughts also tend to be self-fulfilling. If you tell yourself you are going to fail, chances are you will.

Changing Negative Self-Talk

Learning to listen to your automatic thoughts is the first step toward changing them and taking on a more positive view. Once you stop and hear what you are telling yourself, you can challenge the thought, come up with alternative thoughts, and decide which thought you want to keep.

Imagine you are in a store and the sales clerk is rude. You immediately assume you have done something to make the sales clerk annoyed, even though you aren't sure what that could be. Instead, think about alternative explanations. You might think, "She seems very upset; maybe she is having a bad day. Maybe she doesn't feel well. Maybe her boss just yelled at her. Maybe she had a fight with her spouse right before she came to work." There are many different explanations that could explain why the clerk was abrupt with you—and none of them have anything to do with you. By changing the way you look at the situation, you change your reaction. Instead of acting defensively and getting irritated, you approach the clerk with a smile, trying to make her day a little more pleasant.

Automatic thoughts are often based on partial information. You don't take time to analyze the thoughts that pop into your mind. Because they are based on your past experiences and beliefs, they are believable; therefore, you trust them as the truth. Even so, they can be distorted or wrong. For example, if after making a mistake you say to yourself, "I always do something wrong," that would be untrue. It is impossible that you always do something wrong; there must have been times you have done something right. You filtered out those times, focusing only on the times you did something wrong.

In order to have a more balanced and positive perspective, you need to stop, pay attention to your thoughts, and dispute their validity, if necessary. One way to do that is to use your ABC chart.

In Chapter 2, we introduced the idea of problematic thinking patterns, assigning labels to your automatic thoughts and questions to ask yourself to dispute those thoughts. Now you are going to practice coming up with alternate ways of thinking. Use questions listed after each problematic thinking pattern in Chapter 2 to guide you thought this process. It is important to keep in mind that there are no right or wrong answers. The goal is to help you to feel and manage problematic situations better by changing unhealthy perspectives.

The following is an example of using a version of the ABC chart to aid you in challenging your immediate reaction:

A: Situation	B: Belief or Thought	C: Behavior	D: Questions
Your husband rearranges the date for your family vacation based on his work schedule.	This is unfair. He is being selfish. He wants everything on his terms. There is no communication in this marriage. He is trying to bully me or make me feel bad for not agreeing to the dates he wants.	Yell at him Tell him off	Is there a reason he changed the date? Are there other factors that contributed to the situation? Is there other information I need to know? Can I take some responsibility for the lack of communication? How can I talk to him about this without making accusations? How can I focus on specific actions instead of making personal attacks? What are the facts?

In this example, your immediate reaction was to become angry and blame your husband. Based on the problematic thinking processes outlined in Chapter 2, look over the chart and see if you notice personalization and blame, labeling, overgeneralizing, and emotional reasoning in Column B. Notice the types of questions in Column D that can be used to combat these unhealthy thinking processes.

Once you have thought about the questions and challenged your immediate reaction, you may come up with different perspectives on the situation, such as:

- He is forgetful when it comes to social plans. I could have added our vacation to his work calendar so there wouldn't be any work conflicts.

- I know he is going away on a business trip. Maybe he wants to make sure we spend some time together before he leaves.

- We all do things that are convenient for us sometimes. That does not make him a selfish person.

- We communicate well most of the time, on most issues. We need to work on how we can communicate better about our schedules so we both have all the information.

- He did not do this to upset me. On the contrary, he was trying to spend time with me, not hurt me.

When you first found out your husband changed the dates of your vacation without talking to you first, you were hurt and angry. But now, as you ask yourself questions to challenge that reaction, you see the situation differently. Your new conclusion might be: "My husband loves me and wants to spend time with me. We should sit down together to work out a plan so we can make the most of our time off work and spend time together."

Your Turn: Questions to Ask Yourself

Over the next week, as soon as you notice a negative emotion (anger, anxiety, sadness), write down five questions you can ask yourself to challenge your thoughts.

Some examples of questions include the following:

- What emotion am I feeling?

- Where do I feel the emotion in my body?

- What was I thinking right before and when this feeling started?

- What am I afraid might happen?

- Can I imagine myself coping with that outcome?

- What is the self-talk I hear myself saying when I see myself managing the outcome?

Making Assumptions

When you accept your own ideas as true without actual proof, you make an assumption. You fail to ask for more information and don't bother to look for evidence. If you act on your unhealthy thinking patterns without challenging them, it is likely you are making assumptions.

Some assumptions you make are correct; for example, your dog is standing by the door barking. You assume he needs to go outside. Sometimes, assumptions keep you safe; for example, you may be visiting a city you have never been to and assume it is not safe to walk through the streets by yourself.

However, sometimes assumptions can become limiting. For example, when you visit a city and don't feel safe walking alone, you might assume that the only way to be safe is to stay inside your hotel. This limits your behavior. Instead, you could challenge your belief and come up with solutions, such as talking to the concierge about the surrounding area and what places would be safe for you to go alone, signing up for guided tours, or taking a taxi.

Some assumptions are unhelpful. Imagine you text your wife and she does not reply. You continue to text throughout the day and try calling her a few times. She doesn't answer her phone and doesn't text back. You make the assumption that she is ignoring you and are angry. When you get home, you see her phone still sitting on the kitchen table. You realize she hasn't been ignoring you, she forgot her phone. You spent the day angry, assuming something based on partial information—you didn't receive any texts—but without knowing all the facts.

When you make assumptions, you…

- Miss opportunities—you want to invite a friend to the movies but assume she will say no so you don't bother asking.

- Make errors in judgments and decisions—you assume the person in front of you in line is a bad person because of the way he is dressed.

- Misunderstand others—you assume your friend doesn't want to spend time with you because she didn't call you back right away.

- Have a hard time making decisions—you imagine too many scenarios so you don't make any choice.

Assumptions are stories you create to help you understand the people and the world around you. These stories often have nothing to do with reality. Assumptions add to your problems rather than creating a resolution. Sometimes you feel as if you need to make a decision right now and don't bother to wait until all of the information becomes available. You jump to a conclusion based on only the information you have, which is usually not the whole story.

Your Turn: Turning Assumptions Around

There are six steps to turning assumptions around and reacting to the situation:

1. Write down the situational facts you know.

2. Write down the assumptions you are making.

3. Identify your problematic thought processes.

4. Write down any extraneous information you know.

5. Determine the possible actions you can take.

6. Select a response to the situation using on the facts you have.

The next time you find yourself making an assumption, stop and follow the steps. Doing this will insure you don't act rashly based on partial information. Let's look at an example.

Situation: You are expecting a call from your friend Cheryl about meeting after work for some dinner. She said she would call you this afternoon but it is almost time to leave work and she hasn't called yet.

Step 1 Facts:

Cheryl said she would call this afternoon. It is almost time to leave work. She hasn't called yet.

Step 2 Assumptions:

Cheryl is ignoring me.

Cheryl doesn't want to have dinner with me.

Cheryl is still working on the project and doesn't have time to go to dinner.

Step 3 Negative Thinking Patterns:

Fortune-telling—Making an error in reasoning without knowing all the information and filling in information you don't know.

Step 4 Extraneous Facts:

She told me she has a lot of work these days. Her boss is a tyrant.

Step 5 Actions:

I can call or email Cheryl to see if she still wants to meet for dinner.

I can wait a little longer to see if she calls and if not, I can eat at home and meet her another night.

I can make plans with another friend and invite Cheryl to join us if she calls.

Step 6: Response:

I will call another friend. If Cheryl does call, she can join us. I'll keep my cell phone on.

STOP AND THINK

We usually assume people think just like we do, without giving them credit for having their own thoughts and ideas. In order to stop making assumptions, you must accept that others have the right to think in their own way. Your job is not to guess how they are thinking but to ask and listen carefully to the answer.

Tips for Eliminating Assumptions

Just as you need to "catch" the automatic thoughts and make a conscious effort to change them, you can listen to your self-talk and learn not to make assumptions.

Ask questions. When you find yourself making an assumption, ask questions to clarify what you think. Find out as much information about the situation or the person as you can.

Listen. In order to really listen to another person, you have to be willing to put aside your assumptions and focus on what they are saying. Be totally in the present moment; try repeating back their words instead of jumping in with your thoughts.

Give the benefit of the doubt. We often jump to conclusions about what someone else has done—and usually we first consider the negative. In a previous example, you might have jumped to the conclusion that your wife was intentionally ignoring when she didn't answer your calls or text you back. If you gave her the benefit of the doubt, you would have waited until you could speak to her to find out what was going on.

Consider the past. You might ignore the positive aspects of the past and filter only the negative aspects that fit with your current view of the situation. For example, if your wife normally texts you back, why would she ignore you today? Look at the situation as a whole instead of a single incident.

GIVE IT A TRY

Think about a past experience where you based your reaction on what you assumed without gaining more information, or a time where you assumed a bad outcome before the situation played out, only to find out later you were wrong. Ask yourself: what one piece of information would I have wanted to know in order to make a better decision?

Resist stereotypes. Placing a label on someone is making an assumption about his or her character without finding out any information. Prejudice about ethnicity, religion, gender, or appearance is an assumption about a group of people.

Ask yourself if you are making a rational decision or jumping to a conclusion. Ask yourself if you have enough information to make a judgment or a decision, or if you need to gather additional information. Remember, no matter how long you have known someone, you can't know what they are thinking; it is always better to give someone the respect of asking instead of jumping to a conclusion.

Your Turn: Uncovering Your Assumptions

Assumptions are based on unhelpful thinking processes, usually fortune-telling (making predictions without adequate information) or mind reading (believing you know what someone else is thinking). To discover when you most often jump to assumptions, complete the following sentence:

When I am feeling upset, I assume someone is…

- Going to reject me.

- Putting me in a vulnerable situation by…

- Going to say no to my request.

- Planning to criticize me by saying…

- Going to hurt me emotionally or cause me pain by…

- Angry with me.

Think back to a situation when you jumped to an assumption. Was one of these reasons behind the assumption? If so, which one? If not, what caused you to assume something?

Is there an assumption you still hold that is stopping you from moving forward or doing something? What is the reason behind the assumption?

Try using the steps in the previous exercise to work through your assumption and come to a different conclusion. Commit to acting based on information you know. Commit to asking definite questions to find out more information.

Identify Your Core Beliefs

Core beliefs are those beliefs you hold strongly. They indicate how you see yourself and others and how you view the world. They are usually rigid and inflexible beliefs that developed in childhood or because of a significant life event. Negative core beliefs are often related to the following:

- I am not good enough.

- I am unlovable.

- I am bad.

- I am a defective human being.

- I am powerless.

- I am not safe.

Taking the time to analyze what you are thinking helps to identify negative thinking. However, core beliefs are harder to identify as they are hidden below layers of problematic thoughts. You sometimes have to dig deep to find the underlying core belief. Uncovering your core belief goes something like this:

Imagine you didn't get a promotion at work after you took initiative and put in overtime. Your thoughts might be:

- I didn't get the promotion.

- I don't try hard enough at work.

- Because of this I will never get a promotion.

- I will always be in the same position.

- I am not good enough.

There are a few problematic thinking patterns here.

1. You made several generalizations, using "never," and "always."

2. You jumped to conclusions, such as "I will never get a promotion" and "I will always be in the same position."

3. You may have been trying to combat these negative thoughts, but you found they continued to surface because you have not gotten down to the core belief. Until you address the negative belief that you are not good enough, addressing the other issues might not work.

If you have the tendency to use one or two problematic thinking processes, you can create *coping statements* to counter the unhelpful thought patterns.

> **DEFINITION**
>
> A **coping statement** is a statement that counters your most sensitive struggles and gets you to focus on where you have control, who you are committed to, or how you are feeling.

Coping Statements:

1. De-generalize: "Not everything is going to go my way."

2. Don't jump to conclusions: "I have no evidence that I won't get promoted next time. Two people senior to me recently got promoted, so I am next in line."

3. Deal with core beliefs: "Because I didn't get what I want, it doesn't mean I am a failure."

Look over the different problematic thinking processes in Chapter 2. Do you have a dominant style? Create a coping statement to help remind you of the alternate thoughts.

> **IMAGINE THAT**
>
> You may not completely believe your core beliefs, but even those you partially believe impact your behavior. For example, you are going on a job interview and you say, "It will be a good interview; I am going to get this job," even though you don't believe it completely. You think you have a 50 percent chance of being offered the job. Even so, you dress appropriately, are well-groomed, bring along your resume, and act professionally. You don't need to completely believe the interview will be successful in order to make good decisions.

Use coping statements to help you deal with situations that repeat themselves. For example, you are always worried your boss is angry about something you did wrong. Your coping statement might be. "I know my boss is in a bad mood sometimes. It isn't about me." Whenever you notice you are personalizing the situation at work, repeat your coping statement.

Your Turn: Rating Core Beliefs

When challenging your core beliefs, think about how much you believe something. For example, suppose you come home late from a night out with your friends. Your wife is angry that you didn't call to say you would be late and yells at you when you enter the house.

Core belief: I am no good. I can't do anything right.

Ask yourself, how often does your wife think you can't do anything right? How often does she think you are inconsiderate? Rate your answers on a scale of 0 to 100 percent. You might think that your wife thinks you are inconsiderate 20 percent of the time, which means that 80 percent of the time she believes you are considerate.

Your coping statement might be: "Most of the time I am a considerate husband. Most of the time I am doing an okay job."

Develop New Core Beliefs

Just as you challenged other negative thinking processes, you can challenge your core beliefs. Try to gather evidence decrease the strength of your belief.

Core belief: I am not good enough.

Experiences to disprove this belief:

- My boss has complimented my work in the past.
- I have gotten raises on a regular basis.
- I have been asked to do special projects.
- At my last job I received a promotion.

Once you list past experiences that go against your belief, you can look at it in a more balanced way. For example, "I didn't get this promotion but have received compliments on my work in the past, therefore I am good enough."

In Chapter 10, you will learn about behavioral experiments and how to test your predictions and core beliefs. For now, you can create a simple hypothesis about your belief and then gather evidence to proof or disprove your ideas and beliefs about yourself.

Write down a core belief you have about yourself. List any past experiences that go against this belief. Although you may not completely disprove your core belief, you may have to revise it to say it is not always true. For example, suppose you don't have any friends and believe you will always be lonely. You write down a list of all the people you have been friends with throughout your life. You realize that although you don't have any friends right now, you have had friends before; therefore, you can have friends again. You revise your core belief to, "I don't have any friends right now, but I have had friends in the past and can have friends again if I make the effort. I am lonely now, but I won't always be lonely."

The Least You Need to Know

- Automatic thoughts are those that pop into your head without consent. These thoughts reflect how you view yourself, others, and the world around you.
- Listening to and changing your automatic thoughts can change how you view and react to a situation.
- Assumptions are based on partial information. Taking time to gather more information helps you make better judgments and decisions.
- A core belief is a strong belief you hold about yourself. Core beliefs can be challenged just as your thoughts can.

Understanding and Measuring Your Emotions

When you experience surges of emotion, you feel them not only in your brain but also in your body. These emotions connect to your thoughts and behaviors.

For example, imagine you have a test coming up. Whenever you think about the upcoming exam you start to feel nervous. Your brain feels overwhelmed, you cannot concentrate on studying, and you are distracted by a many other thoughts. Your body feels tense, your breathing is little faster than usual, and your hands become clammy.

In this chapter, we'll explore a variety of emotions and how they manifest in your thoughts and behaviors. We'll introduce methods to help you become more aware of your emotions and techniques for managing your emotions when they become overwhelming.

In This Chapter

- Identifying your emotions
- Recognizing helpful and unhelpful emotions
- Measuring the intensity of your emotions
- Feeling and managing your emotions

Naming Your Emotions

How are you feeling today? Are you angry? Annoyed? Anxious? Happy? Embarrassed? Sad? Do you have mixed feelings? Although it is sometimes hard to identify exactly what you are feeling, understanding your feelings helps you manage the reactions to your emotions. This is important because extreme emotions can be harmful to your health and cause you to react in negative ways. Intense negative emotions have been linked to an increased risk of cardiovascular disease, immune system deficiencies, high blood pressure, and chronic pain. When you don't understand and manage your emotions, health, self-image, and relationships suffer.

When you are able to identify both the emotion and its intensity, you have a road map to managing the negative thought process behind the emotion. You can then start your ABCD process by evaluating the negative thoughts for errors and challenging irrational points of view. Then you can change the unhelpful thoughts in order to change how you feel.

STOP AND THINK

Your emotions are your own. They reflect your perspective and past experiences. No one can make you feel anything. When you communicate your feelings, it is more helpful to say, "I am feeling frustrated and angry right now," instead of "You make me angry." Approaching a discussion like this helps to lead to dialogue rather than defensiveness.

Helpful vs. Unhelpful Emotions

All negative emotions are not bad. For example, when someone close to you dies, you feel sadness; your emotion signals "I am experiencing a loss." Depression, however, is an unhelpful reaction because it signals "I cannot cope with this loss."

Unhelpful negative emotions usually signal that you believe you are not able to cope with the problem at hand. You see something in your situation as a threat to your safety or security. When you are experiencing these types of emotions, you usually lack compassion for yourself or for others.

We often use alternate words to express our feelings. These terms might relate to the intensity of the basic emotion, they might be an expression or style of speaking, or they may be a way of more accurately describing how you experience the basic emotion. For example, if you are feeling "nervous" about a job interview, you may not necessarily associate this will feeling scared or in danger. A better description for you might be "I feel jittery" or "I have some concerns." Finding the right term can help others understand you better and build empathy.

Managing your emotions includes the following:

- Determining how you are feeling

- Measuring the intensity of the feeling and describing it accurately

- Deciding if the feeling is helpful or unhelpful

Your thoughts, actions, and physical sensations all give you clues. Look over the following descriptions of emotions. Note the differences between healthy and unhealthy forms of the emotions, the physical sensations you may feel, and alternate words used to describe the emotion. This should help you narrow down your emotion and determine if it is helpful or unhelpful.

Nervousness vs. Anxiety

Nervousness and anxiety are both related to a sense of not being in control. You may feel powerless.

Nervousness (healthy): A situation in the present or the future threatens your sense of safety or security. You feel vulnerable. Low and moderate feelings of nervousness often activate your need to get something done.

Anxiety or Panic (unhealthy): Anxiety or panic is the less healthy counterpart to nervousness. You perceive you cannot cope with the threat. Your *fight-or-flight* response is triggered.

Alternate words: worry, concern, apprehension, fear, agitation, tense, edgy, jitters, panic, uncertainty

Physical sensations: rapid heartbeat, shaking, sweating, stomachache and anxiety, dizziness

> **DEFINITION**
>
> The **fight-or-flight** response is a physiological reaction to stress that results in an increase in heart rate, blood pressure, and glucose levels. Adrenalin levels go up, preparing you to either fight the threat or flee the situation.

Irritation and Frustration vs. Anger and Rage

These and anxiety emotions are based on a sense of unfairness. You feel something must be changed.

Irritation and frustration (healthy): There is some obstacle standing in the way of your perception of fairness and righteousness. This may be something that occurred in your past, is now occurring, or you fear will happen in the future. The larger you perceive the obstacle to be, the higher your level of frustration.

Frustration can be healthy because it signals that something is wrong and needs to be solved. It prevents you from ignoring an issue until it builds and you explode with anger or ignore it, allowing anger and resentment to simmer inside.

Anger and rage (unhealthy): Anger is the unhealthy manifestation of frustration. When you are angry, you don't believe you can handle the obstacle. Anger can lead to rage and hostility.

Alternate words: annoyed, irritated, bad-tempered, enraged, fuming, furious, hostile, livid, miffed, testy, touchy, displeased, cross, outrage, in a huff, hissy fit, mad

Physical sensations: grinding your teeth, clenching your fists, flushing, numbness, sweating, muscle tension

> **GIVE IT A TRY**
>
> Once you have given your emotion a name, look through the other emotions and decide what healthy negative emotions you would like to feel. List what thoughts and behaviors you think would change your emotion to the desired one. Act on those behaviors.

Sadness vs. Depression

Sadness and depression are passive emotions and are a reaction to a sense of loss.

Sadness (healthy): A feeling based on the loss of something valuable and important. Feelings of sadness are temporary. You know eventually you will feel better.

Reactionary depression (unhealthy): An unhealthy form of sadness that occurs after a loss that signals "I cannot cope with this loss." When you are depressed, you stop trying to improve your life situation. You feel a sense of hopelessness. Depression prevents you from accepting and mourning the loss and dealing with your problems.

Reactionary depressions is different from biological forms of depression. When you suffer from biological depression, you have a chemical imbalance that causes you to feel depressed and think of the world as a painful place. In reactionary forms of depression, you are reacting to a particular incident that colors your judgment.

Major depression (unhealthy): A medical condition that affects thoughts, feelings, behavior, and physical health. Depression is a lifelong condition that is much more than a temporary sadness. While some people have only one episode of depression, for many it recurs throughout their lives.

Alternate words: disappointed, hurt, blue, distraught, down, heartbroken, melancholy, sorrowful, deflated, dejected, discouraged, dismayed, let down, grief, lonely, hopelessness, misery, dejection, despondency, gloomy, mopey, in a funk, dismal

Physical sensations: fatigue, crying, body aches and pains, stomachache, headache, changes in appetite

Embarrassment vs. Guilt and Shame

When you feel embarrassment, guilt, or shame, you believe you have not lived up to self-imposed expectations.

Embarrassment (healthy): You feel somewhat responsible for something that has gone wrong. You assume others are judging you and your actions.

Guilt and shame (unhealthy): This is a more extreme and unhealthy version of embarrassment. You believe you should have had control over the situation and you are entirely responsible for the bad outcome. You do not think others will have any empathy for your situation.

Alternate words: humiliated, degraded, discredited, disgraced, dishonored, self-conscious, uncomfortable, condemned, culpable, at fault, inexcusable, reprehensible, unforgivable, remorse, sorry, abashed, contrite, mortified, self-disgust

Physical sensations: blushing, feeling uncomfortable in social situations, insomnia, upset stomach, inability to look someone in the eye

Disgust vs. Contempt

Disgust and contempt are forceful emotions, similar to anger and rage. They result from a disapproval of something you find unpleasant or offensive.

Disgust (healthy): A feeling of revulsion, aversion, or distaste to something that might cause you to withdraw from the object or person.

Contempt (unhealthy): A less healthy form of disgust. You believe you are morally superior of another person; you believe that the person is unworthy of your consideration.

Alternate words: revulsion, dislike, distaste, hatred, abhorrence, objection, loathing, disregard, scorn, aversion

Physical sensations: withdrawal from the object or person, nausea, facial expressions that include narrowing eyebrows, curled upper lip, and wrinkling nose

Stress vs. Shock and Feeling Overwhelmed

Stress, shock, and feeling overwhelmed are all connected to agitation, either from an external event or from an internal struggle.

Stress (healthy): Emotional or mental strain when you are faced with demanding circumstances. The more things you need to deal with, the more stressed you are likely to feel. High levels of stress can lead to feeling overwhelmed. Stress can develop from both good and bad experiences.

Shock and feeling overwhelmed (unhealthy): More intense and negative versions of stress. These signal that you are exhausted and exasperated; you are ready to shut down rather than continue to function.

Alternate words: distress, exasperation, frantic, unease, dismay, dread, strain, tension

Physical sensations: The fight-or flight-response is triggered, causing rapid heartbeat and an increase in adrenalin. When you feel overwhelmed, symptoms increase and can include chest pain, nausea, and dizziness.

IMAGINE THAT

Stress can lead to unhealthy eating habits. According to a survey completed in 2012 by the American Psychiatric Association, almost 30 percent of people skip meals and almost 40 percent overeat or eat unhealthy food as a way to combat stress.

Envy vs. Jealousy

Both envy and jealousy involve believing you deserve something.

Envy (healthy): You want something that someone else has although you don't necessarily want the other person to not have it. With envy, you may be motivated to obtain this thing or something similar for yourself.

Jealousy (unhealthy): The fear that someone else will take something (or someone) you perceive as yours. It is the fear of losing something.

Alternate words: covet, green-eyed monster, resentment, rivalry, lusting

Physical sensations: feelings of unhappiness, tightening of jaw and mouth, pain the pit of the stomach. Feelings of jealousy can include those of anxiety, such as racing heart. You may also feel a lump in your throat and breathlessness.

Your Turn: Discover Underlying Attitudes

Over the next three days, write down four events of the day. They can be as simple as going to work, cooking dinner, calling your mother, interacting with friends or co-workers, studying for an exam, or going on a trip.

Complete this exercise as soon after the event as possible. If you don't have time and are completing it at the end of the day, visualize what happened and replay the details of the event in your mind. Think about and feel the emotion that you felt as the situation happened. Imagine how your body felt and what you were thinking for clues to help the process.

Next to each event, write your emotion, using the descriptive words on the list of emotions to guide you. Rate the intensity of the emotion on a scale of 1 to 10, with 10 being the most intense and 1 being the least. After three days, go back and see if there are one or two emotions you are experiencing more often than others.

You may be surprised at the results. For example, you may not think of yourself as an angry person, but after looking over your list, you realize that nearly half of the emotions you felt were related to anger or frustration. While this doesn't mean you are an angry person or that you spend most of your day feeling angry, you can now address that you are feeling this emotion so often. The evidence shows your underlying attitude is to feel anger when things don't go your way.

If you are having difficulty completing this exercise, you can also track your emotions the opposite way. Divide a paper into seven columns. Write down the main categories:

- Anxiety/Nervousness
- Anger
- Sadness/Depression
- Embarrassment/Guilt
- Disgust/Contempt
- Stress
- Envy/Jealousy

Each time you notice an emotion over the next several days, write down a brief description of the situation and a word that best describes how you are feeling.

As you continue, you may notice that you are experiencing certain emotions more than others.

STOP AND THINK

If you rate your emotions higher than a five, you may be too worked up to manage your emotions in a healthy way. If so, complete an ABCD worksheet to challenge your perspective and come up with coping thoughts. If you still can't calm down, try talking to a close friend, relative, or therapist to help you cool off.

Rating your emotions helps sort out what areas you should focus on. This might not be the area you originally thought needed the most work. For example, you may begin CBT wanting to work on anger, but after tracking your emotions and giving each a rating, you may find that you are experiencing sadness more often. This would be your primary issue and as you change your thinking process behind your depression or sadness, the anger issues may disappear as well.

Mixed Emotions

Emotions are not always straightforward. Sometimes you have mixed emotions: two competing sets of thoughts and emotions about the same situation. Let's say you have been dating someone for a few months. Despite the fact that the two of you get along well and have fun together, you each want different things out of the relationship. While you want to get married, the other person is looking for a more casual relationship. After spending time together, you feel attached, accepted, and perhaps loved, but at the same time you feel rejected, sad, and frustrated that this person does not want the same things. You end the relationship, knowing it's the best thing for you in the long run. However, you still feel upset and lonely. You miss spending time with a person who had become important to you. In this situation, you have mixed emotions: sadness and love.

Behind the emotions, you also have mixed thoughts. You might be thinking:

- This relationship will never be what I want it to be, but I miss him.

- There is someone else I find attractive, but I still want to be with my ex.

These mixed thoughts can be confusing, but they are not unhealthy.

An unhealthy reaction would be to intertwine thoughts and emotions. For example, you might think:

- This person doesn't care about me. (overgeneralization, mind reading)

- This person is an uncaring jerk. (personalization)

- This is evidence that I will never get married. (overgeneralization)

- Things will never work out for me. (black-and-white thinking)

The next time you feel mixed up and confused about a problem, stop and write all the emotions you are feeling and the thoughts connected to each one. This will help you reflect on all your emotions and gain a reasonable perspective that encourages acceptance, plus provide the ability to cope with reality, and allows you to move on.

GIVE IT A TRY

When dealing with an array of negative emotions, take a few minutes to bring yourself back to the present moment. Many negative emotions deal with the past or the future. Dealing with the present moment only makes managing your mixture of emotions easier.

Managing Feelings about Feelings

Sometimes you have feelings about feelings, called meta-emotions. For example, you may be angry at your child for breaking curfew. At the same time, you feel guilty for being angry. You think being angry is wrong. This guilt is a secondary, or meta, feeling. At times the secondary emotion can be so strong it masks the original emotion and makes it more difficult to sort out how you are feeling. It stops you from actively dealing with the primary, or first, emotion you felt.

Meta-emotions are like a "double whammy." Not only do you put off dealing with the primary emotion, you now must deal with the secondary emotion—your feeling about your feeling. Some people grew up believing they should hide their emotions, that large displays of emotion were wrong. If this is the case, when you have strong emotions, you tell yourself it is wrong and try to squelch the emotion. Or, you may be afraid of the primary emotion, worried that you just can't deal with it. When naming and evaluating your emotions, it is important to first identify any meta-emotions and correctly deal with that first.

Your Turn: Create an Emotion Contract

Write down three situations that recently happened where you felt emotional. Write down the emotion you felt and rate each one on a scale of 0 to 100. Include any actions you wanted to take because of your emotions. For example:

Situation 1: My husband forgot to make the mortgage payment. Anger (70/100). I want to yell at him and tell him how stupid and careless he is.

Situation 2: My sister called to tell me that she can't go on vacation with me. Annoyance (50/100). I want to disinvite her to my birthday dinner to show her how it feels to be unreliable.

Does the incident or situation coincide with your level of emotion? Did the intensity of your emotion or what you wanted to do signal that you overreacted? If so, you may be feeling your emotions without thinking about and challenging the negative thought processes behind your feelings.

Create an emotion contract that states for the next week, you will not give in to emotions without thinking about the thoughts behind the emotion. You will keep a thought log and complete an ABCD chart before letting the emotion fester. Sign and date your contract.

As you complete your ABCD log, come up with a new and healthier way of coping. Using the previous examples, you might come up with the following:

Situation 1: Frustration (40/100). Maybe my husband is feeling overwhelmed. Instead of yelling at him, perhaps I should approach him about working together on the household bills.

Situation 2: Stress and Annoyance (30/100). I now have to plan another trip or find someone else to go with me. I will still invite her to my party, but in the future, I won't plan activities that rely on her solely.

The Emotional Process

Your emotions affect you in many different ways. The emotional process involves cognitive, physical, and behavioral reactions. When you understand how these reactions interact, it becomes easy to break the cycle.

You can make changes anywhere in the cycle in order to create positive change. For example, if you are dealing with sadness and mild depression, you may have the following reactions.

Cognitive: You have difficulty focusing or paying attention.

Physical: You have difficulty sleeping or sleep too much.

Behavioral: You avoid going out with friends or stay in bed all day.

Suppose you wake up thinking, "My life isn't any good. I don't even want to get out of bed today." Staying in bed will probably make you feel worse. You might lie in bed, thinking about all the reasons you shouldn't get up and go to work. You may ruminate about everything bad in your life. Later, you feel guilty for not going to work and feel even worse. By the end of the day, your depression has deepened.

Now, suppose that you wake up thinking, "My life isn't any good. I don't even want to get out of bed today, but I know it is best to get up and do something." And so, you do. You get up, you shower, get dressed, have breakfast, and go for a walk. You start to feel better. By changing your behavior you have changed your emotional state. You broke the cycle by changing one area of reactions. Once you did that, it became much easier to change your thoughts and look at the positive in your life.

Cognitive Reactions

In Chapter 2, you learned about the different problematic thinking processes. When you have an unhelpful emotional reaction, it may be because you're using one of these thinking processes.

Black-and-white thinking commonly leads to depression and anger.

- You think, "If this person was my friend, he or she would not treat me this way."

- You believe that you are either a failure or success.

Personalization commonly leads to guilt and anxiety.

- You feel guilty about forgetting to meet your husband for lunch and leaving him sitting alone in the restaurant.

- You forget about plans you made with a friend and spend the afternoon worried that she will be upset with you.

Overgeneralizing leads to depression and anger.

- You think, "Nothing works out for me. This mistake is going to follow me for the rest of my life."

- You think, "He is always treating me this way."

Ignoring the positive can lead to stress and worry.

- You think, "I have so much to do. I will never get it done."

- You think, "I am having a bad day today. I am going to get fired."

Mind reading leads to anxiety and embarrassment.

- You think, "This person does not like me."

- You think, "I can't believe I did that. Everyone will think I am stupid."

Catastrophizing and **fortune-telling** lead to anxiety, worry, and depression.

- You think, "I know this situation will end badly."

- You feel there is nothing you can do to change the outcome of events.

CBTIDBIT

People who focus on the actions of others often feel angry. Those who focus on their own actions may feel anxious or guilty. If you do one more than the other, it is helpful to stop and focus on the opposite point of view.

Physical Reactions

Emotions don't just live in your mind. Research has shown that people feel emotions in their body, too. For example when you feel nervous, you feel "butterflies in your stomach." The basic emotions—anger, fear, disgust, happiness, sadness, and surprise—are associated with bodily sensations and reactions in the upper chest, such as heart rate and breathing. Other physical manifestations of emotions include specific facial expressions and changes in the brain triggered by emotional reactions.

More complex emotions include anxiety, love, depression, contempt, pride, and shame. These are often felt more deeply in the body. The sensations include regions such as the legs, hands, heart, and head.

Review the list of emotions and the corresponding physical sensations at the start of the chapter and take note of the ones you feel regularly. Paying attention to your physical reactions and sensations helps you consciously connect to your emotions and sort out whether your reactions and associated thought processes are helpful or unhelpful. When you experience helpful and healthy emotions, the associated physical reactions help you react swiftly to dangers and take advantage of important opportunities. Consider the following scenarios.

Scenario 1: You're walking along a city street alone in an unfamiliar area and your directions take you down an alley. Your muscles tense, your heartbeat speeds up; your body is on high alert. This is your body's way of telling you to be careful.

Scenario 2: You are asked to give a presentation at work. You feel nervous, your mind feels more focused, and your adrenaline helps you prepare for the presentation and remain focused during the talk.

CBTIDBIT

When writing in your emotional chart, include information on your body's reaction. This helps you in the future to use your body language as clues to what you are feeling and thinking.

While mild physical sensations of your emotions can be helpful, more pronounced physical sensations might interfere with healthy behaviors and reactions. Think back to giving a presentation at work. Instead of feeling mildly nervous, you feel very anxious. Your heart is beating rapidly and your breathing becomes fast and shallow. You feel tightness in your chest, shakiness in your hands, and pins and needles in your legs. The more intense your physical reaction, the more you tell yourself the presentation is going to be terrible and the more you want to avoid it. In a nutshell, the emotions and physical sensation are too intense. Rather than helping you take advantage of the opportunity, they end up contributing to your failure.

By paying attention to physical sensations in your body, you are better able to connect to your emotions and thoughts. For example, you if you pay attention to the butterflies in your stomach as soon as they happen, you are able to recognize that you're nervous and accept it. You can look at your thought processes, which might include, "I am going to bomb this presentation." Instead of giving in to the thoughts and building body sensations, you can use the ABC technique to challenge your thinking.

Your Turn: Where Do You Feel the Emotion?

Use colored pencils or markers to fill the body to show where you feel physical sensations during emotions.

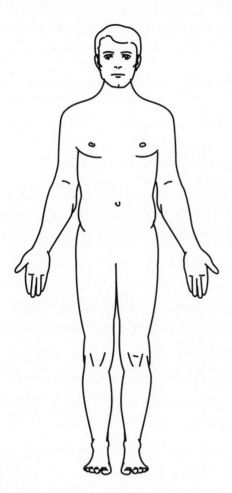

- Yellow: Highest level of sensation

- Blue: Lowest level of sensation

- Green: Mild level of sensation

- Leave areas of no sensation blank.

We store emotions in our body. The more you understand how your emotions feel in your body, the better you become at reading your body language and interpreting your emotions. This exercise also helps you to release the intense emotions through physical exercise or relaxation techniques. For example, anger in the body usually shows up in your hands and you unconsciously make a fist. Recognizing this can help you to counteract the anger by relaxing your hands.

Behavioral Reactions

Your behavior also gives clues as to whether what you are feeling and thinking is helpful or unhelpful. In general, helpful behaviors are those that are constructive and unhelpful behaviors are those that are self-destructive. Obvious self-destructive behaviors include substance abuse and self-harming behaviors, but there are other non-helpful behaviors, too. These include the following:

- Telling someone off or confronting someone without learning the facts of a situation.

- Avoiding a situation or escaping from a situation, such as running out of a meeting or not getting on a plane.

- Not doing anything—not taking care of hygiene, not doing pleasurable things, and with-holding self-rewards.

Instead of giving in to these behaviors, use your emotion contract and add a new, positive action you will perform over the next month. For example:

- Before you confront someone you will go for a 10-minute walk. Then you will ask for information and start a discussion rather than jumping to conclusions and reacting angrily.

- If you anticipate a stressful situation, you will give yourself 20 minutes to relax and prepare. For situations that are prolonged, you will participate for just 20 minutes at first and then add 10 minutes at a time until you are comfortable.

- Instead of giving in to your depression, you will create a schedule that includes activities you enjoy. Sign up for an activity that you can't miss.

Changing your behavior, even slightly, can change your perspective and reduce the negative emotion.

Learning Emotions

Emotions are sometimes triggered through associations and learned reactions known as *conditioning.* For example, suppose you always took your exams in school in a blue room. During the exams, you often felt nervous. Perhaps you had a negative experience, such as failing an oral exam in front of your classmates. Now, as an adult, whenever you sit in a blue room for a meeting, you automatically feel a change in your heart rate, breathing, and muscle tension. Initially, you might connect this with being scared. But the longer you remain in the situation, the more your emotions build. You have fearful thoughts about the meeting and a strong desire to get out of the meeting as soon as possible. The longer you stay in meeting, the more noticeable your thoughts might become. You might think "I don't want to attend those meetings; I always feel uncomfortable. I'm always waiting for something bad to happen." You may or may not be aware that the meetings have anything to do with the room being blue.

> **DEFINITION**
>
> **Conditioning** happens when your brain and body learn to associate an emotion with a set of situations or stimuli. The body sensations become connected to the stimuli or situation, which then triggers the emotion.

Because you may not remember or be aware of the association between your feelings and certain situations, it is sometimes hard to know whether the emotion was learned. Some fears that are frequently a result of conditioning include the following:

- Phobias such claustrophobia, travel anxiety, heights, needles

- Social anxiety

- Depression associated with traumas

- Public speaking

If you are experiencing feelings due to conditioning from past experience, this statement might apply to you "I often feel this way when I'm in in this type of setting. I know I'm not in danger, but I cannot help but feel this way." To determine if your emotions are associated with past experiences, complete the emotion chart from the previous exercises. Write down the date, time, and what you felt. Add facts about your situation, such as where you are, what you are doing, and who is with you. These variables help you find common situations or variables to give you clues about past experiences.

You might write down:

Monday, December 16, 2013. Conference room meeting. I felt very nervous, my hands were shaking and I had an urge to escape. I became sensitive to any critique of my work. Ten people were present; one person in charge who was doing the most talking. The chairs were comfortable; there were windows in the room and blue paint on walls.

Once you write down the details, ask yourself...

1. What was I thinking once the emotion started?

2. Are these thoughts relevant here?

3. Are there negative thoughts about the present situation I can challenge?

Your answers to these questions might give you clues to where your nervousness and fear came from. For example, you might have answered...

1. "When I am in the conference room, I think my boss is going to yell at me and give me a bad report. I don't want to ask any questions or offer any advice."

2. "I know this is not really going to happen and that I am reacting emotionally because I feel anxious. My boss has not yelled at me during a conference before and I have no reason to think he is going to this time."

3. "I can calm down in the conferences because I know that I have been asked to join the meeting. I am a valuable member of the team and have information to share."

You can now look back to see if there were similar situations in your past. What does this situation remind you of? "When I was in junior high, I remember that I took my exams in a small blue room. The teachers walked around the room making me nervous. They openly criticized me. I remember feeling like I wanted to run away and I skipped school sometimes on those days."

If you think you may be dealing with a conditioned emotional response, one way to handle it is through exposure techniques. This method slowly introduces you to a fearful situation until you no longer feel nervousness or anxiety and is covered in detail in Chapter 17.

The Least You Need to Know

- To help manage your emotions, identify and challenge the negative thoughts behind them.
- You can experience more than one emotion at a time.
- Changing your behavior may change how you feel about a situation.
- Paying attention physical sensations can help you identify your feelings.

CBT Techniques

CBT isn't just one simple strategy, it is a combination of different techniques that help you think, feel, and act in helpful and constructive ways. In this part, you learn about many of the techniques you need to put CBT into practice in your life.

Imagery, relaxation techniques, meditation, and mindfulness all help you challenge, test, and change your automatic thoughts and images that cause distress. The different exercises in this section help you practice the strategies so you can use them in many different situations.

CHAPTER 5

Setting Goals for Getting Better

When you picked up this book, what did you have in mind? Do you know what you want to change? You might have depression, anxiety, or anger issues and want to work directly on those. You might have a bad habit of smoking or eating too much. You might not be sure what is going on and feel overwhelmed by situations in your life.

Whatever the case, you know something needs to change. You might not know where you want to end up, but you know you want to feel better. This chapter is about getting from where you are to feeling better. You'll learn how to set goals and how to develop a plan of action.

In This Chapter

- Breaking down a goal into manageable steps
- Using goals to help achieve desired behaviors
- Thinking about pros and cons when making choices
- Committing to change

Setting Goals

Before you can work on improving specific areas of your life, you need to have a goal. Goals should be specific, measurable, and achievable. They should have a time limit and should be stated as positive action—what you want to do rather than what you don't want to do.

STOP AND THINK

You can create goals based on how you want to behave or how you want to feel. When creating goals about feelings, focus on having positive emotions such as happiness, hopefulness, and pride. If you currently experience strong negative emotions, aim toward a less intense reaction: for example, moving from rage to annoyance.

Let's walk through the process of determining and setting a goal with an example. When you created your emotion log, you might have noticed that you become angry easily. You noticed that whenever someone corrects you or gives you feedback you view as negative, you react defensively. Your emotion log might look like this:

A: Activating Event	B: Belief or Thoughts	C: Consequences or Emotions
My boss pointed out some mistakes in my work.	He never liked me anyway. He tries to find mistakes.	Became irritated Snapped at coworkers even though I was mad at my boss
My sister said she liked my hair better the way I had it cut before.	She never says anything nice. I can't do anything right.	Felt insulted Was angry all through lunch Was irritated with the waiter
I spent extra time getting ready and my boyfriend didn't say I looked nice.	He doesn't care. He is selfish and only cares about himself.	Had a fight with my boyfriend Ignored friends who were out with us

As you look over your chart, you see that whenever someone gives you feedback, you feel it is criticism and become angry and irritated. You want to change how you react when other people give you feedback. Because you want your goal to be specific, ask yourself:

- How do I want feel during these encounters?

- How do I want to come across? Open or closed? Flexible or rigid?

- How would I like to behave during these encounters?

- If I'd had a different reaction, how would I see the situation going?

- If I did not get upset so easily, what parts of my life would be improved?

CBTIDBIT

When choosing initial goals, think about which behaviors have the most negative impact on your life and which are most likely to impact other problem behaviors. If you change the first behavior in a chain of behaviors, making one change can result in modifying several behaviors.

Decide how you want to feel and act in this type of situation. You might say:

"I want to feel confident that I can handle feedback from other people. I want to act in a pleasant manner to the people around me."

Using the list in Chapter 2, think about which problematic thought processes you are using. In this example, you are ignoring the positive.

Now you're ready to create a goal:

"When someone criticizes me or gives me feedback, I will first thank them for their feedback. I will then later decide if their feedback is relevant."

You can also create a coping statement, one that you can turn to whenever you begin to feel irritated because someone is giving you feedback. Your coping statement might be:

"It is not a reflection of me as a person. I get plenty of positive feedback."

If you're having a difficult time determining your goals, imagine how your goal would look. Try to put that image into words. What would it look like to be less angry or less depressed? What would it look like to be happy? How would you feel about yourself? How would you relate differently to the people around you? What would you be thinking about?

STOP AND THINK

If you are having trouble reaching your goals, it might be because your current goals are too general. Try being more specific or break down your goals into smaller goals and take one step at a time.

Your Turn: Ladder Rungs

When creating goals, it's easy to be too ambitious. You're eager to make changes in your life and want jump right to the end result. However, unless you create the steps necessary to get there, it will be hard to meet your goal.

In the previous example, your goal was, "When someone criticizes me or gives me feedback, I will first thank them for their feedback. I will then later decide if their feedback is relevant." This is your end result goal, but isn't necessarily where you need to start.

Goals work best when you create a series of steps, with each step moving you closer to the end result. Think of these steps like rungs on a ladder: you must step on each one before moving on to the next. Begin with the most negative extremes. Think about your past actions, list times you reacted poorly to other's feedback. What was your worst reaction? This is your starting point—the first rung on your ladder.

> **CBTIDBIT**
>
> Limit your goals to improving one behavior at a time. You want to focus on one key behavior, such as quitting smoking or losing 10 pounds, rather than monitoring all of the different elements of your health at the same time. Once you accomplish one goal, you can move on to focus on a different area.

Continue to list more moderate behaviors, working your way toward your desired behavior. Each of these reactions becomes a rung on the ladder. Each becomes a goal. The ladder of goals helps you monitor your progress and helps you feel a sense of accomplishment as you move up the rungs.

Define Your Motivation

Everyone knows that change isn't easy. Even when the results are negative, you might fall back to what is comfortable or remain stuck in old habits. When this happens, don't become discouraged. With focus, determination, and the right goals, you can achieve the results you seek.

Suppose you suffer from panic attacks. You dread the dizzy, nauseous, fear-filled feeling when you are in a crowd, so you avoid them. You avoid going in to the city, don't eat in restaurants, and don't go to the mall.

This strategy has paid off—as long as you stay home or go to only selected activities, you avoid the unpleasant feeling of having a panic attack. But this strategy is limiting your life. Your friends enjoy going out for an evening in the city while you stay home. You limit where you work to small companies with only a few employees. You have chosen to compromise your lifestyle in order to avoid having a panic attack.

Think about what your life would be like if you didn't worry about having a panic attack. Where would you go? What type of work would you do? Create an image of what you want. This is your end goal. This is the top rung of your ladder. It is also the beginning of developing motivation to change. The more you develop this image, the more you want to achieve it.

> **GIVE IT A TRY**
>
> Think about broad goals, such as family, relationships, or work. Write down three issues you want to work on and list the pros and cons of working on each goal.

Weighing the Pros and Cons

Without realizing it, you have weighed the costs and the benefits of going to certain places and determined that the cost (a panic attack) is more than you are willing to pay, no matter what the benefit. To change your thoughts, you need to reevaluate the costs and benefits.

A cost-benefit analysis is a tool for weighing the pros and cons of making a change. To get a complete picture, you might want to do two cost-benefit analyses, one for continuing your present behavior and one for changing. Using our previous example, the cost-benefit analysis for using CBT to overcome panic attacks might look like this:

Pros

- I will learn to go out in public without having a panic attack.

- I can try new restaurants.

- I can join my friends when they go out to the city.

- I can look for a better-paying job.

- I can look for a job I like better.

Cons

- I will have to face having a panic attack.

- I will have to face my fears and start going out.

- It will be scary and uncomfortable.

You can use a cost-benefit analysis to show the benefits and disadvantages of just about any decision. It may also help to break down your big decisions into smaller decisions. For example, if you have a panic disorder and it's too overwhelming to think about changing all of your social habits, you might look at changing just one. Imagine you have been avoiding work because of your disorder. Think about the pros and cons of changing just that behavior.

Pros of Staying Home from Work

- I can relax at home.

- I don't need to worry about having a panic attack at work.

- Other people won't think I am crazy.

- I don't need to worry about going out of the house.

Cons of Staying Home from Work

- I like having an income and feeling independent.

- I enjoy seeing my co-workers.

- I enjoy the freedom of being out of the house.

- Going to work gives me opportunities like trying new restaurants or meeting friends after work.

IMAGINE THAT

Cost-benefit analysis can be used in many areas of your life, including behaviors, emotions, thoughts, beliefs, and problem solving. You can modify your analysis to look at short-term or long-term solutions. It works best if you write statements in pairs: What is an advantage of making a change? How would that translate to a disadvantage of *not* making the change?

Be sure to list all of the pros and cons that come to mind. With the cost-benefit analysis, you easily see both sides of an argument and are able to make an informed and rational decision.

Positive vs. Negative Motivation

There are two types of motivation: positive and negative. Positive motivation tends to be more successful because you are working toward something pleasurable. Negative motivation is doing something to avoid pain.

Imagine two people: one goes to work because he doesn't want to get fired and risk losing his home. Another person has the same job and although he doesn't want to get fired, he goes to work because he wants to feel a sense of pride, independence, and financial stability. The first is negatively motivated; the second is motivated in a positive way.

Negative motivation works but rarely leaves you with a sense of satisfaction and well-being. Positive motivation provides an inner force, a reason to keep going. It is looking at what you want rather than what you don't want. Consider your reason for wanting to change; is it framed in a positive or negative way? Sometimes it is a matter of changing the wording:

Negative: I want to change because I don't want to be left behind when my friends go out.

Positive: I want to change because I enjoy spending time with my friends.

Although the statements are similar, notice how one is framed around avoiding a situation (being left behind) while the other is framed around an enjoyable outcome (spending time with my friends.) Your goals, or rewards, can be tangible—a new car—or intangible—enjoyment, respect, happiness. When creating goals, ask yourself, "What do I have to gain?" rather than, "What am I going to lose if I don't do this?"

Your Turn: Create a Cost-Benefit Analysis

Create your own cost-benefit analysis on a current problem you have. Take a piece of paper and fold it in half to create two columns. Label the columns "Costs/Disadvantages" and "Benefits/Advantages." Write down all of the costs and benefits you can think of, no matter how small. Weigh them out against one another to see which option brings the most benefit.

Continue with the cost-benefit, creating one for short-term and long-term pros and cons. Be sure to write the pros as a positive, not as avoiding a negative. This tool is used to determine your personal risk and how both changing, and not changing, impacts your life. Use the positives to help keep you motivated to change.

Your Turn: Create Coping Flash Cards

In a previous exercise, you created a ladder with steps to reach your goal. You are going to focus on one rung of the ladder at a time to keep moving forward to reaching your desired behavior. As you begin to work on each rung, create coping flash cards. These are small cards, such as index cards, that you carry with you to remind you of a positive statement to help you deal with a stressful situation.

To create your coping flash cards, first list every negative thought that may interfere with you completing the goal you are working on. Write one negative thought on each index card. Then turn the card over and write the opposite, positive, and realistic thought to replace the negative thought.

When you notice yourself thinking (or saying) the negative thought, pull out the corresponding card and read the positive alternative you wrote down. Try reading it aloud and repeating it several times.

Maintaining Your Progress

Reaching your goal takes commitment but it doesn't end there. You need to be committed to maintaining the progress you make. This commitment is a promise you make to yourself to make positive changes in your life and to continue using the skills you learn in this book to maintain those changes.

The three levels of commitment:

Mental commitment: A promise you make to yourself. This is the beginning point. Mental commitments alone are easy to break.

Commitment made in writing: A higher level of commitment. When you write a commitment down, you are more likely to keep the promise.

Commitment made by telling others: When you share your goal with at least one other person, you strengthen your resolve to keep your commitment. When sharing your goals, be sure it is someone who will provide positive support and encouragement.

In the beginning, you might not feel comfortable sharing your goals with someone else. You should at least write down your commitment and place it somewhere you will see it on a daily basis. This helps reinforce your goal and your motivation to reach the goal.

The Least You Need to Know

- Goals should be specific, measurable, and achievable.
- Positive motivation is more effective than negative motivation.
- Creating a cost-benefit analysis gives you information to make a rational decision.
- When you write down a goal, you are more likely to follow through.

CHAPTER 6

Visualization and Imagery

Visualization and imagery, while not a type of therapy, are often used in CBT. They are two of the most important and powerful tools you can use to make positive changes in your life. Spontaneous images, much like automatic thoughts, can be a result of a distorted thinking. In this chapter, you will learn how to use visualization when handling difficult situations as well as ways to control your mental images.

Using Visualization

You probably use *visualization* every day without even realizing it. Imagine a co-worker invites you to a party. You might automatically picture a scene of the two of you at the bar, holding drinks and chatting. The more you visualize the image, the more details you fill in. You put your own perspective into the details.

In This Chapter

- How to use your imagination to make situations less stressful
- Consciously changing negative images
- Desensitizing yourself to emotional images
- Coping with spontaneous or automatic images

DEFINITION

Visualization is the act of using your imagination to create mental pictures and images. This happens spontaneously or you can consciously choose to create images in your mind.

How you picture the scene depends on your past experiences, your current mood, and your feelings about parties and the host. You might imagine you don't know anyone except the host. You see yourself at the party, standing alone, feeling out of place and nervous. You picture yourself saying something wrong, dropping your plate of food, or spending the evening sitting by yourself while all around you groups of people are laughing and talking. The more details you put in, the sharper the image in your mind becomes—and the more you don't want to go to the party.

Just as you can change your thoughts, you can change the images in your mind. Instead of picturing yourself standing alone or not knowing what to say to anyone at the party, change the images in your mind. Imagine yourself mingling, meeting new people, talking, and being included in conversations. Make the images in your mind as vivid as possible by including all of your senses. Take a deep breath and imagine what you would smell; imagine the feel of a glass in your hand and the sight of a table full of food. The more senses you bring to your images, the more immersed you will become in the new situation. As you add details and imagine yourself having a good time, you may realize you are looking forward to the party.

GIVE IT A TRY

Imagine a television with a remote control to change channels. Picture an event that causes anxiety or distress on one channel. Change the channel and create another, more pleasurable scene. When you feel anxious, remember you can change the channel to view something else.

Whenever you face a difficult situation, create a scene in your mind. Imagine the problem and imagine yourself dealing with the situation. Picture yourself feeling confident. What do you look like? Are you standing up straight, a smile on your face? What are you wearing? Who is with you? What does the room look like? Imagine yourself combating and challenging your negative thoughts. Practicing CBT techniques through visualization makes it easier to use the strategies when you need them.

Facing Emotional Images

There might be times when you have an image in your mind that provokes anxiety, anger, or sadness. You may try to distract yourself to avoid this troubling image. You don't want to see it and not thinking about it makes you feel better—at least in the short term. Unfortunately, this also reinforces your fear of dealing with the image. It keeps you emotionally connected to the image and prevents you from gaining control over it and the situation it represents.

Many people who suffer from anxiety have difficulty with this. Thinking about, visualizing, or imagining a situation that triggers anxiety often produces just as much anxiety as it would if you were physically in the situation. While visualization can help you learn strategies for coping with situations that produce anxiety, if you avoid the images, you can't practice the needed skills.

Desensitization is a method of regularly facing a scene, either in real life or in your mind. Every time you go through the scene, it becomes a little less emotional. Sometimes it may be necessary to imagine a situation many times until you no longer react with negative emotional intensity. Then, go back through it again, employing CBT techniques and learning ways to cope.

> **DEFINITION**
>
> **Desensitization** is the diminished emotional responsiveness to a negative or aversive situation or trigger. It occurs after repeated exposure to the situation or when an emotional response to the trigger is repeatedly evoked and deemed no longer necessary. Desensitization is a process primarily used to help individuals to unlearn phobias and anxieties.

For example, suppose you have a fear of dogs. Closing your eyes and imagining coming face to face with a dog raises your anxiety level. You start shaking and your heart rate increases. The more vividly you create the scene in your mind, the more your anxiety increases. You can begin to desensitize yourself to this image. To start, write down five images to reflect five levels of difficulty beginning with the easiest level progressing to the most difficult. This allows you to slowly face your fear and slowly become desensitized. Using the example of a fear of dogs, your levels may look something like this.

Level 1: Imagine yourself in a room with a dog that is locked in a crate or small dog run.

Level 2: Picture the same scene, this time with the dog on leash where it cannot reach you.

Level 3: Imagine the dog on a leash but he can reach you.

Level 4: Imagine sitting in the room petting the dog.

Level 5: Visualize the dog sitting on your lap

Each time you do the visualization exercise, commit to picturing the same image for 10 minutes. Hold the image in your mind for 10 minutes before allowing your thoughts to move to something else. Use the same image until your fear subsides and the next image provokes moderate anxiety. This keeps you from moving too fast through the levels and lowers the risk of overwhelming yourself emotionally.

If you find any of the images too upsetting than revise the image to make it slightly less intense and save the more intense image for the next rung in your hierarchy. Add as many levels as you need to reach your goal. Remember, each image should evoke only evoke a moderate level of distress.

Reacting to Spontaneous Imagery

Automatic thoughts may sometimes come as pictures and images in your mind. These spontaneous images are usually related to something that makes you feel unsettled, either from your past or your future. They can range from small, upsetting situations to traumatic events. Flashbacks and nightmares are other forms of spontaneous emotions and thoughts. Because automatic or spontaneous images are usually brief and fleeting, you dismiss the picture as quickly as it appears and may not even be conscious of the image you created.

Suppose you have an argument with your boss. You go home and images of the disagreement keep replaying in your mind. You see your boss frowning and scowling at you repeatedly. You imagine him firing you. This image stops you from requesting a raise, even though you believe you deserve one.

Suppose, instead of imagining your boss yelling at you, you now imagine your boss listening to your reasons for deserving a raise and saying yes. Negative images, as with automatic thoughts, can be changed. There are several strategies you can use to help change the pictures in your mind.

 IMAGINE THAT

Guided imagery, the suggestion of a positive image, has been found to be helpful in pain management, but some research shows that working with spontaneous imagery can also help. Pain can trigger negative images and learning to control those images and change them may reduce the emotional difficulties that come along with pain.

Solving Problems

Instead of feeling overwhelmed by a long to-do list, use visualization to solve problems. For example, suppose you are having your in-laws over for dinner. Your husband was called into work and isn't around to help. You have a list of things that need to get done: go shopping, clean the house, prepare the food. You feel overwhelmed. You tell yourself, "I'll never get this all done," "The dinner is going to be a disaster," and "My in-laws will think I am a terrible wife and daughter-in-law." You picture yourself trying to get everything completed, but all you can see is a messy house and a burnt dinner. Throughout the day, you become more and more overwhelmed. By dinnertime, you are irritable and wish your in-laws would just go home.

Your automatic negative thought process throughout the day was "never going to get it done" and "it is going to be a disaster." The pictures in your mind reflected these thoughts. You went through the day believing these thoughts and images and, even though the dinner did get done, you didn't enjoy it and just wanted it to be over.

Try changing the images to help you solve problems. Picture what you are going to do each time a problem comes up. How are you going to solve it? What are you going to do? Instead of picturing yourself frazzled, imagine yourself working through each step. For example, instead of imagining your in-laws showing up an hour early while your kitchen is still disheveled, imagine them showing up an hour early while you stay calm, and offer them a drink and ask your children to entertain them while you finish preparing the dinner.

Testing Your Image

Sometimes, you base images on your imagination, not reality. For example, if you are an experienced cook, imagining a burnt dinner is not realistic. Likewise, if your in-laws have always been kind and understanding, imagining them being judgmental is not realistic. You can test your images to find out if there is any evidence to back up the image. You might ask yourself:

- Have I ever thrown a dinner party before that ended in a total disaster?

- Based on past dinner parties, is there any evidence to indicate I can't cook this dinner?

- Have my in-laws ever treated me disrespectfully?

- Have there been times in the past when I have burnt dinner?

Once you look at the situation more realistically, you determine that your images are out of line with the situation. You change the images to fit what is really happening.

> **GIVE IT A TRY**
>
> Visualize yourself doing something you think is going to turn out badly. Now visualize a positive outcome. Go out and try the task and see if your positive image comes true. For example, imagine you would like to ask a new co-worker to lunch but are concerned she will turn you down. Imagine the scene playing out in a positive way. Imagine the person saying yes; imagine the person saying no but in a respectful manner. Now go test it.

Changing the Image

Since you create the images, you also have the ability to change them. Images that cause distress are usually those that are exaggerated and not based on the reality of the situation. Take a step back to examine the images you have created and decide how you can change them to more closely reflect what is going on around you.

Your thoughts come in a combination of words and pictures. The most highly-charged memories come in the form of images. When you remember the event, you also remember and experience the emotions all over again. Image rescripting is a way of changing the painful memory, providing a positive and empowering ending. This type of process breaks the negative emotional connection to the previous event.

There are three steps to the process of rescripting:

Step 1: Relive the event. You need to relive the event and the accompanying emotions.

Step 2: Focus on a different ending. Don't change the event itself, but extend the image of the event to include your present or future. For example, if you were yelled at a lot a child but are now an adult, don't just visualize your parents yelling at you. Instead, add to the image and picture yourself leaving home and moving to a safe environment. If this has not happened yet, then visualize yourself leaving one day and securing a safe home.

Step 3: Nurture yourself, but yourself at the age of the traumatic event. For example, if you suffered an abusive event when you were eight years old, you would nurture the eight-year-old child, not the person you are today. To do this, ask yourself what words of reassurance you would have wanted to hear at that age. What information would have made you feel better at the time? For example, "I know one day I will grow up and have a loving family and a happy home. I am a lovable person. The way my parents treat me is not a reflection of my worth."

Twice a day for a week, imagine the extended ending and nurture yourself. Once you have completed the three steps as well as the daily practice sessions, the negative emotions will start to alleviate themselves and no longer be associated as intensely with the event.

> **STOP AND THINK**
>
> The first step of image rescripting is often emotionally painful. It is recommended you work with a therapist or a trusted relative or friend when completing the this process if you are trying to change a particularly traumatic or painful memory.

Changing the Focus

Rather than changing the entire image, you can choose to change the direction of the image. When you are upset, you usually see the situation from only one perspective. For example, if you're concerned about going to a party where you don't know anyone, you probably see either yourself or the faces of others. You might see yourself standing alone and appearing lost, or you might mostly visualize other people across the room talking and laughing while ignoring you. You see things in one direction.

This strategy involves changing your image to look at it from both sides, making both images positive. Using the image of going to a party, imagine other people being receptive and smiling. Imaging yourself walking over to join the conversation.

Completing the Story

As with automatic thoughts, when you are upset, angry, sad, or anxious, you probably stop your image at the worst moment. For example, suppose it is your first day at a new job. You are nervous and you imagine yourself making mistakes. You imagine your new co-workers ignoring you. You imagine your new boss being mean. Then you stop. You carry this negative picture with you as you walk through the door in the morning. This image fuels your insecurities.

> **CBTIDBIT**
>
> Visualization is most effective when you practice it on a regular basis. Take ten minutes each morning to sit quietly and visualize your day. As you practice, you will find it easier to change or adjust your images to fit your goals.

Spontaneous images are often fleeting. They flash before your eyes and then are gone. When these images are negative, they may leave you feeling sad, angry, or depressed: whatever emotion is tied to the image. However, you can make a conscious effort to finish the image—to complete the story and give it a happy ending.

Imagine again it is your first day at a new job. You are introduced to your new boss, who is brusque and sounds angry. You find out that there has been a major mistake made the day before and your new boss is in the process of trying to fix the error. His mood has nothing to do with you. Later, after the mistake is corrected, he apologizes and sits down to teach you the job. He is very patient explaining your duties. It is similar to your previous job and you are sure you will be able to handle the work. Your co-workers are hesitant in the beginning. They aren't sure what to expect from you, but a few ask you to join them at lunch. You enjoy the lunch and are glad to get to know a few of the people you will be working with.

Once you complete the story, you don't feel as nervous. Instead of getting ready for work with flashes of the worst possible outcome, you focus on the finished story, making it a positive experience. You now enter the doors to your new job with confidence and a sense that everything is going to work out fine.

Floating Forward

Often negative images keep you from taking positive action and lead to chronic avoidance. Suppose you want to want to ask your boss for a raise but are fearful he will reject you, so you avoid it. Now imagine yourself one year, five years and ten years from now at the same job, never asking for a raise. Imagine how you feel, picture your living situation, and think about your bills pilling up. This feels pretty awful. While the idea of asking for a raise may still make you nervous, the thought of not asking for a raise seems unbearable. Your negative feelings about not asking for a raise outweigh the negative feelings about asking for a raise.

Your Turn: Creating Your Own Imagery

You can use imagery to prepare yourself for an upcoming stressful situation and desensitize yourself to the pain to better cope. For example, suppose your employer has laid off some of your co-workers. You were told additional layoffs are coming. You know there is a chance you will be next. Visualize the scene when your boss tells you. Repeat the image until you feel less emotional about it. If you do this for several days, when it does happen, you will be better able to cope.

Practice by thinking about an upcoming situation causing you concern. It could relate to your job, your personal life, or a relationship. Create an image of the situation with as much detail as possible. Recall this image several times a day to help you let go of the intense emotion surrounding it. That way, you can approach the situation calmly.

> **IMAGINE THAT**
>
> Even famous athletes use visualization. It not only improves performance but helps relieve fear and anxiety. Athletes such as Michael Jordan, Larry Bird, Tiger Woods, and Roy Halladay have all stated that visualization has helped them perform their best.

Create Coping Skills

Besides using visualization to cope with your current situations, you can use imagery to learn and practice coping skills. This strategy actually combines several different CBT techniques. As with all visualization techniques, you start by creating an image of an action you plan to do. Then, break down the scene to practice each part. This type of technique is good for complex situations such as job interviews or social interactions.

For example, suppose you want to ask your boss for a raise but he is always busy and you aren't sure when it would be a good time to approach him. Now imagine yourself sending him an email asking him to join you for coffee this week. Imagine asking for a raise and having him reply, "Why do you deserve a raise?" Normally, you would become quiet and not assert your needs, but instead, you see yourself acting confident and being assertive by stating your most recent accomplishments at work. You imagine your boss saying he will think about giving you a raise without any indication of when this might happen. This uncertainty makes you feel anxious, so you ask your boss for a follow-up meeting. Imagine your boss says no to your request but instead of feeling defeated and worthless, you now imagine yourself feeling positive emotions of pride and telling yourself "At least he knows I consider myself valuable and has a better idea of my contributions."

Using overly dramatic or exaggerated visualizations can help. Think of a play you have seen; the actors might have exaggerated certain lines in order to make a point. This uses the same concept. You are going to be overly dramatic in your visualizations to emphasize certain behaviors or feelings. Suppose you are going on a job interview and are extremely nervous. You want to give a good impression and convey that you are well-spoken, attentive, and inquisitive. In this type of visualization, you focus on each element individually. First, visualize the interview, focusing on being well-spoken. Imagine yourself as extremely articulate, well beyond the level you need to achieve your goal. Continue this visualization until you are comfortable with the image. Next, work on a different aspect of the interview, such as being attentive. Be overly attentive in your visualization, paying attention to every word and gesture. Continue going through each aspect until you have visualized all of the different parts. Lastly, combine them to create one overly dramatic visualization. This type of visualization helps you break down an overwhelming situation into small parts and practice each part separately.

Visualization can also be used in conjunction with other CBT techniques. For example, if you feel nervous about getting a flu shot, you could use visualization along with the deep breathing exercises described in Chapter 7 to prepare for the shot and manage your anxiety. You might also use visualization when rewriting your inner narration as explained in Chapter 9 or when revising perfectionistic behavior as described in Chapter 12.

Your Turn: Keynote Behavior Visualizations

A keynote behavior is a defining behavior that changes your entire perception and experience in one main action. It is an action that culminates your feelings about a situation. For example, if you are afraid of riding the subway, it may be stepping on the subway train and having the doors close behind you. This is your keynote behavior.

> ☞ **CBTIDBIT**
>
> Many people believe they can't visualize. If you have a difficult time creating images, try this: hold an orange in your hand and look at it for 10 seconds. Close your eyes and try to imagine the orange. Continue until you can bring up a picture of it in your mind. Put the orange away and try to picture it again. Now try to visualize other objects. Continue to practice until you are able to create pictures and scenes.

Visualization is useful in these types of situations. Once you change that one behavior, your perception is changed and further actions change as well. When using visualization to change a keynote behavior, you repeatedly visualize successfully changing that one thing that is most troublesome. In the example of the subway, you would visualize stepping onto the train and the doors closing behind you at least 10 minutes each day and intermittently through the day. Continue for 30 days. To make this process complete, practice completing the action in real life at least two times. While doing so, recall your visualization, reminding yourself that you can do it. As you continue to practice, it will become a habit and you will find that you no longer need to remind yourself that you can do it.

This technique can also be helpful in situations such as...

- Petting a dog.

- Giving your host a hug.

- Confidently shaking hands with an interviewer.

- Initiating a conversation with someone who intimidates you.

The Least You Need to Know

- Visualization is a powerful tool to help you change your perspective.
- You can change the images in your mind, just as you can change your thoughts.
- Visualization can be used to desensitize you to fearful situations.
- Visualization can be used in conjunction with other CBT techniques.

Relaxation Techniques and Strategies

In today's world, stress is inevitable. We spend our days hurrying from one place to another. Our lives are filled with work, family, school, and responsibilities at home. We barely have time to relax. This hurried and stressful lifestyle takes a toll on us, both emotionally and physically. High levels of stress contribute to high blood pressure, heart disease, and digestive issues. Emotional stress manifests as irritability and anxiousness and can lead to anxiety disorders, anger problems, and depression. One part of managing stress is to learn relaxation techniques you can employ in your everyday life. In this chapter, we will talk about meditation and breathing techniques.

In This Chapter

- How breathing properly can help you manage everyday stress and anxiety
- Using meditation to focus the mind and improve health
- Relaxation techniques to reduce tension in your body
- How lifestyle changes can improve your outlook and overall health

The Importance of Breathing

We all breathe—in and out, all day, every day. Breathing supplies our bodies with oxygen and rids it of toxins. No matter how you breathe, you are obviously getting enough oxygen to sustain life, but often, we don't breathe properly. How you breathe affects your health, emotionally and physically. When you take in the right amount of oxygen, you give your body energy, increased focus, and feelings of relaxation and calmness. When you exhale properly, you rid your body of harmful toxins and carbon dioxide, making room for oxygen in the blood.

Proper breathing means breathing both into your chest area (allowing your ribs to get involved) and lower abdominal area (allowing your lower diaphragm to expand and contract). Both lower abdominal area and chest area should expand when you inhale and contract on the exhale.

There are several common ways in which people breathe incorrectly.

Reverse breathers breathe into their chest on the inhale and pull their abdominal area inward and upward. Both areas should move together for proper breathing.

Collapsed breathers breathe into their lower abdominal area only and hold their chest area stationary, preventing their ribs from expanding and contracting. This promotes feelings of depression.

Shallow breathers breathe mostly into their chest region and hold their lower abdominal area stationary. This can cause a feeling of light-headedness and anxiety.

> **IMAGINE THAT**
>
> Many shallow breathers mostly into their pull in their stomachs when breathing, forcing their shoulders upward. This makes them feel as if they are using their abdomens to breathe, even though they are not. Your shoulders should not move when you are breathing properly.

During periods of relaxation or sleep, you breathe more slowly and use more of your lungs. But during times of stress, your breathing changes and you take more frequent, shallower breaths. This is part of the fight-or-flight response and it, along with an increase in adrenalin, is meant to provide a quick burst of energy to deal with an impending threat.

When our ancestors faced physical dangers, such as an animal attack, the fight-or-flight response worked well. Our senses went on high alert to handle, or run from, the threat. Once the threat had passed, our bodies returned to normal. But today's stresses are different; worry about financial problems, relationships, jobs, and security can keep you in a constant state of fight or flight. Your body stays in high alert and your breathing continues to come in short, sharp breaths.

Proper breathing is an essential part of treatment for anxiety disorders. It also helps in learning to manage everyday stress and to combat chronic pain, insomnia, anger, depression, and many other physical and emotional problems. The other relaxation techniques in this chapter—meditation and progressive relaxation—require proper breathing to be effective.

GIVE IT A TRY

Lie down with your right hand on your chest and your left hand on your abdomen. Take a few breaths, paying attention to which hand moves more. If your right hand moves more, you are taking shallow breathes and breathing with only the top part of your lungs. If your left hand moves more, you are breathing correctly.

Your Turn: Breathing Techniques

Proper breathing takes practice. If you have been breathing improperly for many years, your body has become conditioned to breathe that way. You now have to retrain your body to breathe properly. Try using one of the following exercises every day, for 5 to 10 minutes. As you continue to practice, breathing properly becomes automatic.

Feel the Difference

Lie down on the floor, with your spine straight. Place one hand on your chest and one on your abdomen. Breathe in, filling your chest and then stop. Hold for a few seconds and then breathe out. Breath in again, filling your abdomen with air. Hold for a few seconds and then release the air. Feel the difference between the two types of breathing. Understanding and feeling the difference helps you learn how to control your breathing.

Breathe Deeply

Lie down on the floor with your knees bent, your feet slightly apart. (You can also do this sitting upright in a chair. Sit on the edge of the chair, making sure to not lean back, and keep both feet flat on the floor.) Make sure your spine is straight. Place your right hand on your chest and your left hand on your abdomen. Inhale deeply through your nose, bringing the air into your abdomen (your left hand should rise up and your right hand should move only slightly). Exhale through your mouth. Try to slow your breath so you are breathing six to eight times per minute. Count four seconds on the inhale, pause gently, and then count four seconds on the exhale. Pause gently before the next breath starts. Continue for 5 to 10 minutes.

Develop Your Breathing Muscles

This exercise requires a small sand bag or five pound bag of rice.

Lie down on the floor with your knees bent and your feet slightly apart, about the width of your hips, and your spine straight. Place the bag of rice or the sand bag across your lower abdominal area. Relax and breathe naturally. After a few breaths, you will notice that the weight of the rice causes your abdominal area to work a little harder during the inhale and to relax a little more on the exhale. As you notice your breathing getting deeper, slow your breathing. Count four seconds on the inhale, pause, count four seconds on the exhale, pause, and then let the next deep breath begin. In this exercise, you can breathe through either your nose or your mouth, whichever you do normally.

Balloon Breathing

This exercise can be done lying down, as in the previous exercises, or sitting upright on the edge of a chair with your feet flat on the floor. Place your right hand on your abdominal area and left hand on your chest. Start by breathing slowly with your mouth into your lower abdominal area, and then gently breathe into your chest area (count five seconds). When your entire torso fills up with air like a balloon, gently hold the breath for a count of two to three seconds. When you are ready to exhale, purse your lips together slightly and let the air slowly out and watch your chest and belly deflate. When you have fully exhaled, gently hold the abdominal area inward and count for two to three seconds before breathing in again. Let the next breath begin naturally and continue this cycle counting: five-second inhale, two- to three-second pause while holding the air in, five-second exhale, two- to three-second pause before breathing in.

Sighing

Sighing and yawning are your body's way of trying to get more oxygen. You can use sighing to increase your oxygen intake and help you relax. This exercise can be done while standing or sitting. As with the previous exercise, make sure your spine is straight. Breathe in and then sigh, letting the air rush out of your lungs. Repeat several times, feeling your body relax a little more each time.

Meditation

When you think of meditation, you might imagine a monk sitting cross-legged, eyes closed, humming. You might think of new-age religions and wonder if you are meditating in order to find enlightenment or some great universal truth. You might think that only mystics and high priests meditate. However, a great many people, from all walks of life, meditate on a daily basis. Meditation is a useful tool anyone can use to clear the mind. It helps to calm your thoughts and allows you to better control your reactions to the world around you.

What Is Meditation?

Meditation is clearing your mind from the barrage of constant thoughts. When you meditate, you focus your thoughts on a single object (such as your own breath or a photo) or on a *mantra* (a specific word or phrase). Whenever another thought comes into your mind, you bring your focus back to your object or mantra, not allowing distractions to clutter your mind. Meditation is awareness; you are alert, yet your mind is calm.

> **DEFINITION**
>
> A **mantra** is a sound, word, or phrase used to create a mental vibration. Mantras can have specific meanings; for example, the mantra So Hum means "I am." Some people repeat the sound "om" as their mantra. You can choose a mantra with a special meaning to you, use a sound, or find one from ancient meditations.

Many people find meditation difficult in the beginning. It is hard to push aside all conscious thought and remain quiet and still. As you practice meditation, it becomes easier. You may even find yourself meditating for brief periods throughout the day. Some people worry that when they meditate they will lose control and fight the feeling of letting go. However, meditation is safe and you always remain in control.

Why Meditate?

For centuries, monks and high priests have been touting the benefits of meditation, claiming it improves health, well-being, and satisfaction with life. According to recent scientific research, they may be right. Studies have shown that meditation may reduce the risk of high blood pressure, heart attack, and stroke, as well as help to control chronic pain.

STOP AND THINK

While meditation can provide many physical and emotional benefits, it isn't right for everyone. Before beginning a meditation regimen, talk with your doctor. There is some evidence that certain mental illnesses, such as schizophrenia, may worsen with meditation.

In addition to improving physical health, meditation also has a positive effect on your emotional well-being. It helps lower stress levels and improves symptoms of depression and anxiety. One study showed that meditating immediately before a stressful event helped participants cope better during the event. For those without any specific health issues, meditation may improve empathy, compassion, and satisfaction with life.

Your Turn: Simple Meditation

There are many different meditation techniques. The following exercise focuses on concentration. In Chapter 8, we'll go into detail on mindfulness meditation.

CBTIDBIT

Before meditating, take a few minutes to stretch. This helps loosen your muscles and tendons, allowing you to you sit or lie down comfortably.

Step 1: Find a comfortable place for your meditation. This place should be peaceful and free of distractions. Turn off your phone and close your door to avoid any interruptions. While it is possible to lie down and meditate, there is a chance you will fall asleep; therefore, it is better to sit up straight in a comfortable chair or with your legs crossed on the floor while maintaining a straight back. If this is too uncomfortable try kneeling on a pillow placed on the floor.

Step 2: Close your eyes and take a few moments to breathe normally, in through your nose and out through your mouth. You can take a few deep breaths to help relax if you want.

Step 3: Focus on your breathing. Feel your chest move up and down with each breath. Notice how your breath feels coming in and going out. Imagine yourself breathing in all the goodness around you and breathing out any negative thoughts.

Step 4: Continue to focus on your breathing. If another thought pops in your mind, simply refocus your thoughts to your breathing. In the beginning, you may notice thoughts continuously popping into your mind. As you practice meditation, you should notice this happening less often. If you have trouble paying attention to your breathing, use a mantra, repeating it over and over.

Step 5: As you continue breathing, notice the stillness of your mind and relax. Continue to bring yourself back to your breathing or your mantra any time you notice thoughts intruding.

Start with 10 to 15 minutes of meditation per day. Work your way up to about 30 minutes. You can break this up to 15 minutes in the morning and 15 minutes in the evening, or take some time at noon to calm your mind and prepare for the rest of the day.

If you have a hard time staying focused on your breathing, seek out a CD or app that will walk you through a meditation session (see Appendix B: Resources). Especially if you're a beginner, listening to a soothing voice that reminds you to pay attention to your breathing can be helpful.

Your Turn: Kirtan Kriya Mediation

This meditation exercise uses a simple mantra—SA TA NA MA—and stimulates your meridian points. It is a more active meditation that can be helpful for those who have a hard time meditating due to distractions or an inability to relax the mind.

Meridian points are energy points in the body that are often used in acupuncture and acupressure treatments. The belief is that stimulating these energy points improves blood circulation and stimulates nerve endings.

This type of meditation has been shown to improve memory function by increasing blood flow to important brain structures.

Step 1: Sit in chair with your feet on the floor (resist the urge to lean back) or sit on the floor with your ankle to your opposite knee. Keep your spine straight.

Step 2: Touch your thumb to your index finger, middle finger, ring finger, and pinky finger in sequence. As you touch each finger, vocalize one sound of the mantra (SA TA NA MA). Keep a slow steady rhythmic pace.

Step 3: Repeat the mantra and motion out loud for two minutes, in a whisper for two minutes, and in silence for four minutes, followed by in a whisper for two more minutes, and finally out loud for the final two minutes. The total time is 12 minutes.

If you have a hard time doing this on your own, you can download a recording from a website that specializes in spiritual recordings, such as SpiritVoyage. You can also find apps for Android and Apple products, or you can record your own voice to guide you through the sequence.

Relaxing Your Muscles

Progressive muscle relaxation is a technique that involves tensing specific muscle groups and then relaxing them to create awareness of tension and relaxation. It is termed "progressive" because it proceeds through all major muscle groups, relaxing them one at a time, and eventually leads to total muscle relaxation. When your body feels relaxed, your mind can have calmness and clarity. You may want to do this exercise before the mediation or breathing exercise to help your body feel calm.

IMAGINE THAT

Many people don't even realize their muscles are tense. Progressive muscle relaxation teaches you what your muscles feel like when tense and when relaxed. Once you can feel the difference you can take a few minutes, no matter where you are, to tense and relax specific muscles and aid in reducing tension.

Your Turn: Progressive Muscle Relaxation

For this exercise, you may want to tape the instructions and then follow along your recording. There are also apps available to lead you through the progressive muscle relaxation.

Before you begin, find a comfortable position. You can lie down for this exercise. Make sure you are wearing loose, comfortable clothing. Close your eyes and take a few minutes to breath normally, in through your nose and out your mouth.

Forehead: Raise your eyebrows as high as you can to tighten the muscles in your forehead. Hold it for 10 seconds. Then relax, feeling the release of tension.

Breathe in and out, in and out.

Eyes: Close your eyes tightly, holding your eyelids shut as tight as you can. Hold for 10 seconds. Then release, feeling your muscles loosen.

Breathe in and out, in and out.

Mouth: Smile as wide as you can. Tighten the muscles in your mouth and your cheeks. Hold it for 10 seconds. Then release, feeling your face relax and soften.

Breathe in and out, in and out.

Head and neck: Pull your head back as far as you can. If you are sitting, move your head as if you are looking straight at the ceiling. Hold for 10 seconds. Then release, feeling the muscles in your neck lighten.

Let your head and neck sink back into your pillow or the back of the chair. Feel all the stress in your face and head melt away.

Breathe in and out, in and out.

Breathe in and out, in and out.

Fists: Clench your fists, hold for 10 seconds, and release.

Breathe in and out, in and out.

Upper Arms: Tighten your biceps, hold for 10 seconds and then let your muscles go limp.

Breathe in and out, in and out.

Shoulders: Tighten your shoulders, bringing your shoulders back as if your shoulder blades could touch. Hold for 10 seconds and release, feeling the tension in your back and shoulders dissipate.

Breathe in and out, in and out.

Abdomen: Tighten the muscles in your abdomen, sucking in air as you do. Hold for 10 seconds and release.

Allow your upper body to sink into the chair or bed, feeling the limpness in your muscles.

Breathe in and out, in and out.

Breathe in and out, in and out.

Buttocks: Tighten your buttock muscles; hold for 10 seconds and release.

Breathe in and out, in and out.

Thighs: Tighten the muscles in your thighs; hold for 10 seconds and release.

Breathe in and out, in and out.

Calves: Pull your feet toward you, feeling the muscles in your calves tighten. Hold for 10 seconds and release.

Breathe in and out, in and out.

Toes: Curl your toes under; hold for 10 seconds and release.

Let your legs sink into your mattress or chair. Feel how loose your muscles are.

Breathe in and out, in and out.

Breathe in and out, in and out.

Starting with your head, let total relaxation wash over your entire body, from your head to your feet.

Breathe in and out, in and out.

Breathe in and out, in and out.

As with meditation, this exercise takes practice. The first few times you complete the exercise, you may not feel that it did much or that your muscles are still tense. Be patient and continue to practice progressive muscle relaxation every day. As you practice, you will begin to notice it is easier to control your muscles, both tensing and relaxing.

Other Ways to Relax

It can be difficult to give yourself time for hobbies, socializing, and exercise, especially when you feel overwhelmed with other responsibilities. However, all work and no play creates stress overload, which can be harmful to your health. As much as possible, allow yourself time to relax and take pleasure in life. It can be difficult to give yourself permission to put aside other duties in favor of something you enjoy, but keep in mind how important it is for your physical and emotional well-being and give yourself time each day for hobbies or activities you enjoy.

Hobbies

The responsibilities of our jobs, homes, and children often interfere with taking time to enjoy our own hobbies, such as gardening, fishing, dancing, drawing, or reading. We frequently put aside these types of activities for ones we see as more important. However, participating in activities like these, whether alone or with a group, usually helps to lower stress levels and allows you to relax.

If you've been neglecting a hobby that you enjoy, make time to reintroduce to your life. For example, in the past you may have enjoyed painting, finding it relaxing and taking pride it your creations. You keep telling yourself that when your children are grown, when your job is less demanding, when you have more time, you will pull out the paints and start again. Life may never slow down, so it's important to find time now.

Your Turn: Create a Wish List

Write down all of the things that you enjoy doing and that help you relax. Think back over the past and include hobbies or activities you once enjoyed, even if it's been a long time since you took time to enjoy that activity. Include any activities you are interested in learning or starting, even if you have not done it before. This is your wish list.

Next to each item, write down the last time you participated in the activity.

Put a star next to one or two activities high on your list of "wants." Be creative in scheduling time each day or week to submerse yourself in your hobbies.

> **STOP AND THINK**
>
> Ask yourself what has prevented you from doing the activities on your wish list and create a response plan. For example, if you want to exercise but end up working late, then either plan to tell your boss you will do your work at home or come in early tomorrow morning. Or you might plan to work out in the morning. Paying attention to what gets in the way of achieving your goals and creating a plan prevents you from making false promises to yourself.

We all have different schedules and different demands on our time. The trick is finding a way to build activities you enjoy into your schedule. Consider these strategies:

- Wake up a half hour earlier and give yourself a quiet time to pursue an interest.

- Make an arrangement with your spouse that allows each of you to have one evening per week for your own activities.

- Plan to leave work earlier a one day per week and use the time to do something you enjoy.

- Use your lunch hour to do something you enjoy.

- Give up some responsibility at work to take on hobby or personal goal.

Hobbies don't usually overtake your life, but you should work toward a balance. Everyone's lifestyle and responsibilities are different—what works for one person may be too little or too much time for another. Find the amount of time each day or week that works for you and make it a priority to give yourself that time.

Social Activities

Engaging in social activities is an important ingredient to general feelings of well-being and overall happiness. Research has shown that people with strong social connections are better able to manage stress, are healthier, and live longer than those who lead solitary lives.

As teens and young adults, social activities are often a big part of our lives. But as we get older, work and family become more demanding. Your spouse and children may become your sole social outlet. However, having a social network is still very important. Friends fill in the gaps, giving you someone to talk to, to share stories, and to ask for (and give) help.

This can be especially difficult if you have anxiety. You might worry that you won't fit in or find it hard to try new things. You aren't alone. Reaching out to others, while difficult, should help you feel better in the long-term. Start small. Make a goal to add one activity to your weekly schedule. As you gain confidence, you can increase the time you spend on the activity or add a second one. This helps you slowly build your social connections.

If you are having a hard time finding friends outside of your family and co-workers, consider the following ideas.

Look for adult classes in your area. Use the wish list you created in the last exercise to search for interesting classes. This is a great way to meet people with similar interests.

Join a group. Your local paper may have listings for groups in your area. Websites such as meetup.com also offer groups for just about any interest. You can join social or exercise groups, book clubs, or groups that explore spirituality. Local businesses are also a good resource for groups. Specialty stores such as yarn shops, home brewing supply stores, and bookstores often host monthly get-togethers.

Look for community events. Events such as races, fundraisers, and festivals can be a great place to meet new people. Depending on the event, you may be able to bring your children (or your pets), have a fun day, and meet other parents. You can also volunteer and meet other people who are behind the scenes.

Visit a place of worship. Most churches, mosques, and synagogues offer an array of groups, workshops, and events in addition to weekly services.

Volunteer. Try to find organizations in your area based on your interests and passions. Check with the local hospital, senior center, or parks department. Volunteer to spend time with the animals at a local pet shelter. If you want to take small steps, start by volunteering to help at a one-time event and work your way up to volunteering on a weekly basis.

Physical Activity and Exercise Programs

We know that exercise is good for our physical health. It improves how the body functions. Regular exercise lowers levels of anxiety and depression. It improves sleep, concentration, and cognitive function. Between the ages of 19 and 64, you should get at least 150 minutes per week of exercise.

Your Turn: Activity Journal

How often do you do physical activities? Not just traditional exercise or going to the gym, but activities that get your body moving. Exercise doesn't necessarily mean going to "work out" on the treadmill or weight machines. You may actually exercise more often than you think you do.

Start by creating an Activity Journal. Write down the date and any activity you did that day. Maybe you walked in the mall for an hour, did some gardening, took the steps instead of the elevator at work, took your kids swimming, or played golf. Keeping track of these types of activities may motivate you to do even more. At the end of the week, review your accomplishments and set goals for the following week. The goal of this activity is not to become physically fit but to become physically active.

Create a Fitness Program

The first step to creating a fitness program is deciding when you are going to exercise. It's easy to say, "I'll walk three miles whenever I can each day," but that makes it too easy to simply not have the time one day, then the next, until you are no longer exercising. Instead, make a commitment and set aside a specific time each day, even if you start with 10 minutes a day.

CBTIDBIT

Research on patients who had recently undergone hip surgery showed those who made a specific action plan were significantly more likely to exercise and recovered more quickly than those who said they would walk 20 minutes a day. An example of a specific plan is "meet my wife at the bus stop after work and walk home with her."

Structure your exercise time. You might go to the gym and do a specific set of exercises, join a weekly class, or commit to doing a specific routine or workout video at home. Using the right structured program for your needs and your level will help you stick to the program.

You also need to set goals. Setting goals helps you understand your purpose for exercising. Are you trying to lose weight? Be more physically fit? Increase your energy? You can't see any progress unless you know what to look for. Setting specific goals not only gives you something to work toward, but a way to know when you get there. Create a physical goal, such as walking for 20 minutes daily. Set a specific action plan such as, "I will walk home from the train station every day" or "I will spend the second half of my lunch hour walking around the building." Then create an outcome goal. What is one thing that is measurable? Track and record your progress daily or weekly.

Specific Action Plan

Date	Action Goal	Action Plan	Outcome Goal
9/19	Walk 20 min.	Walk from train	Weight = 154 lbs
9/26	Walk 30 min.	Walk to and from train	Weight = 152 lbs

The Least You Need to Know

- Proper breathing—deep breaths from your abdomen rather than shallow breaths from your chest—are at the center of many relaxation techniques.
- Meditation can slow down the constant barrage of thoughts and clear your mind. Regular meditation can decrease symptoms of anxiety and depression.
- The process of progressive muscle relaxation, in which you tense and relax all the major muscle groups in your body, provides a deep feeling of relaxation.
- Physical fitness, social activities, and hobbies are important for your well-being. Make time every day for doing what you enjoy.

CHAPTER 8

Mindfulness

When you practice mindfulness, you live in the moment. Mindfulness helps you look at your thought process, not to change it, but to observe without judgment. While different from many of the traditional CBT techniques, it still plays an important part in understanding and changing behaviors. In this chapter, you will learn what mindfulness is and how to incorporate it into your everyday life.

What Is Mindfulness?

Mindfulness is directing your attention to the present moment and becoming aware of your thoughts, emotions, and sensations. It teaches you to be focused on the present and to remove yourself from the past and the future. It has been said being anxious means being focused on the future; and being depressed is focusing on the past. When you practice mindfulness, you are in the moment. You are experiencing without judgment and you are practicing the art of acceptance, which means simply observing and feeling without analyzing or contemplating. It is accepting exactly what is happening right now, without thinking about what is right or wrong, or looking for solutions. Mindfulness can be described as a way of *being* rather than *doing*.

In This Chapter

- How to live in the present moment
- Learning to distance yourself from your thoughts
- Accepting thoughts in order to move forward
- Developing control of your mental focus

Your brain's autopilot is inclined to default to *doing* mode rather than *being* mode. When you are in the doing mode, you assess for discrepancies between what is happening and what you think should be happening (or should have happened.) Mindfulness exercises enhance your brain's ability to utilize and benefit from the being mode of the brain. This is important because the doing mode can be harmful at times, especially if you are prone to worrying and states of depression, because it can lead to *rumination*.

> **DEFINITION**
>
> **Rumination** is the mental act of reviewing and analyzing thoughts and situations, including why you feel the way you do. When ruminating, you attempt to answer the self-imposed question, "Why?" You then analyze why you feel sad, you think about your shortcomings, and you try to decide how these led to problematic situations. This can be particularly harmful when there is nothing or little to be done to change a situation.

Your Turn: Mindfulness Breathing

When you first start practicing mindfulness, it is common to begin with focusing on your breathing. This is similar to traditional meditation practices, but unlike traditional meditation, you can be mindful while engaging in the world. The purpose of the exercise is to train your mind to focus on one element of your present experience. In traditional meditation, you focus on your breath to begin the journey into your inner wisdom.

Find a comfortable, quiet area where you can sit upright. You can keep your eyes open or have them closed, whichever is more comfortable for you.

As you sit in the chair, start to listen to the sound of your breath without making any changes to your breathing. How does it sound on the inhale and the exhale? Do you make a sound during the moments in between your inhale and exhale? Notice how it feels when air enters your nose, how it feels as you fill your chest and abdomen with air, notice all of the sensations as you exhale. Pay attention to each breath you take, from the moment you breathe in until the moment the air leaves your body.

Continue this exercise for 10 minutes. Each time you notice your thoughts becoming distracted or wandering, take notice of those thoughts and then bring your attention back to your breathing. Don't judge yourself for letting your attention wander and don't look to change your breath. Remember, you are observing without analysis or judgment.

Practice this exercise once a day for a week. As you continue to practice you will notice your thoughts wandering less often and you will be able to keep your attention on your breath with greater ease.

A Thought Is Just a Thought

When you observe and accept a negative thought or emotion, without reacting to it, it is easier to move on to other thoughts. In other words, you allow a negative thought to exist without fixating on it or giving it any weight. The attitude you are adopting is "it is just a thought" and of course not all thoughts are true or permanent. Once you accept this "just a thought' perspective, the thought no longer has any hold on you.

Imagine you are waiting for an important call. You have the thought "he is not going to call me." Instead of ruminating on the thought or testing the validity of the thought, you let it go. The person calls and you move on as though the thought never occurred. You don't need to stop and analyze your negative attitude each step of the way. This is mindfulness.

Mindfulness allows you to activate the "being mode" by producing a change in perspective known as distancing. This technique changes not just the way you think about something but also nature of your thoughts. Distancing helps you gain control of your thoughts because it allows you to see the thoughts as "just thoughts" rather than as reflections of reality that need to be worked out. Distancing is particularly helpful if you obsess over situations you have little control over or things of minor importance.

The Role of Mindfulness in CBT

Many of the techniques and strategies used in CBT are meant to change your thoughts and your behaviors. Mindfulness, although used in CBT frequently, works in a different way since it's not about challenging the thoughts themselves but changing your focus and controlling the content. It's not about how you think about a situation but more about what you think about it. The more you learn to distance yourself from certain thoughts, the more you learn to let things go. You no longer spend unnecessary time analyzing information that doesn't really matter; instead, you move on. Distancing helps you gain control of your thoughts. By allowing yourself to see thoughts and feelings without judgment and analysis, you reduce the tendency to relapse into states of depression.

IMAGINE THAT

While mindfulness has its origins in Buddhism, most major religions include some form of it. In Buddhism and Hinduism, it is known as *Samadhi*, in Islam as *zikr*, and in Christianity as *recollection*.

Acceptance Does Not Mean Settling

When introduced to the concept of acceptance, you might confuse it with the concept of settling. Mindfulness does not mean you have to settle for less than what is ideal; it gives you the space to pause and prioritize what you issues you want to address. In the example of waiting for the call, if you didn't practice mindfulness you might have invested unnecessary energy into a fleeting thought.

Unproductive thought processes often follow one of two paths. Once you have a negative thought you feed into it, giving yourself an entire narrative to back up your negative thought. Imagine you are preparing to take a test. You have the automatic thought "I am going to fail." If you stop and give in to this thought by ruminating, then your negativity feeds on itself and you remember every test you have failed. You continue chaining negative thoughts until you have worked yourself into a frenzy. The second path is to try to avoid the negative thought—pushing it from your mind—but this technique rarely works because the more you try to ignore a thought, the more it pops back into your mind.

Mindfulness gives you a third option. It allows you to see and accept the negative thought and then move on because you are recognizing that "it's just a thought." The thought itself cannot hurt you. It also cannot really help you beyond reminding you to move. It is similar to watching television. You become engrossed in the show and when a commercial comes on you tune it out. You know it is there, but it is "just a commercial." When the show comes on, you once again become engrossed and no longer think about the commercial.

Controlling Urges

When you first start mindfulness, you will notice that it is very difficult to simply notice a thought, feeling, or urge without responding to it. Practicing mindfulness helps you accept challenging emotions and urges without acting on every one. For example, imagine you are trying to lose some weight. You go out to eat and have the urge to order chocolate cake for dessert. You finish your meal and the waiter approaches to ask if you would like dessert. You notice your urge for chocolate cake but instead of ordering it you think, "I am having a craving for chocolate cake, but just because the thought and feeling are there, that doesn't mean I need to give in to it." You tell the waiter "No, thank you." This is mindfulness at work.

> **STOP AND THINK**
>
> When you first start practicing mindfulness, you might become frustrated because you can't seem to stop the unwanted thoughts or distractions. Be persistent and keep trying. As with anything, mindfulness takes commitment and practice. The longer you work at it, the easier it becomes and the more you will realize the benefits.

Your Turn: The Raisin Experience

This exercise is a good way to begin practicing mindfulness. By focusing on the raisin and the experience of eating the raisin, you develop your ability to be mindful in other experiences.

Place a raisin in your hand. Look at it. Examine how it feels in your hand. Notice the smell, texture, and color of the raisin. Lay the raisin on your tongue. Close your eyes. Notice again how the raisin feels. Notice how it tastes as it lies on your tongue. Notice any urges you have to eat the raisin. Just notice them. Don't give in to the urge to eat the raisin. Just notice how it feels. Then, after one minute, start to chew the raisin. Notice every sensation as you chew. Don't swallow. Notice the urge to swallow without giving in. Then, after one minute, swallow the raisin. Notice any body changes as you swallow the raisin including the changes in facial, hand, and body muscles. Notice the differences in muscle tension in your face and throat after you swallow the raisin. Notice any thought and sensation after you swallow the raisin.

Your goal is to become completely immersed in the experience of eating a raisin.

Being Present in the Moment

Today is the only important day. This moment is the only important moment. You have heard this many times. Even so, you probably spend most of your time thinking about what happened yesterday or sometime in the past or worrying about what will happen tomorrow or the next day. Even though you are living this moment, you are not present in it—unless you focus on it.

You might wonder how it is possible or even helpful to only live in this very moment. After all, you have goals and dreams for your future. If you live only in this moment, how can you take steps you need to take to reach your goals? But, it is only the present moment you can control or cope with. And, it is this moment that shapes your future. If you live by focusing only on your future, you miss the moment you are in right now and the opportunity to experience it in a way that works for you. Instead, learn to experience your emotions and recognize the future will take care of itself when you handle the present moment.

> **GIVE IT A TRY**
>
> Stop and notice your surroundings. What do you see? What do you smell? Use all five senses to take in your surroundings. Notice how your clothes feel. What noises do you hear? Notice if you are hot, cold, or comfortable. Notice if you are relaxed or tense. What are your points of tension? Take some deep breaths and feel the tension leaving every time you exhale. Pay attention to what is happening in this very moment.
> Do this daily, on your commute or as you run errands. Instead of just going through the motions of life, learn to take in the experience.

Practicing mindfulness on a daily basis helps you incorporate it into different parts of your life, including times when you face difficult or uncomfortable situations. There are times in your life when you anticipate feeling uncomfortable. During these times, you probably anticipate every possible difficulty. Instead, be mindful of yourself and the situation. This helps you to distance yourself and cope more easily.

Suppose you are afraid of flying and are about to board an airplane. Instead of worrying about all the possible disasters and thinking that you will not be able to handle being on a plane, try focusing on your body's sensations. Notice each thought that passes through your mind. Identify thoughts about uncertainty and those about your discomfort. Once you observe these thoughts and emotions, you should begin to feel grounded. You feel more in control of your feelings and better equipped to manage the situation.

> **CBTIDBIT**
>
> Anticipating discomfort is one of the primary causes of anxiety. This means instead of being in the present, your brain focuses on the future.

Tips for Living in the Present Moment

Spend 10 minutes a day practicing mindfulness. Pick a basic task that you often do mindlessly, such as brushing your teeth, commuting to work, or washing the dishes. In each of these experiences, pay attention to all five senses. Notice any thoughts and emotions. Just notice without reacting. The more you practice, the more you will find yourself stopping throughout the day to appreciate the moment.

Don't rush. If you are rushing through the process, you are probably more focused on what comes next than the moment at hand. Use slow, deliberate movements. You may need to give yourself additional time to complete each task or remove some of your tasks from the day. However, you put more into each task you complete and find more satisfaction.

Reduce the activities that don't promote mindfulness. Turn off the television, shut off your computer. Eliminate things that distract you from paying attention to the moment. If you find yourself reacting negatively to the people around you and what they are doing, focus on accepting them for how they normally behave. Instead of judging their actions as "wrong," just notice them, as you notice your own thoughts and your own body sensations.

Take the time to be present in conversations. Listen to what the other person is saying and respond thoughtfully. Don't rush to express your own opinions.

GIVE IT A TRY

Imagine the last time you were with someone who was endlessly complaining—about their health, their job, their spouse. Chances are you tried to address the problem and offered advice. Instead, let go of your desire to solve the problem and become mindful. Sit back and listen. Notice their body sensations and their energy; listen without giving advice. Tell yourself, "I cannot resolve this problem. That is okay. Listening is enough." Your friend will feel heard and you will feel less frustrated.

Watch Your Thoughts Sail By

One of the main concepts of mindfulness is to become aware of your thoughts without judging them. Think of your thoughts as sailboats. Instead of trying to fix them, just notice them sailing by. When you see a sailboat in the ocean you don't try to jump on board or tell the captain how to drive the boat. You sit back and take pleasure in watching them sail by. Remember, your thoughts are not good or bad, they simply are. Practicing this helps when going through a difficult or emotionally charged situation. You can recognize that you are feeling sad, frustrated, or angry but know that the feeling will pass just as the sailboat sails out of sight; it is a temporary feeling. As you practice watching your thoughts sail by, it will get easier to say, "I am angry but this is a passing thought and I will get through it."

Your Turn: Observing Thoughts

Sit back in a comfortable chair, with your back upright. Spend a few minutes focusing on your breathing, paying attention to how your breath feels as it enters your body, fills your abdomen, and then leaves your body. Don't change your breathing, just notice it. Then start to pay attention to your thoughts, recognizing they are simply thoughts. Do not make any judgments, just notice the thought.

Use this technique daily to help gather information about what is on your mind and gain a sense of your autopilot mode. You are practicing "being" rather than "doing" which helps build mental dexterity, the ability to direct your attention as needed. The point of this exercise is not to try to dismiss your thoughts or make them go away, but to let your thoughts happen. It helps you understand that thoughts come and go.

Accepting Upsetting Thoughts and Moods

When feeling sad, upset, or angry, you may try to analyze your thoughts. You might ask yourself:

- Why am I feeling this way?

- What did I do to cause this feeling?

- Did I act differently than I usually do?

- What other times have I felt this way?

You probably ask these questions in an attempt to feel better, but often analyzing your thoughts leads to ruminating—remembering past times you were sad and angry or blaming yourself for feeling this way. As you delve into answers about your mood, you often feel worse and instead of helping the thought or emotion go away, it exacerbates it.

Instead of "solving" your mood, try accepting it and all it encompasses. Our moods usually come with physical symptoms. For example, feelings of anxiety are often accompanied by a racing heart, shortness of breath, an upset stomach or trembling. When noticing your thought, stop to pay attention to your body's reaction. Pay attention to your body sensations and focus on everything you are feeling. Allow yourself to feel the emotion, paying attention to the changes in your body and your thoughts as you let the emotion go through you. Your feelings may ebb and flow. For example, you may feel sad for a little while, then, as your thoughts change, it may disappear only to return again later.

Describe or write down the facts of what you're feeling.

- My stomach feels like it is in knots.

- I have a headache.

- I feel sad.

- I am having a hard time breathing.

Writing down your thoughts in a factual way helps you create distance; the thoughts are no longer a part of your emotions but instead are facts. You can see them as part of the process, rather than the process itself.

In mindfulness, you should be aware of everything that is going on, including the good. Notice the good in your environment. You may be sad, but maybe it is a beautiful day outside or a friend calls to see how you are. Maybe you are comfortable in your home. These things need to be included in your experience. They help you keep balance in your emotions.

Incorporating Mindfulness in Everyday Life

Mindfulness practice sessions are important and give you an overall sense of well-being. But don't leave mindfulness in your chair. There are plenty of opportunities throughout your day to be mindful.

While brushing your teeth. Pay attention to the taste of your toothpaste in your mouth and how it smells. Notice how the toothbrush feels going across your teeth; be mindful of each tooth. Notice the sound of the toothbrush as you brush your teeth. Pay attention to how your arms move. Ignore the urge to look in the mirror, check your hair, or multitask getting ready for work. Pay attention to only the task of brushing your teeth.

When waiting in line. In our hectic lives, there are usually times throughout the day when you have to wait in line—at the bank, waiting for lunch, buying groceries, sitting in traffic. These times are often frustrating; you just want to get done and get back to your routine. Standing in line stops you from doing other things. Instead of becoming impatient, take the time to breathe deeply. Pay attention to where in your body you feel tense. Instead of focusing on your frustration, take this as a time to be quiet and still for a few moments.

When eating. Enjoy the entire process of eating. Notice how the food looks on your plate, the different colors and textures. Pay attention to the smell of the food. Savor each bite, noticing the texture, temperature, and taste of the food. Notice how the silverware feels in your hand. Pay attention to those around you and focus on what they are saying.

While taking a shower. Pay attention to the how the water feels on your body, how the soap or shower gel smells and feels. Feel the temperature of the water and listen to how it sounds. Notice the feel of the shower floor on your feet.

> **CBTIDBIT**
>
> Mindfulness is most effective if you practice it in short bursts throughout the day. Start your day with five minutes of mindfulness and then take several mindfulness breaks throughout the day.

No matter how hectic your day is, there is always time to be mindful. Stop several times during the day to pause for a few minutes, take several deep breaths, and be in the present moment. Write down five things you notice at this moment for each of the five senses. Just taking five minutes can leave you feeling more refreshed and more connected to your environment.

Your Turn: Diary of Mindfulness Exercises

It's good idea to develop a daily habit of practicing mindfulness. Any of the exercises introduced in this chapter are a good way to start. As you continue, these exercises will become habit. Keep a journal of your mindfulness exercises. Record the following for each exercise you do:

- Date

- Mindfulness activity

- Location

- How easy it was for you to be mindful, on a scale of 1 to 10

- Whether or not you were distracted

- One word that describes what you observed during your mindfulness activity

During times of stress you might find it harder to be mindful. Instead of judging yourself as a failure or retreating back to bad habits, accept this is a part of stress. You will find that it becomes easier with time. Remind yourself that this is why you practice.

The Least You Need to Know

- Practicing mindfulness helps you view your thoughts without judging them or labeling them as right or wrong.

- When you accept that your thoughts are just thoughts, they no longer have the power to control your actions.

- Mindfulness helps to reduce anxiety and depression by focusing on the present moment, not looking back to what already happened or worrying about what is yet to come.

- Thoughts and feelings come and go. Accept negative thoughts and then let them go and move on.

- When you notice your senses, you are able to be present and accept what is happening in this moment. Acceptance is needed for adjustment and peace.

Your Inner Narration

Your inner voice talks to you every day. It tells you what it likes and doesn't like. It tells you what you are doing wrong and what you are doing right. Even if you don't like what it says, you can't turn it off. It is always there. In this chapter, you learn how to change the words and tone of your inner voice. You learn how to recognize and then respond to inner criticisms and replace those thoughts with more positive perspectives.

Self-Talk

As you go through your day, you constantly think about the world around you. You narrate your activities and interpret your environment. Your self-talk guides you and your decisions. This self-talk is sometimes positive, "I am definitely getting a raise." Sometimes neutral, "I need to call my client to reschedule the missed meeting." Sometimes negative, "This meeting is not going well."

Generally, there are three ways you internally narrate what is happening around you:

Situational: Narrating a situation, including your expectations and assumptions

Others: Creating opinions and judgments based on what you expect from others in the situation with you

Me: Making judgments and assumptions about yourself based on your core beliefs

As a human being, you automatically accept your self-talk as the only version of reality. Most of the time, you don't double-check what you are thinking or ponder what someone else's perspective might be. You approach a situation based on whether your internal narration is positive, negative, or neutral.

Negative: You are likely to approach the world in a closed off, impatient, or cynical way. Your self-talk might center on "I am going to fail," "No one will help me," or "The world is a bad place." This limits your attempts at problem solving.

Positive: Your attitude reflects the belief that "I can handle this," "Someone will help me," or "There is a solution to this problem." You approach situations with the expectation that you will get through it just fine.

Neutral: You see a situation as neither positive nor negative. "I need to attend several meetings today." You approach situations with a matter-of-fact attitude and are open to whatever happens.

You might notice your self-talk not as sentences but as short fragments that reflect your attitude or feelings toward a situation, such as "Great!" "Now what?" or "Oh, no."

STOP AND THINK

If you have positive or neutral self-talk, you are more likely to approach life with curiosity, openness, and tolerance.

You probably don't even notice many of these thoughts; they happen automatically and come quickly as you do your job, take care of your children, relate to your spouse, run errands, etc. You might think about the "big picture" but don't necessarily pay attention to how you narrate the small moments of your day. Although you might tend to use one type of internal narration more than others, you probably bounce from one to the other, depending on the situation.

Your Turn: Recording Your Inner Dialogue

Now it's your turn to become mindful of your self-talk. This is the first step in changing your negative self-talk.

Over the next day or two, set an alarm to signal you every hour. When the alarm goes off, take five minutes to review the past hour; write down what has been going on and your thoughts. Determine if your inner dialogue was positive, negative, or neutral. Write down how you felt and give your emotion a rating of 0 to 100.

Example:

8:00 A.M.   Dropped kids at party

Thoughts: The other moms are so shallow with their nice clothes. I will never fit in with them. I am such a slob.

Negative

Embarrassed, less than 50

9:00 A.M.   Went to grocery store with husband

Thoughts: He has to inspect the grocery bill at the register and hold up the line. The people behind us are angry. I am so embarrassed.

Negative

Annoyed, 40

If your dialogue was negative, rewrite your narration of the events as if you saw them in a neutral or positive way. For example:

8:00 A.M.   Dropped kids off at birthday party.

Thoughts: The other women were well dressed. They seem interested in fashion. I have nice clothes I can wear. Getting up and dressing nice might motivate me to improve myself.

or

Thoughts: The other women were well dressed. They seem interested in fashion. That doesn't interest me but I can try to fit in and relate to them in other ways. If not, I have other friends.

Types of Negative Narrations

Negative narrations usually fall into one of four categories. Read the following profiles to see which one sounds most like your inner dialogue:

The Worrier

The theme behind your thoughts is "What if..." This type of self-talk can lead to anxiety or depression. You might...

- Anticipate and have images of the worst-case scenario.

- Overestimate the odds that something bad or embarrassing will happen.

- Underestimate the likelihood that things will turn out okay.

> **GIVE IT A TRY**
>
> As soon as you realize you are worrying about something, ask yourself five questions:
>
> 1. Is this situation as bad as I am imagining it to be?
>
> 2. What is the worst that could happen?
>
> 3. What is the best that could happen?
>
> 4. What is most likely to happen?
>
> 5. How important is this going to be in five years?
>
> Often, taking the time to look at the situation from different points of view helps you calm your worrying.

Your inner voice is always on guard, vigilant of others and situations. You are always ready to point out any sign that something is going wrong. The most common problematic thinking processes in this type of inner dialogue are catastrophizing, overgeneralizing, and fortune-telling.

Some examples include the following:

- "Oh no, my heart is racing. What if I have a heart attack?"

- "I feel nervous. What if they judge me?"

- "This is hard. What if I fail?"

- "What if something bad happens and I am alone? I won't be able to handle it or get help."

- When you have no facts or information: "I bet something bad happened."

- When something bad happens: "Things will always stay this way."

Even when things go good, you are skeptical. When things are going well, you think "I should not be too happy, because it won't last or I'll jinx it."

Self-Critique

This type of inner dialogue breeds low self-esteem. The underlying theme is "I am never good enough. Why should I even try? It won't work anyway." This type of self-talk contributes to not meeting personal goals because as soon as you make a mistake, such as cheating on a diet, you give up entirely. You use this self-talk to make excuses and avoid having to try.

Examples include:

- "What a disappointment I am. That was stupid."

- "I already cheated on my diet (smoked a cigarette, etc.). Why bother?"

- "Can't I ever get it right?"

- "Look at her and how capable she is! I'll never be like that."

- "I could have done better."

The critic inside your head judges what you do and say. You are quick to point out your faults and limitations. When you narrate your world this way, you constantly remind yourself of your failures and compare yourself to others. Common problematic thinking processes for this type of self-talk include discounting the positive, self-blaming, labeling, and over-generalizing.

The Victim/Blamer

This is the inner voice you hear most often if you have depression. It leads to feelings of hopelessness and helplessness. The theme is "I can't. I will never be able to" or "It's my fault."

Some examples include:

- "I'll never be able to do that, so why try?"

- "I feel physically drained today; why bother doing anything?"

- "Maybe if I had done that 10 years ago, but it's too late now."

- "I'm hopeless."

- "I've had this problem for too long; it'll never get better."

- "I can't believe I did that."

- "This wouldn't have happened if I had…"

Common problematic thinking processes of the victim/blamer are blaming others and catastrophizing.

> **IMAGINE THAT**
>
> When your self-talk includes problematic thinking styles of "blame" or "should" toward others, you don't take any personal responsibility. By focusing on your responsibility, you gain control.

The Perfectionist

You criticize your abilities as a way to push yourself to do better. This inner voice lets you know you aren't trying hard enough or doing enough. You tell yourself "I should have" or "I must." This inner voice comes from the part of you that wants to be the best, but doesn't tolerate when you make a mistake or fail to miss a goal. It convinces you that your worth comes from external sources, not from within.

Examples of perfectionism are:

- "I should always be on top of things."

- "I should always be considerate and unselfish."

- "I must get this job (that raise, my parents' approval, etc.)."

- "I'm not worth much if I am not the best."

- "I must complete all of my goals even if it costs me my happiness."

- "I cannot relax and take a break."

When the perfectionist takes over, you are pushed into high levels of stress and exhaustion. The problematic thinking patterns include *should* and *must*.

Checklist for More Positive Inner Narration

After you identify the negativity in your inner narration, you want to reword your thoughts. The following questions can help you:

Is my thought specific or general?

Create statements that are specific to individuals or situations. Rather than "I don't get along with anyone at work," you can say, "Tom and I do not agree all the time." Be as specific as possible.

Is my thought flexible or stable?

Consider that situations can change. Instead of "I am not good at my job," you can say, "With some training, I can do this job." Focus on how situations can change and improve with time.

Is my thought external or personal?

Create statements that are neutral or external rather than making events and situations about you. Instead of saying, "Everyone else is dressed much better than me; I have no sense of style," make it more neutral, "Fashion is not my strong suit, but that shouldn't interfere with my ability to do my job."

Is my thought about what I can control or about what isn't working?

Change your thoughts to focus on what you can control within a situation rather than what is wrong with a situation. Instead of "No one seems to want to talk to me," say, "I can start a conversation with someone."

Your Turn: Which Category?

When going through a difficult situation, listening to your inner narration can help you.

Divide a paper into five columns:

1. Situation

2. Thoughts

3. Category (Worrier, Self-Critique, Victim/Blamer, or Perfectionist)

4. Problematic Thinking

5. New Thought

Use the following examples as a guide:

Situation: I ordered take-out for dinner.

Thoughts: I am a bad mother; good mothers cook healthy dinners every night.

Category: Perfectionist, Self-Critique

Problematic Thinking: labeling, overgeneralizing

New Thought: I make dinner most nights; there are limits to what I can do. There isn't anything wrong with take-out once in a while.

Affirmations

Your inner dialogue reflects your beliefs, many of which you learned in childhood. Some of these beliefs are no longer relevant in your life. You can use *affirmations* to help change to a more relevant and positive way of looking at yourself, your life, and the world around you. Affirmations are a choice to think positive thoughts.

> **DEFINITION**
>
> An **affirmation** is a positive statement you purposely tell yourself. You use affirmations to develop a more positive perception of yourself, to change negative behaviors, or accomplish goals.

Change isn't always easy. Imagine you don't have many friends and you think you are unlovable. This is a belief you have carried with you for many years. Creating a positive affirmation, "I am a lovable person. I can meet some new friends," is going to be hard for you to say. At first, you aren't going to believe it and might feel a deep resistance. Your subconscious finds it easier and more comfortable to stick with your old belief.

Continually repeating your affirmation, stating it aloud, with conviction, slowly chips away your resistance. The more often you state your affirmation, the more you begin to live and behave as though it is true. This challenges your previous belief. You are slowly replacing your negative and faulty core belief with a more positive inner truth. Positive affirmations "reprogram" your thoughts. They are about creating ideas to change your future. When you act on your affirmations, you start looking at everything in your life in a more positive way. Small starts, even changing one belief, snowball into many positive changes.

Combating the Idea of Lying to Yourself

When you first start using affirmations, you won't completely believe your new thoughts. That is okay. Suppose you are shy and avoid parties and get-togethers. You feel uncomfortable standing alone. You think everyone is judging you. You decide that you are going to try using positive affirmations to help you overcome your shyness. You write down your negative thought:

> When I go to a party and don't know anyone, I think everyone is looking at me and judging me.

And you write down a positive affirmation:

> I enjoy going to parties and meeting new people. Everyone enjoys my company.

You repeat this statement several times every day, but each time there is a nagging feeling that tells you it isn't true. You are lying to yourself. After a few days, you give up. You know it isn't true. You know you don't like going to parties and don't like meeting new people. Positive affirmations are nothing more than telling yourself lies, you think. Your subconscious is rejecting your statement.

Making Affirmations Believable

It helps to soften your affirmation and create one that your subconscious isn't going to reject so easily. You might start out with an affirmation of "Meeting new people is fun and interesting." You can look into your past, remember some times that you have met someone new and enjoyed talking with him or her. Your subconscious can back up your statement that meeting new people is a good thing. As you say this statement every day, you begin to believe it. You might start looking forward to meeting new people. You might look for opportunities to meet new people.

> **GIVE IT A TRY**
>
> With practice, you can become less critical of yourself. Use a piece of paper folded in half, lengthwise. On the left side, write down some areas where you are hard on yourself. On the right side, write a positive statement. Fold the paper in half so you can only see the positive statements. Pin it up in your room, on the refrigerator, or somewhere you will see it every day.

Sometimes it helps to listen to your arguments. For example, when you say, "I like meeting new people," what are the automatic thoughts that pop into your mind? Are you quickly telling yourself, "I am not interesting," or "No one wants to talk to me"? Create affirmations to change those negative thoughts. You might start out with an affirmation that says, "I am an interesting person." This combats your negative thought process.

If you still find yourself having difficulty or resisting when you repeat your affirmations, try including words like "choose" or "potential" to make them more realistic. For example, you can state, "I choose to meet new people," or "I have the potential to get the job promotion." These words help create a willingness to make a change and a sense of empowerment, that you are making a choice to make positive changes in your life.

Seeing the Big Picture

For some people, seeing the big picture and making affirmations to reflect your final goal works best. You imagine what it is you want to be and then begin telling yourself you are already there. It is the "fake it until you make it" philosophy. For example, you may want to lose 20 pounds. You create an affirmation that says, "I am thin and beautiful." You create in your mind the reality you want to achieve.

Your mind doesn't know the difference between reality and make-believe. If you are able to tell yourself repeatedly that you are stupid or useless and believe it, you are able to tell yourself the opposite and believe it as well. Affirmations are a way to tell yourself what you want to believe, and then saying them repeatedly until you do believe it.

Some people have a hard time with "big picture" affirmations. They become more depressed or uneasy because they feel like they are simply making things up. Their automatic thoughts take over, and after repeating an affirmation, they tell themselves it is not true and never will be. If this happens, it might be best to break down your affirmations into small pieces and work on one affirmation at a time, building up to the bigger picture.

Tips for Creating Affirmations

The wording of your affirmations can make the difference between helping you to feel better or making you feel worse. Begin creating affirmations by writing a series of "I am" statements that describe what you want to have or experience. Even though your wants are in the future, you should write them as though they are already true.

Don't write:

> I want to be happy.

Instead write:

> I am happy.

When you write affirmations in the future, such as "I want" and continue to repeat it, you leave yourself feeling as if your present life is lacking something—the thing you want. The intention of positive affirmations is to make you feel as if you already have what you want.

For personal growth affirmations, begin with a list of "I am" statements focusing on your positive attributes. Are you a hard worker? Are you smart? Are you attractive? A good friend? A good listener? When you think of yourself, you might dwell on negative characteristics and traits, ignoring or skimming over your positive attributes. Creating affirmations about the positive traits and repeating them every day helps you appreciate who you are and boosts your confidence.

Write affirmations in a positive tone. Don't write what you want to avoid or what you want to eliminate from your life. Instead of writing, "I am no longer worried about my finances," write, "I have a comfortable lifestyle," or "I have the money to meet my needs." In other words, imagine that you have already accomplished your goal and write your affirmations from that point of view.

Use counter-statements to create affirmations to dispute characteristics you see as negative. If you believe you are lazy, then you probably act in ways that reflect that belief. Write a counter-statement, such as "I am a hard worker."

Write down your affirmations and post them in several places—the bathroom mirror, the front of the refrigerator, on your car dashboard. Whenever you see the affirmation list, read it aloud. The more you state your affirmation, the more it becomes part of your belief system.

Keep your affirmations short. While some people write longer affirmations, it is easier to remember and repeat one sentence.

Decide if you want your affirmations to reflect the "big picture" or if you want to start small. Many people prefer affirmations that have some truth in them.

Piggyback one affirmation on another. If you find you are resisting your affirmations, such as "I am a worthy of love," try stating something you do believe about yourself first and then add the second affirmation.

Make stating your affirmations fun. Make the affirmation rhyme or sing it aloud in the shower. The more fun you make it, the more likely you are to continue.

Affirmations are personal. Write affirmations about what you want to change in your life. You cannot write affirmations about someone else.

When writing affirmations, avoid the following:

Ambiguous words—keep your affirmations as precise as possible.

Comparatives—don't use words like "more" or "better." Instead of "I want to be a better person," write "I am a good listener."

Changing thinking patterns takes time. Be patient and continue repeating your affirmations as often as possible. You will see results and feel the difference.

The following are examples of how to start affirmations:

I am happy…

I am at peace…

I am a loving person…

I have…

I own…

In my life I have…

I am grateful for…

I appreciate…

Affirmations are most effective when they bring about feelings. Just saying the words might not work; you want to create the feeling you would have when this thing comes to be.

The Least You Need to Know

- Self-talk is the inner dialogue through which you narrate and interpret your experiences.
- Self-talk can be positive, negative, or neutral. Changing your negative self-talk to neutral or positive statements can help to improve your outlook on life.
- Negative self-talk can manifest as worry, self-criticism, self-blame, and perfectionism.
- Affirmations are positive statements that help change the way you look at yourself and the world around you.

CHAPTER 10

Testing Your New Beliefs

In CBT, you use reality testing to test your old thoughts and beliefs and reinforce new beliefs. It helps you compare old and new beliefs and decide which are more helpful in your life. The preceding chapters have helped you to become aware of your thoughts, analyze them to find the negative thought processes, and come up with alternative thoughts and beliefs. In this chapter, you will take things one step further by creating experiments to test out those new beliefs and thinking styles—in essence, to test out your new reality.

Reality Testing

On paper, as you complete your thought logs, you come up with different ways of thinking. And, on paper, these may seem to make sense. Even so, you might not be convinced. You probably need some proof to fully accept the new way you think about yourself, others, and the world. *Reality testing*, also called behavioral experiments, allows you to be interactive in the CBT process.

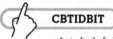

DEFINITION

> **Reality testing** or behavioral experiments are concrete actions that seek to prove your new way of thinking and disprove your old way of thinking.

To create a behavioral experiment, start with your ABCD log:

A: Describe the situation and identify a particular problem.

B: Record your negative beliefs.

C: Record what you assume will happen.

D: Identify your problematic thought processes (refer to Chapter 2 if you have trouble identifying these) and write down ideas that challenge your these views. Where are you catastrophizing, mind reading, or overgeneralizing?

Now add column E for evidence testing—creating an experiment to test out your predictions and beliefs.

E: Write down an alternative outcome. Think about other ways in which the situation might develop. Record how much you believe in this new outcome using a scale of 0 to 100 percent.

CBTIDBIT

> It is helpful to measure the success of your plan by using a grading system (0 to 100 percent). This keeps you from falling back into old patterns of thinking. Measure both the success at carrying out your action plan and how close your prediction came to the outcome.

Once you've completed the chart, create an action plan to test out your new outcome. Write down specific actions to take that will increase the chances of your prediction occurring. For example, if you are going to a party where you don't know anyone, instead of writing "I will be friendly," write down "I will smile and say hello to at least five people." Once you create a plan, put your plan into action. Write down exactly what happened and then review the information. Ask yourself:

On a scale of 1 to 100 percent, how close did I follow the plan?

On a scale of 1 to 100 percent, how close was the outcome to your new prediction?

When reviewing your results, try to look at them from a positive perspective. Pay attention to your thoughts to be sure you aren't reverting back to negative thinking patterns, such as looking at the situation as black and white or overgeneralizing the results. The skills you learned in

Chapters 1 and 2 should help you to look at the results more objectively. Reality testing should reinforce your new beliefs and give you a reason to continue making changes in your thinking and behaviors.

The following is an example of how you can use reality testing:

A: You are attending a dinner party.

B: You predict you won't know many people. You predict the evening will be a disaster. You think you will feel left out and that others will find you uninteresting.

C: You are anxious and don't want to go to the party.

D: I am overgeneralizing and fortune-telling about all parties and all people. After all, the person who invited me is a nice person. I do not have any information to prove the people at the party will reject me. I have been in new situations before and they turned out okay. If I am not enjoying myself I can leave after the cocktail hour. I do not have any evidence that I am not capable of holding a conversation with others or successfully attending a party. I am only responsible for making polite conversation.

E: I can go to the party for at least one hour and talk with at least two people. This will prove that I can navigate a dinner party as successfully as most people around me.

Behavior Plan/Strategy:

- Bring a bottle of wine and thank my host for inviting me.

- Make small talk with a few guests.

- Smile and say hello to everyone.

- Ask other guests questions, such as "Where do you work?" and "What do you like to do on the weekends?"

- If I stay for dinner, I will talk to the people sitting on either side of me.

Once you have created a plan, do your best to follow through. Then review and rate the results. For example:

I would give the overall outcome a rating of 80 percent since I enjoyed myself but also felt a little awkward.

I would give myself a 90 percent for carrying out the plan. I did bring the wine and said thank you for inviting me. I talked to most of the people at the party but not the couple sitting across from me. The person to my left was busy talking to the man on the other side so we did not get a chance to talk about his work.

Overall: Based on my experience, I have to say that my original prediction did not come true and I can have a good time, even if I don't know anyone where I am going. I can have conversations with people I don't know.

An experiment such as this helps you review your original beliefs. Before going to the party, you believed you weren't very interesting and no one would find talking to you enjoyable. You now have to reevaluate that belief. Your experiment disproved it. Although you may not be ready to believe that you are always going to enjoy parties when you don't know anyone, you have to accept that it can sometimes happen. Your new belief might be:

I can sometimes enjoy parties even if I don't know anyone.

STOP AND THINK

There are two types of goals: measuring success and measuring each step, called intentional goals. To be successful, you need to focus on both. For example, if you want to lose 10 pounds, this is your overall or success goal. The steps you need to take, such as changing your diet and exercise habits, are your intentions. If you measure the success at your intentions on a scale of 0 to 100 percent, it is easier to see where you can improve and you are less likely to give up.

Comparing Behaviors

You can use planned experiments to test behaviors as well as beliefs. Suppose you want work on how you handle fights with your partner. Your overall goal is to resolve the fight and have a healthier relationship. You want to know what types of behaviors you could use to help reach this goal. To start, list several different behaviors. These are your intention action goals. You might list the following:

- Not talking to one another for one hour and then just moving on from the argument.

- Acknowledging his side of the argument without getting defensive and criticizing him. Using the sentence "I can understand why you are upset because…."

- Writing a letter to your partner explaining what is upsetting you.

- Giving each of you a few minutes to cool down and then talking without interrupting each other.

You can now try out different behaviors to determine which works best for you. Keep a report card and use the same rating system, giving each action a score from 0 to 100 percent for how well you executed the action and then rate how much it contributed successfully to the outcome goal of resolving the fight.

Report Card:

Not talking to one another for one hour and then just moving on from the argument.

How well I did this: 60%

How effective it was: 80%

Notes: This was effective when I was able to do it, but was harder to do than I expected.

Acknowledging his side of the argument using the sentence "I can understand why you are upset because…." without getting defensive and criticizing him.

How well I did this: 80%

How effective it was: 90%

Notes: This was easier than I expected. Having a specific response gives me some control. This strategy opened the door to him having empathy for my side.

Writing a letter to your partner explaining what is upsetting you.

How well I did this: 99%

How effective it was: 40%

Notes: This strategy was easy for me to do, but it just reignited the fight.

Giving each of you a few minutes to cool down and then talking without interrupting each other.

How well I did this: 40%

How effective it was: 90%

Notes: This strategy was incredibly hard to pull off, but when I did, it helped.

By keeping a self-rated report card you can note which behavior you used and how well each contributed to the outcome. After a while, you can look back to determine which behavior gives you the most desirable outcome: in this case, resolving the argument and feeling more satisfied in the relationship. After you have reviewed your different approaches, you can draw a conclusion:

"Overall, when my husband and I fight, the best course of action was to use a preplanned statement and acknowledge his feelings and point of view. This ultimately leads to him wanting to know how I feel as well. We both end up feeling that the other person has listened."

This type of experiment also helps when you are trying to create a level of comfort for a task you find difficult. Suppose you have anxiety when you fly in an airplane and you have a trip coming up. You want to lower your level of anxiety. Start by creating small steps, each one leading you closer to being comfortable flying.

Your actions and goals might be:

Actions	Goal
Take a ride to the airport.	Don't panic; chat with friend.
Go on a tour of an airplane hangar.	Feel relaxed.
Take a short flight with a friend.	Read the paper during the flight.

Use the same report card system to chart your progress. Rate each action and each goal on a scale from 0 to 100 percent. Don't move on to the next step until you have completed the task by at least 80 percent and the goal by at least 90 percent.

GIVE IT A TRY

Think about how you drink your coffee each morning. Do you rush through, drinking it as you get ready for work? How much do you think you would enjoy it if you used mindfulness and slowly drank the hot coffee? Make a prediction and give it a rating from 0 to 100 percent. In the morning, wake up 15 minutes early to sit down and practice mindfulness while drinking your coffee. How much did you enjoy it? Did it match your prediction?

Feedback

Another type of behavioral experiment is to create surveys and ask for feedback. Surveys work best in formal settings, such as work or school. In less formal settings, you will need to settle for informal feedback. This type of experiment is helpful if you worry about how other people react to you.

Formal Surveys

Suppose you feel you must be perfect at work in order to get promoted. You try hinting to co-workers or your boss for feedback on your performance, but don't seem to get the information you are looking for. You feel judged for every mistake you make. You don't think your co-workers are being honest when they say something positive. You can create a survey to test this negative thought process while gathering some constructive information on your performance.

You might include questions such as the following:

- How would you rate my overall performance in the last six months?

- Was there a time in the last six months when you thought I was not doing enough? What specifically could I have done differently?

- What do you consider to my areas of strength?

- What do you consider to be areas that need improvement?

- What skill would you like to me focus on developing over the next six months?

- What are your expectations (what is the policy) when it comes to responding to emails and calls during my personal time, such as nights, weekends, and vacations?

- How would you describe my communication with clients?

- How would you describe my communication with co-workers?

Then, set up a meeting with your boss and ask her to complete the survey. Ask other important team members to complete it as well. You now have specific information to prove or disprove that your boss and co-workers are negatively judging you at work.

> **IMAGINE THAT**
>
> Sometimes you may find your original prediction is correct. For example, your original belief may be "My boss doesn't want to hear my ideas." Your experiment may prove this to be true. You then need to think about whether the results say something about you or about your boss. Maybe he is simply close-minded or intimidated when others have good ideas. While you may not like the results, you can now make a decision about what is best for your life.

Informal Surveys

In many situations, a formal survey may seem unusual and may not be an effective way to get feedback on your negative beliefs. In these cases, informal surveys are useful. They work well with friends, significant others, and family.

Situation: I'm single and would like to develop a committed romantic relationship.

Problem: I cannot seem to get passed the first date.

Beliefs: I am ugly and overweight. This is why no one is interested in going out for more than a first date. I am never going to get married.

Challenges to problematic thinking: I know people who are heavier than me who are happily married. I have been asked out and obviously those people already know my size. Therefore, some people must find me attractive. Maybe it is just that I have not found the right person.

In this situation, your plan of action might be to invite a few close friends over for dinner and explain your concerns. Ask them for feedback on your appearance, how you dress for a date, your conversation style, and on the people you have been dating. Let them know you are looking for constructive feedback, such as suggestions on what to change and ideas on how to make those changes. Let them know this is not a pep rally nor is it an opportunity to tear you down. Keep the conversation focused on specific topics, such as what clothing might be flattering to wear or what behaviors you should avoid on a date. Let your friends know that they can be honest, and that you appreciate their feedback.

Write down everything they say and try not to react defensively. Initially, you might not want to hear the information, but after you've had time to reflect on the feedback, you can refer to your notes and make changes you think are appropriate. Recognize that although you are not perfect and your friends' feedback is not the letter of the law, you now know some areas where you can improve and feel reinforced about some things you doing right.

Observation

There may be times when you're not able to directly measure the results of your prediction by planning an experiment or taking a survey. Instead, you may record your observations. Suppose you recently moved into an apartment building. Many of the neighbors have stopped and said hello, but one neighbor won't acknowledge you, even when you are both in the elevator at the same time. You immediately think this neighbor doesn't like you. Each time you see him in the hall he ignores you and you are more convinced that he does not like you for some reason.

You decide to test your theory and determine if it's correct. First, come up with a few possible reasons for your neighbor's behavior.

* He does not like me.

* He is shy.

Because you can't determine what he is thinking and it is inappropriate to ask him directly, you decide to observe his behavior with some of the other neighbors. You watch as he gets his mail and another neighbor is also getting her mail. You notice they don't speak and barely look at each other. On the elevator, you talk with one neighbor but your unfriendly neighbor doesn't join in the conversation. After days of observing, you notice that he seems to speak only to the people who work in the building; he barely nods to the other neighbors and only responds when someone speaks directly to him.

Your original theory has been proven incorrect. It isn't that your neighbor doesn't like you; he keeps to himself and doesn't speak unless it's necessary. The theory that he is shy seems to fit better.

> **STOP AND THINK**
>
> When reviewing your results from your reality testing, be sure to use your ABCD chart. This helps you avoid reinforcing old beliefs.

Observations help when you are trying to discover which theory best fits a situation. This type of experiment helps you create alternative theories and opens you up to the possibility that there may be more than one explanation. Your observations may support or disprove your original theory.

Each type of reality testing—formal, informal, or observation—has benefits. You need to decide which type is practical for your situation and which gives you the feedback you need to make positive changes in your thinking and in your life. No matter which type you choose, there are three key components that will help you create successful experiments.

Expectations: Establish clear expectations for what you want to achieve. You do this by breaking your overall goal into steps, the more specific, the better.

Feedback: Feedback is necessary. Use the 0 to 100 percent self-report card and ask for feedback from others. Avoid becoming defensive; others may not want to be honest if you are defensive.

Reward: Reward yourself for carrying out each step and moving closer to your overall goal. You might use a star system for each step. When you achieve 10 stars, give yourself a concrete reward.

Your Turn: Testing Your Predictions

Use the ABCDE log you created in previous exercises. Fill in each column.

A: What is the situation or problem?

B: What negative beliefs do you have about the situation?

C: What do you assume will happen?

D: What are your problematic thought processes and how can you challenge them?

E: Which type of reality test would best fit this situation? What action plan can you use to prove your old theory wrong? What action plan can you use to achieve your overall goal?

Determine a reward for each action goal and for achieving your overall goal.

Remember, feedback does not necessarily need to be from other people. Rating your goals with the 0 to 100 percent scale is also feedback. Keep a notebook with all of your reality tests so you can refer to the results when a similar situation comes up.

The Least You Need to Know

- When you test your new beliefs, you are like a scientist looking for evidence to prove your beliefs and thinking process.
- Your experiments should include identifying problematic thinking processes and ideas to challenge those thoughts.
- Reality testing can help you choose what behavior will best help you reach your goals.
- Feedback is essential to understanding errors in your thinking patterns.

CBT for Personal Growth

Your thoughts have an impact on every part of your life. They reflect how you feel about yourself, how you interact with others, and how you handle stressful situations. When you use negative thoughts and words to describe yourself, it creates negativity in all these areas. CBT helps you to reframe and restructure your thoughts into more positive views. With practice and commitment, these changes are lasting and permanent, helping you gain more satisfaction from your life.

In this part, we discuss areas of personal growth, such as boosting self-esteem, improving communication, letting go of perfectionism, and building relationships. Finally, we talk about learning to manage the stress in your life by giving you step-by step ways to break problems down and solve them one at a time. As you focus on one area, you might notice the other parts of your life improving as well.

Increasing Your Self-Esteem

Do you like yourself? Are you happy with who you are? Your self-esteem reflects what you think about yourself. If you are like many people, you may not like yourself all the time. But it is possible to choose to like yourself. In this chapter, you will learn what self-esteem is, identify some of the obstacles to creating a healthy self-image, and discover ways to improve your self-esteem and learn self-acceptance.

What Do We Mean by Self-Esteem?

Self-esteem refers to your opinion of your overall value and self-worth. If you use negative words, such as failure, loser, idiot, stupid, or lazy when you think about yourself, you probably have low self-esteem. You may use external factors to measure your self-worth, such as your looks, your job, or your relationships, but self-worth is not just about what you offer to others; you have your own value as a person.

In This Chapter

- Learning to accept yourself as you are
- Why self-acceptance can be difficult
- How to creating a positive self-image
- How to overcome guilt and shame

Self-esteem is how you feel about yourself. It is your opinion of your value and self-worth.

If you think of low self-esteem as something to improve, you might believe that you need to develop high self-esteem. After all, high is the opposite of low. But both low and high self-esteem are the product of self-judgment. The opposite of low self-esteem is self-acceptance—to accept who you are and understand that while you are fallible, you are a complex human being with both strengths and weaknesses.

Self-Acceptance

Self-acceptance is unconditional. It is recognizing your weaknesses, your faults, and your limitations, and accepting that these do not define who you are or your self-worth. Self-acceptance means liking yourself, your whole self. It is accepting faults as areas to improve rather than judging them as failures.

Your level of self-acceptance often determines how happy you are in life. In his book, *Happiness Now*, author Robert Holden explains that you allow yourself to experience happiness only to the degree that you believe you are worthy of it. If you don't accept yourself, you don't believe you deserve to be happy; when you do accept yourself, you open yourself up to enjoying life.

Your level of self-acceptance might vary in different areas of your life. For example, you may feel confident at work, having mastered the duties of your job. When you make a mistake or miss a detail, you quickly move into problem-solving mode because your overall belief is that you are capable and competent. At the same time, you might feel inadequate in your relationships. You could feel guilty for not spending enough time with your wife and children or for not being considerate enough. You might think you are not a good husband. Your confidence level is high when at work but drops significantly the moment you walk into your home.

Self-acceptance allows you to take responsibility without becoming defensive. You see negative feedback as a critique, not a criticism, and you are open to growth and learning for a lifetime.

Negative views of yourself are limiting. If you believe "I am a failure. I will never be a good parent. I am not worthy of my children's love," you may give up trying. After all, no matter how hard you try, you believe you won't be successful. These types of negative views take away your motivation to change and improve. With self-acceptance, you look at yourself more objectively and take responsibility for your limits. For example, you make a choice to miss your child's dance recital in order to finish an important project at work. Your child is not happy. You might think, "I am doing the best I can. I thought I made a good choice based on my family's financial needs. I realize that this recital was more important than I thought. I can apologize and learn to communicate better with my child to prevent an ongoing pattern."

Obstacles to Self-Acceptance

There are two main components to developing self-acceptance:

- Recognizing your strengths and successes.
- Recognizing and being comfortable with your shortcomings and mistakes.

Recognizing your strengths may be easier, but even this can be difficult. The problematic thinking processes discussed in Chapter 2 interfere with learning to see your positive traits. For example, you focus only on the negative, ignoring or minimizing achievements and accomplishments. Other negative thinking patterns also become obstacles to self-acceptance.

Equating Acceptance with Giving Up

One of the myths about self-acceptance is that once you accept a fault, you must resign yourself to it. You think you must just give up and accept that it is part of you. But self-acceptance doesn't mean giving up or giving in, it means accepting your limitations and mistakes and working to improve them. Suppose you freeze up when taking a test. You want to go back to school but are concerned that your test anxiety will cause you to fail. You can accept that you aren't good at taking tests and allow it to limit you by not going back to school, or you can accept that you aren't good at taking tests and find strategies to help you better cope with the anxiety.

Measuring Your Worth on External Factors

You might equate your worth with external factors, such as your job, achievements, financial holdings, social status, attractiveness, or love life. But these situations are often temporary. You might go through several jobs in your lifetime, some better than others, some lasting longer than others. You might spend some time being unemployed. Your financial worth might not be where you want it to be. You might go through several relationships or you might be in a long-term relationship that has its ups and downs. The problem with linking your self-esteem to these situations is that when the situation ends or changes, your self-esteem suffers.

Overgeneralizing

Another common thinking process that contributes to low self-esteem is overgeneralizing. When you make one mistake, you believe you are a failure. You overgeneralize specific situations and rather than seeing them as temporary or one-time situations, you globalize them, making them about your entire life. For example, you make a mistake at work and miss an important deadline. Your boss is angry. You believe you are a failure, you can't do the job, and you are pathetic and incompetent. You fail to recognize that this as one single incident and not representative of your job performance as a whole.

Maintaining an Outdated Self-Image

Life is ever-changing. What you feel, think, and do today is probably much different than what you felt, thought, and did five or ten years ago. Even so, your opinion of yourself is probably the same as it was in the past. You don't take into consideration what you have learned and experienced through the years. If you were unpopular in high school, you still see yourself as unlikeable.

Basing Your Self-Worth on One Aspect

Human beings are complex. There are many facets to your personality. You have varied abilities and talents. You might show different sides of your personality and take a different role in different areas of your life. For example, at the office you could be a leader and with your friends you are more passive. You might be great at swimming but not so good at catching a ball. You might be good at cooking but not as competent at housework. You might enjoy some parts of your job but find other parts tedious and boring. Yet, you base your self-worth on limited aspects of yourself. For example, you may have beautiful eyes but hate your nose. You think you are ugly because you only see your nose.

Your Turn: Self-Assessment

For each of the following categories, write down a few short statements that describe you.

- Physical appearance

- Interpersonal skills (how you relate to others)

- Problem solving

- Creativity

- Sexuality

- Productivity at work or school

- Personal productivity

- How others see you

Once you have completed the list, go back and look at each word. Circle each one you see as a positive quality or a strength.

For each negative word or shortcoming, think about which problematic thinking process you are using. Look over the list in Chapter 2.

- Are you overgeneralizing?

- Ignoring the positive?

- Thinking in terms of black and white?

- Using mental filtering?

- Being specific without considering the whole situation?

Change the wording of your negative assumptions about yourself to a more positive thought process.

Rewrite your list to reflect the new language you have used. Read the list aloud at least once every day.

Steps to Improving Self-Esteem

It is impossible to rid yourself of shortcomings. The idea of self-acceptance is not about making yourself perfect. It is about accepting who you are. It is accepting that you are a unique individual. It is knowing that you have something to offer to others. Accepting shortcomings doesn't make you less of a person or less valuable to yourself and others.

IMAGINE THAT

People who have accepted themselves focus on growth and improvement, while people with low self-esteem focus on not making mistakes.

Monitor and Adjust Your Self-Talk

The self-assessment you completed in the previous exercise identified your negative self-perceptions. Learning about your self-talk and the negative messages you send yourself is the first step to improving your self-esteem. You can now reword your messages so they are more positive and relevant to your life.

Suppose under work performance you wrote down the following:

- I am careless; I make a lot of mistakes.

- I am not talented; I don't have the natural skills others do.

- I am lazy; I leave at work earlier than many of my co-workers.

As you completed the assessment, you realized that you used mental filtering, overgeneralizing, and black-and-white thinking, as well as personalizing and labeling statements. You focused only what you did wrong, compared yourself to others, and held yourself to an impossible standard without considering what else you have going on in your life.

Revised statements might look like this:

- I am usually conscientious about my work, but sometimes there is so much happening I feel overwhelmed.

- I just started to learn this new task. Just because I don't know how to do it right now does not mean I cannot learn.

- I try hard. I get in an hour before others do and often work over the weekend.

As you go through your day, pay attention to how often you repeat one of your negative self-assessments. Immediately change your thought to your revised statement.

STOP AND THINK

When revising negative self-talk, be sure to use accurate and logical language. Your mind will fight your thoughts if you come up with statements that are illogical or positive hype. For example, if you are new at your job, don't combat a negative thought with, "I am the smartest person at the office." Instead, create a positive but accurate thought, such as, "I am competent and with training I will do this job well."

Review Your Expectations

When you set a goal or create expectations for a situation and you fall short or the reality of the situation is much different than what you expected, your self-esteem takes a hit. You feel you have failed. It could be that your expectations are unrealistic. Suppose you have just started a new job. You set an expectation that you will learn the job within one week. At the end of the week, you feel disappointed in yourself because you haven't learned all the aspects of the job yet. You think, "I will never learn this job; I am stupid and unqualified." Your expectations were unrealistic and set you up for feeling bad about yourself.

> **CBTIDBIT**
>
> Look at situations with self-efficacy. This is the belief that you can handle a situation. It doesn't necessarily mean you know what you are going to do but that you have the resources and capabilities to figure things out.

Don't Compare Yourself to Others

Your self-esteem suffers if you are constantly comparing yourself to others. You can always find someone who is better at something than you are, someone who has a nicer car, a bigger house. When you compare yourself to someone else, you unconsciously put yourself down; you state that what you have or can do is not good enough.

Focus instead on your own goals. Reward yourself each time you reach a goal. Be proud of your accomplishments. Think "in the grey" instead of putting yourself and others in categories of either successful or failure. Think of each person, including yourself, as an individual with positive and negatives. Remember, you don't know someone else's story or what is behind their success. You could believe someone is "talented at work" without realizing that their health or family life is suffering as a result. When you compare yourself to others, you assume you want to be like them without considering the consequences.

Adjust Your Self-Image to Fit the Present Moment

We often turn to an old, outdated image of ourselves. We focus on what we used to be and create our self-image based on that. Suppose you struggled during school and never thought of yourself as being one of the "smart kids." Although you now have a successful career, you still think of yourself as less intelligent than others. Instead of carrying around your old belief, you need to make adjustments to fit today's reality. Make a list of all the ways you have changed. If you did not have many friends in high school, start thinking about all of the people in your life who matter to you now. If your list does not have enough to change your view, add some activities you can do to increase the list and reach your goal.

Add Self-Esteem Activities

Your beliefs about yourself might stop you from trying new things or participating in activities that would improve your self-esteem. Suppose you believe that you have no friends, and that you are too shy to take part in social gatherings.

You consider signing up with a local hiking group to meet new people, or at least be around other people, but then you think, "I'm no good at small talk; I'll just act shy, be unlikeable, and won't gain any friends." This is the self-esteem loop that keeps you trapped. Instead, adjust your expectations. Limit your exposure by committing to a short hike rather than an entire weekend, and commit to doing an action at least two times.

Your goal might be:

I will go on two hiking events. I will go for the shortest hikes so I don't feel trapped. I will say "hi" to people and ask them one question. I don't expect that I will share personal information like a phone number by the end of the hike. This is just for me.

Your Turn: Create Mini Action Plans

Keep track of your thoughts about yourself and create small actions to help counter negative thoughts or images about yourself. Remember to be specific, flexible, and positive in your thoughts about yourself and the behavior actions you plan.

GIVE IT A TRY

Get out a piece of paper and set a timer for five minutes. Write down five positive things about you in the following categories:

- Strengths
- Achievements
- Activities you enjoy
- What you admire about yourself
- What makes you feel good about yourself

Don't worry about grammar or spelling. Simply focus on the positives in your life.

Accepting Bad Behavior

Learning to change your thought process, while never easy, may seem impossible if you feel guilt and shame over a large error you have made. Suppose you…

- Stole money or items at your job.

- Had an affair.

- Lost your temper and physically hurt someone.

You might believe you are a horrible person and think that changing that belief is impossible and wrong. How can you have any self-esteem when you have treated people so terribly? Your guilt overrides any positive statements you try to make.

Self-acceptance means accepting yourself, flaws and all. It means you accept that you are fallible and imperfect. You make mistakes. It means you accept that these mistakes do not define who you are. At the same time, you must accept your mistake, take responsibility for it, and learn from it.

When you accept your mistake, you accept that this mistake does not make you worthless. It does not make you a terrible person. It makes you a person who has made a mistake. And everyone makes mistakes. Remember that you have many good qualities that define who you are.

Suppose you had an affair and you lied to your partner. When your partner found out about the affair, she was hurt. You feel guilty and believe only a bad person would do such a horrible thing. You can't get past the guilt and shame you feel at causing your wife such pain. Even though it is hard, you must accept that your behavior was wrong. Your actions caused someone pain. However, you also have many good qualities. This mistake is not who you are.

CBTIDBIT

It isn't possible to change the past, but it is possible to change how you perceive it and how you respond to it going forward. Look objectively at what happened to make you feel guilty, and reframe the memory to include what you learned and how you changed.

Think about what you can learn from this mistake. Why did it happen? What negative thoughts and feelings brought about this behavior? What can you do to make sure this type of mistake doesn't happen again?

You must also take responsibility for your mistake. Acknowledge the pain the other person feels. Apologize and accept the consequences of your actions. Avoiding facing the mistake only increases your feelings of inadequacy and shame. If you have hurt someone, you need to apologize. If you have taken something, you need to make amends. However, this only works if you are sincere in asking forgiveness. Remember, you cannot control whether someone forgives you; you can only control whether you forgive yourself.

It is difficult to come to terms with a major mistake, especially when it hurts other people, but it is possible. Continue to focus on your self-talk and monitor it for negative thought patterns. Continue to work on adopting a more helpful way of thinking.

The Least You Need to Know

- Self-acceptance means liking yourself despite your faults and limitations.
- Your self-image may be outdated or based on previous situations.
- Unrealistic expectations can lead to low self-esteem.
- Making mistakes does not make you a bad person; it makes you a person who has made a mistake.

CHAPTER 12

Overcoming Perfectionism

Striving for excellence is an admirable trait. It propels you to do your best. But there is a fine line between striving for excellence and the need to be perfect. In this chapter you will learn what perfectionism is, how it can negatively impact your life, and strategies to lessen your expectations while still trying to do your best.

Defining Perfectionism

Perfectionism is placing pressure on yourself to meet exceedingly high standards. Having goals and standards is important. People without goals often don't get much accomplished; they work hard but feel like they are spinning their wheels. This is because they haven't created a goal or an end result. They don't know what they are working toward and therefore don't know when they have achieved it. On the other hand, having extremely high standards means nothing is ever good enough. Trying to achieve perfection can cause frustration, anxiety, and depression.

In This Chapter

- Understanding the need to be perfect
- Identifying perfectionist behaviors
- How to stop seeing the world in black and white
- How perfectionism can cause procrastination

> **DEFINITION**
>
> **Perfectionism** is having self-imposed, extremely high standards and constantly working to attain these standards, even when it interferes with your ability to do the task or other areas of your life.

Imagine you are completing a report for work. You spend several hours compiling the information. You want to make sure it is correct and spend hours double-checking the research you already completed. You then ask a co-worker to check your work, just to make sure there aren't any errors. When you receive it back, you do the research again, checking for mistakes. Your boss gave you one day to complete the report, but because you needed to check the work repeatedly, you took three. Your boss is upset that the report was not completed on time. Although your work may have been perfect, it didn't matter because you didn't turn it in when it was needed.

You could be a perfectionist in everything you do or have high standards in only a few areas of your life. For example, suppose you play baseball. You are passionate about the sport and want to win every game. You spend hours practicing hitting and throwing the ball. You expect your teammates to do the same and are annoyed when they don't even show up for practice. You blame yourself if your team loses, believing if you had hit the ball farther or run a little faster you would have won. You spend even more time practicing after a loss. Because of the time you spend on baseball, your work and relationships suffer. All of your goals center on being a perfect baseball player.

Perfectionism comes with a cost. You devote a tremendous amount of time and energy trying to reach unrealistic goals. Although you may be doing some or most things well, perfectionism will take a toll. The following are some of the ways perfectionism can negatively affect your life:

- You lack free time.

- You neglect some areas of your life.

- Achievements feel empty or do not satisfy you.

- You blame yourself when things don't go right or the way you want them done.

- You blame others when things aren't done "the right way" or your way.

- You don't believe others can do the job as well as you.

- You waste time by doing things several times to make sure they are done correctly.

- You feel others judge you if things are not perfect.

- You constantly worry about not being good enough.

- You procrastinate or avoid doing things because you don't think you will do them perfectly.

STOP AND THINK

Perfectionism has been shown to have both negative and positive effects on your health. When you use perfectionism to provide motivation to succeed, it has a positive effect on health. However, when you believe others are judging you as perfect or not perfect, there is a negative effect and results in a higher risk of developing physical illness.

It is important to set goals and to have high standards. However, if your quest for excellence interferes with other parts of your life or causes you frustration and anxiety, you need to learn ways to scale back your expectations.

Your Turn: Are You a Perfectionist?

Read the following statements and think about how they apply to you. Respond with *always*, *frequently*, *rarely*, or *never*.

1. Making mistakes always causes problems.

2. I spend so much time making sure I complete tasks correctly that I often don't have time to finish the rest of my work or do other things.

3. I feel it is important to do things right the first time.

4. I avoid doing tasks I don't think I can do perfectly.

5. I believe other people think badly of me if things are not done right.

6. I need to do everything well, even those things that I know I am not good at.

7. When I do accomplish something, I don't think it is enough. I always think there is something more I could have done.

If you responded "always" or "frequently" to most of the statements, chances are you have problems with perfectionism.

Perfectionist Thought Patterns

Problematic thought patterns are inaccurate ways of interpreting the world around you. Many of the common ones are listed in Chapter 2. Those common in perfectionism include the following:

Black-and-White Thinking

Everything is either good or bad. You don't see any grey area. Therefore, if a situation is not perfect, it is unacceptable. Some examples of this type of thinking pattern in perfectionism include the following:

- If it isn't perfect, it is a failure.
- If I can't do it perfectly, I might as well not try at all.
- I am either a loser or a winner; I'm either successful or a failure.

Catastrophizing

Every problem ends in disaster. You believe any little mistake is unacceptable. Some examples of this type of thinking in perfectionism include the following:

- If I make a mistake, everyone will think I am stupid.
- I can't handle the humiliation of making a mistake.

> **GIVE IT A TRY**
>
> Do something badly. Go out, try something new and intentionally fail at it. Learn from your mistake. You should learn two things: one, how to do it better, and two, nothing happened. You didn't die, you didn't stop breathing, everyone didn't stand in a circle around you, pointing and laughing. Life went on. Go on, go out and do something badly.

Personalization and Blame

Everything that goes wrong is your fault or you blame others because they didn't live up to your high standards. You say things like this:

- We would have won the baseball game if I had practiced more during the week.

- We would have won the baseball game if the other players took it seriously and showed up for practice.

- Why can't my employees just listen to me and do things correctly?

- I am better off doing everything myself; others are just lazy and stupid.

"Should" and "Must"

Everyone needs to live up to your high standards and you are frustrated and angry when they don't. You feel guilty if you do not do everything exactly right. This type of thinking may lead to statements such as the following:

- Mistakes are bad; I should never make a mistake.

- I should always make sure my work is perfect before I hand it in.

- Everyone should work as hard as I do; I work over the weekends, why shouldn't they?

Mind Reading

You assume other people follow the same rules as you do. You feel angry when other people live by different rules. You lack empathy and consideration for how others think.

- My co-workers don't check emails over the weekends and evenings—what is wrong with them?

- My friend didn't invite my husband to join in; I would never do such a thing. She is rude and inconsiderate.

Adding Flexibility to Your Life

You have certain "rules" you live by. These might include, "It is important to be kind to others," or "Lying is wrong." You follow these rules most of the time but also understand that they are flexible. You might not be kind to people every moment of every day and yet you still consider yourself a kind person. Rules such as these are important and usually are helpful in your life. The rules become unhelpful when they are rigid or inflexible; for example, you might think you are a failure if you do not follow a rule exactly.

Revising Rigid Rules

Think about your expectations for yourself and others. Do you have high expectations? Do you get hurt, angry, anxious, or disappointed when things don't go your way? Is it difficult for you to revise your goals and expectations when they seem unreasonable or unattainable? If you have a hard time doing so or find you are judging others for not living up to your standards, you probably need to revise the rules you live by.

> **CBTIDBIT**
>
> When trying to be more flexible or to see something from a different perspective, change your physical environment. Go for a walk, sit in a different chair, or move to a different room. Sometimes, literally changing your perspective helps you think differently.

Rigid rule: Others should not ask personal questions until they get to know me better.

Flexible rule: Sometimes people ask personal questions as a way to get to know me.

Rigid rule: Everyone should work as hard as I do.

Flexible rule: It is my choice to work this hard. Others can make their own decisions.

Rigid rule: I cannot make a mistake or I will look foolish.

Flexible rule: Everyone makes mistakes. It is okay if I make a mistake.

Rigid rule: I must do everything completely and perfectly before letting someone else see it.

Flexible rule: It is okay to show someone a draft or a work in progress.

When you find yourself feeling disappointed in your own behavior or the behavior of others, think about your expectations. Is it rigid or flexible? Write down your rule and then create a more flexible version of the rule. The ABCD charts you completed in previous chapters can help you discover your rigid rules and modify your expectations and thoughts.

Perfectionist Behavior Checklist

Perfectionism shows up in your behaviors, leaving you feeling overwhelmed. Review the following statements and check off any behaviors that are relevant in your life:

❑ Indecisive; you are unable to make a decision because you are afraid of making the wrong decision.

❑ Overly organized; you write and rewrite lists, you believe everything has its place and feel uncomfortable when things are not put away properly.

❑ You must have your workspace organized before you can start work.

❑ You check over your work several times to make sure it is correct.

❑ You ask others to check your work to make sure it is acceptable.

❑ You avoid tasks you think you can't complete perfectly.

❑ You correct other people when they make a small mistake such as mispronounce a word or say something incorrect.

❑ You comment when you think someone says something politically incorrect and try to persuade them into thinking like you.

❑ You clean your bathroom and kitchen with antiseptic cleansers every day or several times to make sure there aren't any germs.

❑ When giving directions, you fill in every possible detail.

❑ You keep paperwork, such as bank statements and tax returns, for years and years, just in case you need the information.

❑ You do all the work yourself, at home and at work, because you don't trust anyone else to do it correctly.

❑ You redo other people's work because "it's just not good enough."

❑ You demand that others do things your way.

STOP AND THINK

Perfectionism often interferes with relationships. Your need to be perfect puts you at odds with your partner. You need to be the best, sometimes creating a rivalry between the two of you. You also demand perfection in others, making your partner strive to live up to your unrealistic expectations—and always fall short.

These are some examples of perfectionist behaviors. You might notice others in your life. When you find yourself behaving in these ways, stop and ask yourself if you are doing so because you are trying to meet your extremely high standards. If so, try to modify your behaviors to reflect thinking that is more flexible.

Introduce Shades of Grey into Your Life

Problematic thinking that leads to perfectionism usually contains absolutes. You think that something must be done a certain way or it is wrong; you believe that if you don't do something perfectly, it isn't worth doing. Changing perfectionism doesn't mean giving up on your standards, it means introducing shades of grey into your life.

Perfectionism may not show up in all areas of your life and may not interfere with some areas as much as others. To start, consider where consider where your quest for perfection is causing the most problems. For example:

- Do you have trouble getting things accomplished at work accomplished because you want everything to be perfect?

- Is your relationship in trouble because you expect your partner to do everything your way?

- Do you exercise or diet constantly because you need to have a perfect body?

- Do you neglect certain parts of your life because you spend too much time on others? What are those areas where you spend too much time?

Once you decide where you want to start, think about the standards that are the most important to you. Remember, the goal is not to settle but to limit your standards to things that really matter.

Your Turn: Shades of Grey

Make a short list of your expectations for a given task. Once you meet those standards, stop and let go of any unwritten standards. This prevents you from wasting times seeking the "best" or "most perfect thing." For example, suppose you are shopping for a pair of running shoes. Make a list of three important features you want in your new shoes. You might want...

- Proper fit.

- Good for cross training.

- No more than $60.00.

Keep your short list with you when you shop. Once you find a pair of shoes that fit your criteria, buy the shoes and end your shopping trip. Don't go into several more stores to see if you can find a better pair. You know you have a product that meets your high criteria. You are not settling, you are just preventing yourself from wasting time "making it perfect." Follow this example to limit your criteria instead of reaching for the impossible.

> **👉 CBTIDBIT**
>
> Limiting your choices requires you to choose between what is available rather than endlessly searching for the perfect choice. For example, if you agonize each morning trying to find the perfect outfit to wear to work, try taking out several outfits on Sunday evening. In the morning, choose from one of these outfits rather than going through all of your clothes.

Cost-Benefit Analysis

At first, lessening your expectations feels uncomfortable. You fight the urge to continue to live up to your high standards. You might find it helpful to list ways that a particular high standard has had negative consequences in your life. In the preceding example, you might write down these things:

- Spent my entire day going from shoe store to shoe store.
- Wasted gas driving around.
- Spent extra money buying coffee and lunch to keep my energy up.
- Missed out on getting together with friends because I was so wrapped up in shopping.
- Ended up going over my budget.

Reminding yourself of the negative consequences of your perfectionism keeps you motivated to change. Reward yourself, even if it is a virtual pat on the back, each time you follow your new standard. Remember, everyone makes mistakes, so if you slip and go to one extra shoe store, don't judge yourself, just review your goals and commitment to change and start again.

Procrastination and Perfectionism

If you are a perfectionist, you might avoid doing things that you can't do perfectly. You prefer not to do something than to fail at doing it. You procrastinate.

IMAGINE THAT

Approach avoidance is a classic perfectionist pattern. You start with a bang, putting forth strong effort and energy and then fizzle out. For example, when a college student starts a new semester, he starts with a vengeance, staying up late, completing every assignment. By the end of the semester, he avoids studying, skips classes and doesn't bother showing up for the final exam.

Imagine you have to complete a report for work. There is no specific deadline but you know your boss is waiting for it. Yet, you keep putting off starting. It is a project you don't have much interest in and don't think is important. Still, you want it to be perfect; anything less is a failure. Day after day you avoid starting the report. You think, "Maybe it is better to not do it at all than to a basic job." When you find yourself avoiding a task, ask yourself these questions:

- Am I striving for excellence or demanding perfection?

- Is the result going to matter in my life next month, next year, five years from now?

- Do I want to do well because this is something that matters to me or because I want others to think well of me?

- What is the worst thing that could happen? How am I going to manage that?

Use the following strategies to help you deal with procrastination:

Create a clear beginning to your project. Select an exact time to start instead of waiting until you "feel like doing something."

Set a specific ending time. Don't allow yourself to review or redo tasks to make them better. End at the time you set.

Use a timer. Give yourself a specific amount of time to work on a task and set the timer to go off five minutes before to warn you time is almost up. Then reset it to go off at the ending time. When the second timer rings, stop working.

These strategies might feel uncomfortable at first. You might worry about the quality of your work. With practice, it gets easier to not double check or redo tasks.

Your Turn: Taking One Step at a Time

When working toward a goal, it is beneficial to break it down into steps. The stepladder approach outlined in Chapter 5 works well for overcoming perfectionism. Start with the top and bottom rung of the ladder. On the bottom rung, list your perfectionism behavior you want to change. On the top rung, write down your goal—how you want your behavior to look. Create intermediate goals on each rung. Suppose you check your work three times and have a co-worker check it once before handing it in, your ladder may look like:

Check work once and hand it in.

Check work twice and hand it in

Check work twice and have co-worker check it

Check work three times and have co-worker check it

Rather than trying to reach your goal in one step, you have a plan of action. Depending on your goal, your ladder may have more or fewer steps. Remember, when you first begin, you might feel some anxiety. Hang in there and resist the urge to resort back to your perfectionism behaviors. If you do give in, you might find it even more difficult next time.

The Least You Need to Know

- Perfectionism is created from self-imposed standards.
- Categorizing things as "good" or "bad" leads to perfectionism.
- Consider the costs of perfectionism to find motivation to change.
- Procrastination is sometimes the result of perfectionism.
- Limiting your expectations can help you manage perfectionist tendencies.

CHAPTER 13

Improving Your Relationships

Relationships can bring a great deal of joy to your life. When there are problems, however, these same relationships cause pain, anxiety, and stress. This chapter identifies some of the common types of problems that can occur in a relationship and provides strategies for dealing with them. Although this chapter focuses on the relationship between partners, the concepts and skills can be applied to any relationship.

In This Chapter

- What to do when you blame one another
- How to frame demands as preferences
- Ending the cycle of arguments
- Tips for improving communication skills

Who Is to Blame?

Your relationship isn't working, or maybe you are going through a bumpy patch. You love your partner but feel neglected, misunderstood, disrespected, or criticized. You aren't sure what went wrong, but lately you seem to argue more than talk. When you attempt to resolve differences, you end up fighting instead or you both ignore each other.

You might think:

- I cannot seem to communicate with him. Why bother trying?

- She never listens to me anymore. She doesn't care about my opinion. This is hopeless.

- He wants everything done his way. I am sick of it.

- She turns down my advances all the time. I am not loved or attractive.

- I was just trying to help him. What a waste of time.

- Get off my back. She is always telling me I am wrong.

No matter what is wrong, chances are you blame your partner for many of the problems in your relationship. You think if you could fix him, everything would be okay. But fixing a relationship isn't about fixing the other person. Both people are responsible for the health of the relationship and both people are responsible when things aren't working. It is best when both people work together to solve problems within a relationship. However, rather than focusing on what the other person can do, you need to focus on what you can do to improve the relationship. Try taking responsibility for your own limitations, mistakes, and contributions to the problem.

> **STOP AND THINK**
>
> You might use blame to protect your self-esteem. It is easier to make someone else wrong than it is to accept responsibility. Most people, even those who blame their spouse for marriage problems, understand that they must take at least partial responsibility but it is difficult for them to do so. Often those who blame are the partners unwilling to see a marriage counselor or work on improving the marriage.

Choose Your Reaction

Your significant other gives you some negative feedback. You feel upset. "He's so critical of me. He makes me so angry," you think. You want to tell him how wrong he is and defend yourself. You keep going over his words and actions in your mind, blaming him for getting you mad. In reality, no one can upset you. You must take responsibility for your feelings. You choose your reactions—you choose to be upset or furious. Your first reaction is "He is putting me down; I need to stand up for myself. I need to defend myself and point out how horrible he is." Instead, you can choose to be empathetic, compassionate, and flexible. Think, "Does he have a point? Why is he upset by this; did he have a bad day at work or is this something that really bothers him? I don't like how he started the conversation but I am not always perfect in how I explain myself."

GIVE IT A TRY

The next time your partner criticizes you in some way, instead of defending your position, pause and ask yourself these questions: What point is he trying to make? What else might be going on today? Can I hold myself accountable for anything he is saying?

Problems usually have two components: practical and emotional. When you become angry or anxious, you are probably focusing more on the emotional reaction than to the practical problem. For example, it's your night to make dinner for you and your partner. Your partner calls after you have already put the food on the stove and tells you he is going out for a drink with an important client and some other people from the office and won't be home for dinner. Your initial reaction is to feel angry and think, "I am not important. He is so disrespectful and inconsiderate. He always does something like this. Wait till he gets home!" These are all emotional reactions and are likely to escalate the problem. Instead, focus on the practical parts of the problem. Recite the facts without adding judgment or your opinion: "I spent $50.00 on groceries. I was looking forward to spending time with him and now I will have to eat alone. I had some important things to tell him." Now you can problem solve. "I can save the leftover food for lunch tomorrow. It's important that he meets with the client and could mean a larger bonus. I can catch up with one of my girlfriends on the phone and talk to my husband tomorrow about the things I wanted to discuss."

When you separate the emotional reaction from the emotional problem, you can look at it more objectively. It allows you to discover the problematic thinking process, change your thoughts, and then change your reaction.

Making Demands

You grew up with a certain image of what the perfect relationship looked like. This image might have come from your parent's marriage, observing other couples or watching television. You created certain expectations in your mind; you have ideas of how you expect your significant other to act. In the beginning, you are willing to relax your expectations because you are in love. But as your relationship continues, these expectations become demands—the "shoulds" and "musts" in your life.

CBTIDBIT

"Should" and "must" statements reflect inflexible or rigid thinking. When questioning these types of thoughts, ask yourself what you would tell a friend. For example, if a friend called, upset because her boyfriend was late and hadn't called, what would you say? Would you reassure her? Tell her he is probably stuck in traffic or held up at work? You might tell her not to worry or not to be too hard on him for forgetting to call one time. Consider your advice to a friend when restructuring your thoughts.

A "should" or a "must" is a demand you put on yourself or others or on the circumstances.

For example:

- He **must** call me when he knows he is going to be late.

- I **must** be a perfect wife for him to love me.

- Marriage **should not** have any problems. When there are problems, it means the marriage is doomed.

Your "musts" and "shoulds" might be masked under your emotions. For example, you get annoyed when your partner does not give you his full attention when you are talking. You get angry when he does not stop what he is doing to listen. The underlying reason, however, is that you have made a demand, "He must listen to me; I must have his full attention when I want it." Additionally you have attached an emotional response to this demand; "If he doesn't listen to me he doesn't love me, or he is not a good husband."

Use an ABC chart to help identify your underlying should or must demands.

A: Activating Event	B: "Should" or "Must" Statement	C: Emotion
Husband continued to watch television while I was talking.	He should listen to me when I am talking.	Angry

Once you identify your "should" or "must" statement, create a healthier way to look at the situation. "I would prefer he give me his undivided attention when I talk to him, but this is not always possible. If I need his undivided attention, I can tell him and we can make sure there aren't any distractions." Once you change your demand to a preference, your anger diminishes.

 IMAGINE THAT

The term MUSTerbation is sometimes used to refer to emotional and cognitive demands placed on yourself, others, or a group of people. MUSTerbation uses terms such as "must," "should," "need," or "have to." It is often the source of conflicts.

When disputing "should" and "must" statements, remember the following:

- Your partner is an individual with free will.

- Your partner has the right to make his or her own decisions.

- Your partner does not always need to do what you want and does not need to agree with you at all times.

- When your partner does not follow your expectations, it does not mean he or she does not love you.

You might find it helpful to turn your expectation into a question, such as, "Why must he listen with undivided attention every time I talk to him?" While it may be unpleasant when your partner does not agree with you or meet your expectations, you are an adult and can handle the disappointment.

Your Turn: Sharing Preferences

Over the next week, use the ABC chart to record anytime you feel frustrated or disappointed in your relationship.

Use the information to determine your "should" and "must" expectations.

Rewrite each into a preference.

At the end of the week, cross out any preference you think is unreasonable for your relationship.

Set up a time to talk with your partner about the preferences left on your list. You can start the conversation with "I have some ideas about how we should treat each other. I want to share these ideas with you and would like to hear your input."

Ask your partner to write down his preferences. When he shares his list, be sure not to interrupt or correct him until it is your turn to give feedback.

Breaking the Cycle

Unmet expectations in your marriage might start a vicious cycle. For example, you are upset that your partner works late most nights and you don't spend much time together. By the time he arrives home, you are hurt and annoyed; you ignore him, trying to punish him for working late. Your partner feels your anger. He doesn't feel that home is a pleasant place and whenever his boss asks someone to stay late, he volunteers. This cycle continues until you and your partner are barely speaking to one another.

While it is best to work through relationship problems together, with both partners involved in the solution, it is possible for either partner to make changes and stop the cycle. By changing your perception, behavior, and reaction to the situation, you change the dynamics. Let's look at the scenario again.

You are upset that your partner has been working late and not coming home from dinner. You react by saying, "We have not been having dinner together lately in the evenings. I miss that time together and I miss you. I enjoy seeing you in the evenings. I could make a special dinner for us one night this week. What night works best for you?" In this response, you have let your partner know how you feel without making demands. He is more likely to be responsive to your request. You have broken the cycle of avoiding each other without an argument.

CBTIDBIT

When you and your partner are in a rut, or when arguing, one of the best things to do is give your partner a compliment. It is easy to focus on the negative elements of your partner and your relationship. Instead of falling into habit, tell your partner something you like about him. If an argument is going in circles, take a break and tell each other something you like about the other person. This helps break the cycle and remind you of why you are together.

Communication Skills

It is impossible to have any long-term relationship without having conflicts. It is how the problem is handled, not the problem itself, that creates either a disagreement or a solution. Just as important as what you say is how you communicate. Effective communication is the cornerstone of any relationship.

Listening

How closely do you listen when your others talk? Do you focus on what your friend is saying? Or are you forming a response before she is even finished talking? Many people believe they are listening and don't even realize that they are thinking about what to say next. Listening effectively means you hear the words spoken and understand the feelings behind the words.

The following are some guidelines for effective listening:

- Maintain eye contact.

- Don't interrupt. If you feel a response is needed, nod, smile or use other body language to indicate you are listening.

- Reflect back what you heard. Reword and repeat important information to let your partner know you are listening.

- Ask clarifying questions to make sure you understand what the other person is saying.

- Pay attention to your partner's body language and other nonverbal cues to get a better sense of their feelings.

- Monitor your body language. Show you are listening by leaning in, nodding, smiling, and making eye contact.

STOP AND THINK

When listening, avoid giving advice unless the other person specifically asks for it. When you listen, the other person feels worthy, appreciated, interesting, and respected. It helps prevent misunderstandings. You always learn more when you listen than when you talk.

Keep any criticism or judgments to yourself while your partner is talking. You want to foster an environment of open and honest communication, so even if you don't agree, keep your opinions to yourself while your partner is speaking. Try to understand his or her point of view.

Speaking

There may be times when you feel that your partner is the one who needs to learn how to listen. You might feel frustrated, feeling that you aren't heard. How you approach a conversation is important. The following are guidelines to being heard:

- Find the right time. Don't try to have an important conversation when the television is on or either person is preoccupied with other issues. If you need to, schedule a time so you are both prepared to have a discussion.

- Avoid attacking or cross-examining. This is your turn to state your opinion.

- Keep your body language consistent with the message you are trying to deliver.

- Edit what you want to say. Stop if you begin rambling, going off topic, or repeating yourself.

- Pause occasionally to allow your partner to ask questions. Ask for feedback to make it a two-way conversation.

Let your partner know your intentions before you begin the conversation. For example, you might want advice or you might want to vent without getting advice. You might want to work together to problem solve. Each of these requires a different response. State in advance which response you are looking for so you aren't disappointed or frustrated. If you are asking for advice, however, be ready to accept advice graciously. That doesn't mean you need to take the advice, but don't be critical or harshly dismiss the advice.

Nonverbal communication

When communicating, you say a great deal through your *nonverbal communication* or body language. Your body language helps your partner understand the feelings behind the words you are saying. Becoming aware of your own body language and the body language of your partner makes you a better communicator.

> **DEFINITION**
>
> **Nonverbal communication** is the process of communicating with someone through nonverbal means. We routinely enhance our communication through gestures, facial expressions, touch, tone of voice, body movements, and eye contact. Some experts believe that around 90 percent of all of our communication is conveyed with nonverbal cues.

Pay attention to eye contact, gestures, tone of voice, muscle tension, facial expression, and body movements. These are all part of natural nonverbal communication. The following tips will help you notice and use nonverbal cues to improve your communication.

Notice when the nonverbal cues don't match up with the words. Maybe your partner says he isn't upset, but he has his arms crossed and is looking away from you. His nonverbal communication is sending a different message. When this happens, ask questions to find out more. Unexpressed anger often turns into resentment.

Use eye contact. When you are unwilling to make eye contact, it gives the impression you are trying to hide something. Too much eye contact can seem confrontational. Be sure to make eye contact without trying to stare down your partner.

Don't focus on one small gesture. You can better understand the meaning behind nonverbal communication if you look at more than one movement or gesture. When a group of nonverbal cues reinforce an idea or an emotion, you are probably reading the signals correctly.

IMAGINE THAT

Touching or smiling can change the tone of any negative situation. If you and your partner just had an argument and you are still replaying the argument in your mind or are unable to let go, try holding hands, hugging, snuggling together, or giving a simple smile or touch. This immediately changes the dynamics of the situation and makes it more positive.

As with an oral conversation, if there is something you don't understand, it is better to ask for clarification than to assume you know what he is thinking.

The Least You Need to Know

- You can choose your reaction to problems. You can choose to be angry or choose to show empathy.
- "Should" and "must" statements are inflexible and rigid thinking. Changing these statements into preferences makes them more flexible.
- You can be involved in a negative cycle if you have unmet expectations. Changing your perception can help break the cycle.
- All relationships have conflicts. Learning effective communication skills helps you work with others to find resolutions to problems.

CHAPTER 14

Building Assertiveness

You know what you want but usually keep it to yourself. You don't want to make waves or disappoint others, so you remain silent when others take advantage of you. You feel like a pushover. This chapter will show you how to speak up for yourself effectively, while still being respectful of other people. You will find out what happens when you aren't assertive and how to use a few simple steps to speak your mind and let others know what you think and feel.

Defining Assertiveness

Assertiveness is expressing your needs, wants, beliefs, opinions, and feelings in a way that is respectful to you and to others. When you are assertive, you…

- Express your point of view.
- Express your feelings.
- Ask for what you want or need.
- Say "no" without feeling guilty.
- Set boundaries.
- Stand up for yourself and your rights.

In This Chapter

- The difference between being assertive and being aggressive
- How not being assertive affects your life
- Ways in which you can be assertive
- What you can gain from criticism

> **STOP AND THINK**
>
> Being assertive is not the same as being aggressive. When you are aggressive, you make demands. When you are assertive, you ask for what you want.

When you are not assertive, you...

- Say "yes" even when it is inconvenient, a burden, or unfair to you.
- Have difficulty expressing positive feelings.
- Feel embarrassed or humiliated when criticized.
- Allow people to take advantage of you.
- Go along with the crowd even if you don't agree.
- Become aggressive when someone has taken advantage of you.

Some people are naturally more assertive than others; however, it is a learned skill. You can be assertive with practice.

Steps for Assertiveness

There are no strict rules for assertiveness; it looks different depending on the person and the circumstances. There are steps you can take to build assertiveness:

Step 1: State your point of view. Briefly describe the situation as you see it, including what you expected.

Step 2: Discuss how you feel.

Step 3: Ask for what you prefer. Be specific; ask for something that is measurable, actionable, reasonable, and timely.

Step 4: Point out how complying with your preference will benefit everyone involved. Ask for the other person's understanding.

Suppose a close friend invites you to spend the holidays with her and her family. At the last minute, your friend tells you there isn't any room and you can't attend after all. You are hurt and angry. You go back and forth, one minute wanting to tell off your friend, the next wanting to ignore the situation. A better way to handle the situation is to follow the four steps. Start by calling your friend and setting up a time to talk. Come up with a script of what you'd like to say, following the four steps.

Step 1: Jill, when you invited me to the holidays I was excited to be a part of your celebration. I spent a lot of time baking cookies and bought small gifts for your family. I also didn't make any other plans because I was spending the day with you.

Step 2: When you cancelled our plans, it made me feel hurt and like I'm not important to you.

Step 3: Next time you invite me to something and you cannot accommodate the invitation, I would prefer that you let me know at least three days before so I have a chance to make other plans.

Step 4: I care about you and our relationship. It's necessary that we both respect each other's time and feelings. Can you understand where I am coming from?

Being assertive isn't easy, especially if you are used to being passive and staying quiet when others take advantage of you. In the beginning, it is scary. When you first start, use the steps and create a script you can follow.

> **IMAGINE THAT**
>
> If you lack assertiveness, you may be using one of these problematic thought processes:
>
> Mind reading—you assume others know what you are thinking and feeling.
>
> "Should" statements—you assume others should know better without you having to express yourself.
>
> Fortune-telling—you assume the other person won't care about your feelings.
>
> Catastrophizing—you predict if you are assertive, it is going to end badly.

Rights and Responsibilities

It's important to stand up for your rights, but your rights come with responsibilities. Effective assertiveness requires balancing your needs and rights with those of the people around you. The following table outlines some basic rights and the responsibilities that go along with them:

Rights	Responsibilities
To be respected	To show respect to others
To make choices	To accept the consequences of your choices
To make mistakes	To accept the consequences of your mistakes
To express your opinion	To respect that others also have the right to express their opinion, even if you disagree
To say "no" without feeling guilty	To accept "no" from other people
To be honest about your feelings	To not expect others to know how you are feeling unless you clearly state your feelings

Your rights often vary depending on your situation; for example, you might not have the right to say "no" to your boss when given a request, unless the request is demeaning or discriminatory. You do, however, have the right to say "no" if a friend asks you to do a favor that is inconvenient or a hardship. You choose when to be assertive.

> **CBTIDBIT**
>
> You might find it hard to say "no" because you feel guilty or don't want to disappoint someone. However, always saying "yes" can overload you. Decide on your limits and then stick to it. Politely and calmly explain you don't have time right now or the request doesn't fit with your values. Don't apologize and make excuses. Use assertiveness techniques such as rephrasing your assertion if the other person isn't willing to accept "no" the first time.

When You Aren't Assertive

You are your best advocate. There isn't anyone else who knows what you feel, think, want, and need. If you don't let others know how their actions make you feel, chances are they don't know. When you aren't assertive, you frequently end up feeling angry and resentful at the other person, even though you didn't speak up.

If you aren't assertive, you may...

- Feel embarrassed or humiliated when given any type of criticism.

- Develop a need for perfection so no one has a reason to criticize you.

- Feel you never get what you deserve.

- Resent others for taking advantage of you.

- Have low self-esteem because you think you should stand up for yourself more often.

Being passive, or timid, affects your life in many different ways, both significant and insignificant. You might be at a restaurant and your food is undercooked or burnt, yet you eat it anyway because you don't want to tell the waiter. You might have items at home that should be returned or exchanged but you end up giving them away or throwing them out because you don't want to have to explain why you are returning them. Or maybe you've accepted working for years without a raise because you can't bring yourself to talk to your boss about a promotion. Instead, you go over the situation in your mind, thinking about what you could have or should have said and feeling like a failure because you didn't.

> **IMAGINE THAT**
>
> Being passive is accepting the other person's terms. When the outcome isn't too important to you, this is okay. For example, your partner orders Italian food but you wanted Chinese. You don't speak up and think, "We can order Chinese next time." Passive-aggressive is when you agree but inside you are resentful. Passive-aggressive behaviors include sarcasm, slamming doors, making cunning remarks, rolling your eyes, or planning retaliation.

Choosing the Middle Ground

Assertiveness is choosing the middle ground. On one end is passivity and on the other end is aggression. Imagine you are standing in line at the grocery store. Someone comes along and jumps in front of you in line. If you react passively, you do nothing. If you react aggressively, you make a scene. An assertive response would be to say, "Excuse me, I was already in line. Could you please move to the end of the line?"

Being overly or regularly passive creates resentment and low self-esteem. You go through life wanting to do something but lacking the courage to go ahead and try. Something always stops you from getting what you want, or maybe you wait for someone or something to push you forward, never taking that first step on your own. When you are passive, other people probably don't know what you want. Aggressiveness is overreacting. An aggressive person uses demands and force—violence or the implied or overt threat of violence—to get what he or she wants. When you are aggressive, others might resent you. Assertiveness accepts that your wants, feelings, and needs are valid and that you can stand up for your rights while still treating the other person with respect.

Helping Others to Be Assertive

Sometimes other people in your life lack assertiveness, which can lead to frustration and confusion on your part because you want to be responsive to their needs. What they say and do might be contradictory to previous behavior or they may not state their needs clearly. One way of overcoming this problem is to help them become more articulate with their needs and desires.

Imagine your partner gets upset when the credit card bill comes in the mail and he sees expensive purchases you made. You always ask before buying something expensive and his answer is always, "Yes, you should get it." You feel frustrated and confused. You might say, "Honey, the last few months, you have been upset when the credit card bill comes. But when I ask you about buying something, your answer is always 'yes.' This is confusing and I am concerned about buying anything else. Can we talk about budgeting? I want us to be on the same page so I don't worry every time I buy something."

Restating the message you are getting from the other person gives them a chance to voice their needs.

Types of Assertiveness

Assertiveness is standing up for your rights; therefore, being assertive usually means using "I" statements. You are letting someone know what you think and feel. There are several different ways of using assertiveness.

Compliments, Praise, and Information

Assertion is not just about complaining or setting boundaries. Offering compliments or information is also a form of assertiveness. Keep your statements brief and to the point. Don't embellish.

"I enjoyed your presentation."

"The cost is $150.00."

"I like your new outfit."

"You look nice today."

Self-Disclosure

Stating how you feel sometimes helps to lower the intensity of the emotion or diffuse the situation. Use "I" statements to explain how you feel without attacking the other person.

"I feel angry."

"I am nervous about today's presentation."

"I am unhappy with your behavior."

GIVE IT A TRY

Body language is an important part of assertiveness. Your body should be relaxed, your voice neutral. You should stand or sit up straight to reflect confidence. Your arms should be at your sides, palms open. You should make eye contact. Practice being assertive in front of a mirror. Pay attention to your body language. You want your body to give the same message as your words.

Empathy

When you have empathy, you show you are aware of someone else's feelings but still expect certain behavior. Showing empathy for the other person's point of view helps lower tendencies toward aggression and gives you time to imagine the other person's position. Pay attention to your tone of voice when using this type of assertive response; it can sound passive-aggressive when delivered with sarcasm.

"I understand you don't agree with the procedures but appreciate that you are willing to complete the job."

"I understand you are busy but are willing to complete the job by the end of the day."

"I understand that is your job to tell the boss about my mistake, but I would prefer you let me tell him myself."

Discrepancy Assertiveness

This is used when there is a discrepancy either between what was said previously and what is now happening or a discrepancy between words and actions in the present. State the discrepancy without making accusations; instead, try to clarify information or misunderstanding.

"Yesterday you said you wanted to go out to dinner tonight, but I see you are making dinner. Did something change?"

"You say you don't want a committed relationship, but sending flowers and wanting to go out every weekend makes it seem like you want more than a casual relationship. Can you help me understand?

Conflict Resolution

Sometimes just stating what you want does not get you what you want. The other person involved has his or her own opinion or side of things. Instead of arguing or feeling as though you cannot get what you want, try negotiating.

Let's say your partner wants to spend the day sightseeing and you want to relax on the beach. You might say, "I understand why it is important for you to see these things, but I'm really tired today. Can we spend the morning relaxing on the beach and then we go to the museum this afternoon?"

Try to figure out a way for both person's needs to be at least partially met.

Rephrasing Your Assertion

Sometimes others don't accept your first response and continue to ask the same question or act in the same way toward you. Saying exactly what you have said before and continuing to repeat the same statement is likely to make you frustrated. Instead, ask how you can clarify better or help them to understand where you are coming from. Suppose you are in a store and a sales clerk is pushing you toward making a purchase.

Sales Clerk: "This yellow dress would look wonderful with your skin coloring. Why don't you try it on?"

Response: "No thank you, I am just browsing today."

Sales Clerk: "It won't hurt to try it on, just to see how it looks."

Response: "I am just browsing today. Is there some way I can just signal you if I want help?"

You can combine this technique with other types of assertiveness or start mildly and become more assertive (but not angry or aggressive) each time the other person doesn't accept your position.

Consequences

Use this technique as a last resort. Make sure to keep an even tone of voice, relax your body and face, and maintain eye contact. Without this type of body language, this technique can be taken as threatening.

"If you continue to ignore my requests, I am going to have to talk with your supervisor."

Assertiveness is a learned skill and therefore takes practice. Try using the techniques at times you don't feel emotional. This will give you time to get used to speaking up for yourself. Keep a log of the times you use one of the techniques. Write down facts about the situation, what you said, and how the other person reacted.

Acting Assertively

Sometimes expressing what you want is not enough. You need to act on needs. The following are some examples of how you can act assertively.

You and a friend are out to dinner. You have an early meeting at work and want to go home. Your friend wants to go out for a few more drinks. He continues to insist that you come along despite your objections. You might say, "I know you don't have to work tomorrow, but I do. Thank you for the invitation, but I really do need to go home. Good night." Then, you leave.

You and your roommate walk to class together each morning. She is usually running late and you don't want to walk into class late again. "I can't be late for class again. I will be sure to save you a seat." Then, you go to class.

You are traveling with a friend and are on a tight budget. She wants to go for an expensive massage and insists you should join her. She tells you it is okay to max out your credit card. You might say, "I am sorry I can't join you. It would be fun but it isn't in my budget. I will meet you back at the hotel. Enjoy your massage."

STOP AND THINK

When you are passive, you work with a "you win, I lose" philosophy. When you are aggressive, you work operate with the idea "I win, you lose." When you are assertive, the goal is "I win, you win."

You and your partner are arguing. The fight is going in circles. You are exhausted and think the fight is going to go downhill from here. You might say, "I need to pause right now. I am exhausted and can't talk about this anymore. Can we talk again later when we are both calmer?"

In these examples, you are using assertiveness for self-care. When doing so, make sure you are not hurting the other person. Keep your body language calm. It helps to acknowledge the other person's position.

Some tips for practicing assertiveness are as follows:

- Politely ask to talk.

- Be aware of your environment; if necessary, ask to talk in private.

- State what you think, feel, and want. Give facts without judging or blaming.

- Speak respectfully. Avoid intimidating or upsetting the other person. Never use violence or the threat of violence.

- Use "I" statements. Never attack the other person.

- Stick to your point, your perspective, and your feelings.

- Remember that no one can make you feel anything. Take responsibility for your feelings.

- Give the other person a chance to voice his or her opinion. Make it a discussion rather than one, or both, of you trying to win an argument.

- Accept that sometimes the issue can't be resolved and you must agree to disagree.

Assertiveness, however, is not a guarantee that you will get what you want. For example, suppose you request a meeting with your boss and ask for a raise. You explain why you believe you deserve the raise and point out your achievements. You are assertive. Your boss might turn down your request but might respect your initiative and be inclined to give you a raise later.

Accepting Criticism

Criticism is pointing out a mistake, fault, or an area to be improved. It is impossible to go through life without being criticized at some point. Often, criticism is seen as a negative, a judgment against your abilities or you as a person. Sometimes, though, criticism isn't meant as a negative; it gives you information to grow and learn. It is meant as a critique.

> **DEFINITION**
>
> **Criticism** is pointing out a mistake, fault, or an area to be improved. It differs from critique in that criticism usually looks for what is wrong, while critique looks for what is working.

The first step to learning to accept criticism is to see it as a chance to learn how others see you. Suppose your boss sets up a meeting to discuss your work performance. He talks about your strengths but also points out several ways you can improve your performance. He says he notices you miss details and would like you to double-check your work. Because of the careless errors, he isn't sure you are ready to take on more responsibility. You have two choices: become angry and defensive or consider what your boss said and use the information to become better at your job.

If you have a difficult time accepting criticism, try the following:

- Look for any part of the criticism you agree with. Sometimes you might agree with only a very small part of what the other person has said.

- Show empathy by agreeing to that one point.

- Ask for more information on how the other person views that one part.

- Express your point of view with "I" statements.

In the previous example, you might say, "You are saying sometimes I am careless when completing my work. I think that is true. Can you give me some guidance to help me improve my work?" By agreeing on one point, you open up the possibility of learning and growing in your job.

If you find it hard to respond to criticism on the spot, accept the criticism gracefully. Later, when you have time to think about it, decide what points you want agree with and take steps to improve those areas. The rest you can simply reject or accept as another person's opinion.

Misconceptions About Assertiveness

You might be afraid to be assertive and worry about what other people will think of you. It's common to feel that being assertive will have negative consequences. The following are some common misconceptions about assertiveness.

Misconception: I will look selfish.

Reality: When you are assertive, you are standing up for yourself. You are putting your needs on an equal level with the other person's wants and needs. That doesn't mean you aren't considering their needs or seeing their wants as not important as your own. You are simply stating what you feel or want.

Misconception: People won't like me.

Reality: Think of people you know who are assertive. You might have observed them and wished you were more like them, more able to speak up for yourself. Are these people unlikeable? Or, are they respected and well liked? People usually like and respect those who stand up for themselves.

Misconception: The other person will get angry.

Reality: This is fortune-telling and jumping to assumptions. You are assuming you know how the other person will react and are assuming their reaction will be unreasonable. When you are being assertive, you are being reasonable, not aggressive.

Misconception: I get too nervous to be assertive.

Reality: Being assertive, especially if you aren't used to doing so, can make you nervous. Although difficult at first, as with many things, it gets easier as you practice. Start by practicing with people you know well, friends and relatives, until you feel comfortable stating your opinion or feelings.

Assertiveness is give and take. You need to state your opinion and feelings. You also need to take the time to actively listen to the other person's point of view. You can get what you want through intimidation, but you will gain respect with assertiveness.

The Least You Need to Know

- Assertiveness is standing up for your rights, wants, and needs.
- When you are aggressive you make demands; when you are assertive you make requests.
- Assertiveness requires you to balance your needs with the needs of others.
- Criticism gives you information on how others see you.

CHAPTER 15

Managing Everyday Stress

In today's fast-paced, high-achievement world, it is easy to become stressed. Each day you must deal with family and work, find a way to balance both, and still find time for you. With everything going on around you, it's no wonder you feel stressed much of the time. In this chapter, you will learn what stress is, where it comes from, and ways to cope with it.

What Is Stress?

Stress is internal pressure you put on yourself. It occurs when faced with difficult, overwhelming, or challenging situations. When you're stressed out, you don't think you have the ability or resources to deal with the situation. You feel burdened, either emotionally or physically. Stress is unique in each person. You might handle certain situations calmly, feeling completely in control, while someone else might feel frazzled when faced with the same situation.

In This Chapter

- Defining stress
- Discover your triggers to stress
- Stress-free problem solving
- Techniques for lowering stress

Stress is unavoidable. From the time you were a child, you have learned to deal with stress. It pushes you to try harder and achieve more. This type of stress is short-term. For example, you feel stress when you have an important test. You study and prepare, but once the test is over, the stress is gone. Other times stress lasts much longer and becomes harmful. You are frustrated and irritable. You have trouble sleeping, get headaches or stomachaches, have nightmares, or have difficulty concentrating. When this happens, it is referred to as distress. Chronic, or long-term, stress can be debilitating.

IMAGINE THAT

Everyone experiences stress at some point in their life, but distress is avoidable. This is when you feel completely overwhelmed and shut down because you perceive your situation as too much to handle.

Identify Your Stressors

Most people juggle several areas of their life each day. Stress can develop in any one of these areas. Some common causes of stress include the following:

- Working long hours

- Pressure to succeed

- Job uncertainty

- Friction with co-workers or supervisors

- Poor working conditions

- Lack of career prospects

- Relationship problems

- Illness

- Financial difficulties

- Moving

- Having a baby

- Starting a job

- Traveling

- Planning a large event

Sometimes identifying your stressors can be easy; you might look at the previous list and quickly see several areas that are stressful for you. Maybe you are working long hours or facing losing your job. Maybe you are going through problems in your relationship and considering divorce. At other times stressors are harder to figure out. Maybe there isn't anything big going on in your life, but you feel overwhelmed managing you household, taking care of your children, and cleaning your house. Or maybe your stressors are hiding behind denials, excuses, and blaming others for your problems.

STOP AND THINK

The most stressful events usually revolve around transition periods, such as getting married, having a baby, moving, starting a new job, death of a partner, and divorce.

Take time over the next week or two to write down what situations and events cause stress or tension in your life. Note whether this was a one-time event, such as a job interview, or an ongoing situation. For each stressor that is an ongoing situation, place it into a category, such as work, family, illness, pain, or social situations. This helps to separate short- and long-term stress and to identify the areas of your life that are causing the most difficulty. It gives you a place to start managing your stress.

Problems vs. Problematic Thinking

Once you have a list of common stressors in your life, decide whether each one is the result of a problem or problematic thinking. Is there a specific problem and possible solution? If so, sit down and write a plan of action for solving the problem. If not, reread the problematic thinking processes in Chapter 2. Are you creating stress in your life thinking negatively?

Suppose you wrote down that you feel stress when your wife works late. You think, "There is so much to do. I have to cook dinner, straighten up the house, help with homework, and get the children ready for bed. It's going to take forever and I have a report to read for work. This is a disaster. I'm doing all of this alone; she should be here to help. She only thinks about herself. I can't do this." In this example, you are:

- Catastrophizing ("This is a disaster;" "I can't do this.")

- Overgeneralizing ("This is going to take forever.")

- Using "should" statements ("She should be here to help.")

- Blaming ("She only thinks about herself.")

If you slow down, take some deep breaths, and restructure your thinking, you can approach the situation differently, looking for things that are practical and solvable. You realize that it isn't really a disaster. You can take care of your children; you have gotten them dinner and ready for bed in the past. You realize that you and your wife are partners and that means you both take responsibility for your home and children. Once you see the situation from a different perspective, you start problem solving. You check the refrigerator for something for dinner, you get everyone settled with homework, and you don't worry about straightening up—that can wait until tomorrow. By the time your wife arrives home, everything has been taken care of, your children are ready for bed, and you can focus on work.

Your Turn: Problem Solving

Write down the problem in one or two phrases or sentences. Focus on the actual problem, not how you feel. In the previous example, you would write, "my wife arriving home late when I have work to do" instead of "my wife doesn't care about me." Writing the problem helps because trying to solve things in your head is difficult. The solutions and ideas get cluttered and create confusion. Solutions become much clearer when you put the problem on paper.

> **CBTIDBIT**
>
> In CBT, you are encouraged to look at problems from a different perspective. One way to do this is to pretend to solve the problem for someone else. When faced with a challenging situation, imagine you are talking to a friend or a young relative, 10 years in the future. What would you tell him to do? What advice would you give?

After you've written your problem, list all of the possible solutions. Don't worry about whether the solutions are all practical or realistic right now. Write down every solution you think of. For example:

Problem: Car making a strange noise; needs to be taken to a mechanic.

Solutions:

- Buy a new car.

- Ask a co-worker for a ride to work while the car is in the shop.

- Take the bus to work.

- Rent a car until the car is looked at.

- Work from home.

- Take a day off work to take the car to the shop.

Once you have list all the possible solutions, go back and cross out any unreasonable solutions. You might cross off "buy a new car" because it isn't in your budget and "take the bus to work" because the bus route is inconvenient.

Keep the top two or three solutions and write down the pros and cons for each one:

Ask a co-worker for a ride to work.

Pro: least expensive

Con: need to have co-worker pick me up and it is out of his way

Rent a car.

Pro: gives the most flexibility

Con: might be expensive

Take a day off work and take car to shop.

Pro: can take car to shop and wait for it to be done

Con: have to use a vacation day

You can now decide which choice is best for your situation and create a plan of action. Some problems are more complex. For those, you will need to break your plan of action into steps and work on one step at a time. Then, monitor your progress and, if needed, change and revise your plan until you reach your goal.

GIVE IT A TRY

When going through a stressful situation, ask yourself these questions:

- What are the facts?
- Is the situation bad or do I feel bad about what is going on?
- What evidence supports my feelings? What evidence disproves my feelings?
- How big of an issue will this be in five hours? Five days? Five years?

Remember, feelings are temporary. No feeling lasts forever, not even the good ones.

Stress Reduction Strategies

You manage your stress, or your stress manages you. Stress has been linked to diseases, such as heart disease, diabetes, high blood pressure, and stroke. Managing your stress improves your overall feelings of well-being and increases your longevity. The following are some techniques for managing every day stress:

Prioritize. If you have a long "to-do" list each day and worry about whether it is every going to get done, take time each morning to prioritize your tasks. Write down everything you want to accomplish. Rate each one. You probably have several tasks on your list that are only mildly important or nonessential. Cross these out. You might have four or five items that need to be completed. This is your new "to-do" list. Accept that the other tasks might not get done.

Think in action steps. Instead of thinking in terms of an entire project from start to finish, break your projects into actionable steps.

Build an oasis. When feeling stressed, take a few minutes to build your own private oasis. Find a quiet area and take a few deep breaths. Use visualization or positive imagery, as explained in Chapter 6, to imagine yourself in a serene and calm place. As you practice this, you will find it easy to simply close your eyes and go to the quiet space in your mind for a few minutes of peace.

Determine the probability. During stressful times, it is easy to catastrophize. Take a few minutes to determine the probability of your anticipated outcome occurring. Usually, the likelihood is much lower than you imagine. Make a list of all of the steps that would have to occur in order for your situation to be as catastrophic as you image. Assign each step in the sequence a percentage of how likely it is to occur and multiple all the percentages by each other. This is probability of your outcome occurring.

For example, imagine your boss has sent you an email criticizing an aspect of your performance. You immediately assume you will be fired. Look at each event that would lead to that outcome and realistically evaluate how likely it is to occur.

I will be put on probation. (30 percent chance of occurring)

I will make another mistake. (10 percent chance of occurring)

I will be fired. (50 percent chance of occurring)

Multiply those numbers together: $.3 \times .1 \times .5 = .015$

There is a 1.5 percent chance that you'll get fired. This is not something you need to worry about.

List what you can control. Sometimes you feel stressed about situations and events over which you have no control. Think about what you can control and ask yourself if there are any concrete steps you can take to improve the situation. Remember, even when the situation is completely out of your control, you can choose to control your reaction.

Use relaxation techniques. In Chapter 7, you learned different relaxation techniques such as deep breathing and meditation. Focusing on relaxing your body can help to lower your stress levels.

Pay attention to your negative thought patterns. Use the list in Chapter 2 to help you identify your negative thought patterns and use the ABCD worksheets to come up with more helpful ways of looking at situations.

Create a stress coping phrase. Find a coping phrase you can repeat any time you feel stressed. You might use "I feel calm," or "I can handle this," "I am doing the best I can" or "she is doing the best she can" This is a good way to silence the negative self-talk.

Make time for yourself. Schedule time every day for pleasurable activities and relaxation time. This helps create a balance in your life and helps you put difficult situations into perspective.

Do a muscle relaxation exercise. Tighten and relax each muscle in your body for at least 10 seconds. Progressive muscle relaxation exercises are explained in detail in Chapter 7. Learn your body's stress signals. Paying attention to how your body reacts to stress, such as tight muscles, helps you identify stress early and take steps to change your perspective.

Ask for help. When you are approaching distress it is possible you need help. If you have a hard time with this, review the assertion strategies in Chapter 14.

Schedule a vacation. Shut the cell phone off and just tune out. In today's busy world with cell phones, tablets, email, and social media, it can be hard to take break. Your mind is constantly going, checking for the next communication. You don't have to take a trip; just schedule an hour, a day, or a weekend where you shut off your electronic devices and rejuvenate.

Your Turn: Create a Stress Worksheet

Create a worksheet you can complete each time you are feeling overwhelmed. Write one to two sentences for each of the following:

What is the situation?

What is my immediate reaction?

What emotion am I feeling?

Evidence I have to support any distressing thoughts:

Evidence I have that disproves any distressing thoughts:

Balanced statement:

What emotion am I now feeling?

When filling in your worksheet, remember: moods can usually be described in one or two words. Thoughts are more complex and require phrases or sentences.

Exercise Your Stress Away

Regular exercise has been shown to reduce stress levels. It releases muscle tension and gives you a chance to break the cycle of negative and stressful thoughts. Some people find exercise to be a form of mindfulness meditation—they get "in the zone" when exercising and forget about problems for a short time. During exercise your body produces endorphins, sometimes called the feel-good brain chemical. It may even change how your brain releases and uses chemicals, making the effects of exercise on stress last long after you have stopped.

When beginning an exercise program...

- Talk to your doctor if you have any health conditions. Be sure exercise is safe and ask what types of exercises are best.

- Schedule exercise into your daily routine. Other tasks and responsibilities might seem more important, but remember, exercise helps you better manage stress and can improve cognitive performance and memory. You might find that you feel better and more energetic when tackling other tasks.

- Find the right exercise program for you. Choose something you like to do. You are more likely to stick with an exercise program if it fits into your lifestyle. Consider your time and budget.

According to the U.S. Centers for Disease Control and Prevention, adults should have a minimum of two and a half hours of moderate aerobic exercise per week. You can spread this out over the week and even spread your daily exercise into several sessions each day. You do want to make sure that each exercise session is at least 10 minutes long.

> **CBTIDBIT**
>
> If you don't already exercise, start small. Even 10 minutes of exercise each day has been found to lower stress levels. When first starting an exercise program, many people get carried away, overdoing it and then feeling tired and sore. Then they stop. Instead, start slowly and increase your activity level in small increments each week.

The Least You Need to Know

- Stress occurs when you don't think you have the ability to handle a difficult situation.
- Identify your stress triggers to discover what areas in your life are creating the most problems.
- Solving problems sometimes requires you to look at the situation from a different perspective.
- Regular exercise is an important part of stress reduction.

CBT for Specific Conditions and Situations

Research has shown that CBT is an effective way to manage depression, anxiety, and other disorders. Studies indicate that those using CBT techniques often reduce or eliminate the need for medication in their treatment. CBT provides lasting change and gives you the skills you need to become your own therapist.

In this part, we address how CBT can help you manage depression, anxiety, addiction, and obsessive-compulsive disorder. Choose the areas you find most problematic in your life to concentrate on; however, you will probably find useful information in the other chapters in this section as well. It is important to note that some of the issues discussed in this section are medical issues. You should consult with your doctor or therapist for help. However, many therapists use CBT techniques and this book can be used in conjunction with outside therapy.

CHAPTER 16

Overcoming Depression

Depression affects about one in ten adults in the United States. It makes you feel helpless and hopeless about your future. Depression is different from feeling blue. In this chapter, you'll learn how to recognize signs of depression and the negative thought processes that lead to depression. You'll learn how to stop the cycle of negative thoughts and how taking care of your physical needs can lessen feelings of depression.

In This Chapter

* Distinguishing sadness from depression
* Finding your motivation
* How to stop ruminations
* Focusing on your physical needs

Sadness vs. Depression

Everyone feels sadness at times. It is a normal human reaction when faced with loss or disappointment. Sadness, although painful, is temporary. Depression, however, can last for weeks, months, or years. It is sometimes described as "extreme sadness," but there is more to depression than sadness.

Consider these key differences between sadness and depression:

- Sadness is usually a result of circumstances.

- Depression does not always have a rational or logical cause.

- Sadness temporarily reduces your ability to enjoy parts of your life, but you are usually still able to cope and participate in activities.

- Depression usually lasts longer, is more intense, and is often debilitating. It interferes with your ability to function and care for yourself.

- Sadness is not constant. You can have interspersed moments of laughter.

- Depression can be chronic; it is something you experience almost daily for at least half of the day.

- Sadness fades with time or once your problem is resolved.

- Depression usually does not resolve itself without some type of intervention.

IMAGINE THAT

According to the U.S. Centers for Disease Control and Prevention, approximately 1 in 10 people report having symptoms of depression. Women are more likely to have depression than men, as are people with less than a high school education, those previously married, and those between the ages of 45 and 64 years old.

While profound sadness is one of the symptoms of depression, there are other symptoms:

- Lack of interest in activities you previously enjoyed

- Changes in appetite—either overeating or loss of appetite

- Agitation and irritability

- Insomnia or sleeping too much

- Loss of energy, fatigue

- Trouble concentrating

- Indecisiveness

- Feelings of hopelessness or worthlessness

- Thoughts of death or suicide

Sadness is a normal human emotion, while depression is an illness. You can't "snap out of it." If you are depressed and are having trouble taking care of yourself, not connecting with others in your relationships, or experiencing some of the symptoms listed, you should speak with your doctor.

The Role of CBT in Treating Depression

Research shows CBT to be effective in treating mild and moderate depression. CBT techniques work to...

- Change negative thought patterns and replace them with positive, balanced ways of looking at situations and events.

- Stop ruminations.

- Schedule activities.

- Overcome shame and hopelessness.

While CBT is sometimes used alone as a treatment for depression, your doctor might recommend medication. CBT and medication can be used together. This might be needed if your depression is severe. It is important to talk to your doctor, discuss all treatment options, and together decide which is best for you.

In CBT, the term *cognitive triad* refers to depressive thoughts in three areas:

1. Thoughts about yourself: I am a failure; I am not loved; I have no control.

2. Thoughts about the world or situations you face: The world is cruel; This situation is unfair.

3. Thoughts about the future: My future is hopeless and bleak.

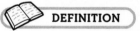 **DEFINITION**

The **cognitive triad** was first proposed by Dr. Aaron Beck, the founder of CBT in 1976. It states that depressive disorders are characterized by negative views of yourself, your life experience (the world around you), and your future.

Suppose you are dating someone and he breaks up with you. If you are prone to depression, your thoughts might be similar to the following:

1. I am ugly. I am not loveable. I can't cope with this. I am alone.

2. This is completely unfair. He hurt me without reason.

3. I will never be happy again. I will never find love. I won't be able to cope.

These types of thoughts…

1. Ignore the fact that you have friends and family who are there to support you during this time. You ignore the times you have coped with difficult situations.

2. Blame your ex rather than considering that you and your ex wanted different things out of the relationship, and you are now free to find someone whose relationship goals more closely match yours. You fail to take any responsibility for the problems in the relationship.

3. Assume there is no one else out there for you. Assume no one will want to stay with you long-term. Assume you won't find happiness again. Assume you need another person to survive.

You can use the ABC chart to think in a more realistic way. While you might still feel sadness over the end of the relationship, you are no longer depressed.

A: Activating Event	B: Thoughts or Beliefs	C: Coping Thoughts
Breaking up	I am ugly.	I am single. I would rather be in a relationship but am still likeable and attractive.
	I am not loveable.	When I make an effort, I usually meet someone who wants to get to know me.
	I can't cope with this. I am alone.	I have friends who accept me and will help me through this time.
	This is completely unfair.	Not every relationship is meant to be forever.
	He hurt me without reason.	We were not a good fit because we wanted different things from the relationship
	I will never be happy again.	I feel sad now but I have felt sad at other times in my life and have gotten over it.
	I will never find love.	I will feel better if I keep a positive attitude, spend time with friends, and focus on my job right now.
	I won't be able to cope.	I can take a short trip.

The "Do Nothing" Syndrome

One of the hallmark symptoms of depression is the lack of motivation to do anything. You might withdraw from family and friends and barely be able to pull yourself out of bed each day. You might have stopped going to work or spending time on hobbies you enjoy. You may put off household chores or responsibilities. The problem is this type of behavior worsens your depression. It makes you feel more useless and more hopeless.

One of the goals of CBT is to gradually increase your level of activity. If you have been staying in bed all day, it is unreasonable to assume that one day you are simply going to get up and be active all day. But if you set realistic goals for your activity, you slowly build up your activities. For example, the first day you might set a goal of getting out of bed and getting a shower. It is important to start your goals from where you are now, not from where you think you should be.

CBTIDBIT

When creating your daily schedule, be sure to include pleasurable activities. Include something fun or indulgent. The important thing is to not just schedule boring, work-related tasks or chores that keep you isolated. Try going out to lunch, getting a manicure or a massage, taking the dog to the dog park, going on a trip, taking a yoga class, or going to the movies.

Create a daily activity schedule. Planning activities increases your motivation to follow through. Use the following template, breaking your day into one or two hour increments. Make a list of activities that you feel you can do now and those that you want to do. Rate them from easiest to hardest, for example, you might put "take a walk" and rate this as easy and "meet a friend for lunch" and rate this as very difficult. When you start creating a schedule, begin by adding the easy tasks.

Time	Activity
8–9 A.M.	Get up and shower
9–10 A.M.	Have breakfast
10–11 A.M.	Rest
11–Noon	Straighten the house
Noon–1 P.M.	Eat lunch
1–2 P.M.	Rest
2–3 P.M.	Read
3–4 P.M.	Rest
4–5 P.M.	Pleasure activity: Go to Dog park
5–6 P.M.	Have dinner
6–7 P.M.	Watch television
7–8 P.M.	Watch television
8–9 P.M.	Read
9–10 P.M.	Go to bed

Be sure to include eating and sleeping on your schedule. Each day or every few days, add another activity to your schedule. Don't overload your schedule as you may get overwhelmed and give up, going back to not wanting to do anything. The goal of creating a schedule is to gradually become more active. Keep a notebook with your daily schedules so you can monitor your progress.

Avoidance

You might be tempted to fill your schedule with activities that take the place of going out of the house. Suppose you fill your schedule with "read" or "watch television." If you haven't gotten out of bed, adding these activities are a good start; however, they can also be a way of avoiding other, more challenging activities, such as those that require you to leave the house. Avoidance usually leaves you feeling worse than you did before. You may feel isolated and alone.

What do you avoid? Review the following list and check the items you have avoided.

- ❑ Seeing friends

- ❑ Answering the phone

- ❑ Looking at or answering emails

- ❑ Household chores and responsibilities (cleaning, paying bills, etc.)

- ❑ Hygiene (showering, bathing, washing clothes)

- ❑ Taking part in hobbies

- ❑ Going to work

Look over your list. Do you have avoidance behaviors? Try to switch one avoidance behavior for a healthy behavior each day. Complete the following chart to help you come up with alternatives:

Avoidance Behavior: Not seeing friends

Effects: I feel isolated and more depressed

Alternate Behavior: I can get together with a friend once a week

Benefits: I will get out of the house. I will have the support of my friends. I will not feel so isolated.

Obstacles: No one is available; when I call my friends they often already have plans.

Steps: I will call two friends at the beginning of each week and ask to see them over the weekend for an hour. I will make plans to meet a friend for lunch once each week. I will sign up for a class at the local community center to make new friends.

GIVE IT A TRY

If you are having a hard time getting yourself out of the house, talk with a few close friends or relatives. Ask for help. Let them know you want to do more but are having a hard time getting motivated to leave the house. Good friends will understand and provide encouragement. Remember, everyone feels down sometimes; you are not alone.

Some people with depression shy away from friends and family because they feel "they aren't good company right now." They worry that they will have nothing to say or seem pathetic. Choose to spend time with people that are supportive and understanding and explain a little about what you are going through so they are sensitive to your needs. When you are with your friends, start by talking about superficial things. Ask questions and listen to what they have been doing. Resist the temptation to compare your life to theirs. Don't think, "Look at all the great things she is doing; I am such a failure." Allow yourself to simply enjoy the social interaction.

Ruminations

When depressed, people tend to ruminate. Ruminating is when your thoughts play in one continuous loop in your mind. You repeat the same scene, constantly trying to sort out what is going on. You can't seem to shut off the thoughts. Ruminations often center around the following:

- What if…?

- If only…

- How did this happen?

- Why me?

- Why do I feel this way?

- Why didn't I do things differently?

- I feel bad. I am always going to feel this way. I am hopeless.

Ruminations are all-consuming. Once you begin ruminating, you can't seem to stop. You might find that you have been sitting and thinking about something for hours on end, without realizing how much time passed.

When you notice the same thoughts going through your head, write down the time, where you are, and what you are thinking. Keep track for a few days and use this information to help you break the habit of ruminating. For example, you might find that you ruminate in the morning when you are still lying in bed. You start thinking about your situation and realize that you have been lying in bed for an hour, going over the same thoughts. Or you might lie awake at night, ruminating about your situation.

To stop ruminating, you must make a conscious decision to break the chain of thoughts. Don't worry about the content; it is the process of rumination you are trying to stop. Make a list of activities you can do whenever you find yourself ruminating. Your list might include the following:

- Exercise for 15 minutes.

- Do a mindfulness meditation exercise.

- Read a magazine or book.

- Do a puzzle.

- Do a breathing exercise.

Select one item from the list and make that the activity you automatically go to when you start ruminating. Be sure the activities you choose occupy your mind. Activities like walking or gardening might not be adequate to keep your mind from wandering. The idea is to give you alternative thoughts. The more absorbed your mind is, the less likely you are to continue to ruminate. Become mindful in whatever activity you choose and concentrate fully on the activity instead of the thoughts you have when you ruminate.

CBTIDBIT

If you find it impossible to stop talking or thinking about the topic, schedule a time each day you will indulge in thinking about the problem. Contain it to 15 minutes.

Your Turn: Reduce Your Ruminations

To help reduce rumination, create a list of problems going through your mind. List thoughts in all three areas: yourself, the world, your future. Then, create a coping statement in response to each problem.

Suppose you are feeling depressed. You are reevaluating the state of your life. Your list might look like this:

Career

>   **Myself:** I hate my job. No one wants to hire me.

>   **The world or situation:** Everyone is out for themselves in my company.

>   **Future:** I will never be successful.

Finance

>   **Myself:** I am poor and I have no money. I should have gone to college.

>   **The world or situation:** Everyone makes more money than me.

>   **Future:** I won't be able to retire.

Social Life

>   **Myself:** I have no friends. I am too shy.

>   **The world or situation:** No one wants to hang out with me.

>   **Future:** I cannot make friends because of my shyness.

These thoughts are negative and not helpful. Repeating them over in your mind will only make you feel worse and stop you from finding solutions to your problems. Follow the following steps to challenge your negative thought processes.

Step One: Use the ABCD method to label and challenge your negative thoughts.

Step Two: Use behavior experiments, as explained in Chapter 10, to challenge and find solutions.

Your new list of thoughts would look like this:

Career

> **Myself:** I don't like what I am doing at work but it gives me a steady income.

> **The world or situation:** No one at work seems to have time to train me on new areas, but maybe I could take an online course or ask someone to spend a few hours on a Saturday morning to go over the new system. I can offer to review the inventory system in return. I know that system.

> **Future:** Learning new skills can help me move up the ladder, get a raise, and show my boss I have initiative.

Finance

> **Myself:** I have enough money right now to pay my basic bills. If I get a second job or do some freelance work, I could have some extra money.

> **The world or situation:** I don't need to compare my income to other people. I can focus on myself.

> **Future:** I can start a retirement account and put a little bit of money from the second job aside.

Social Life

> **Myself:** I get along well with the people at work.

> **The world or situation:** I know people get busy with their own lives.

> **Future:** I can start asking someone to join me at lunch instead of eating alone at my desk. I can bring my lunch but eat in the cafeteria with my coworkers.

Step Three: Select one area to work on. Once you make progress in that area, you can move on to other areas. Consider which area might be easiest, the most important, or might help you resolve multiple problems. You might decide:

I will start my asking someone at work to trade training time; this will make me feel better about my finances and give me a social activity while we are training. I know at least three people who want to learn about the inventory system at work and they all have expertise in other areas at the company.

Step Four: Create *coping statements*—short, one-sentence statements that challenge your negative self-talk. Often when you are depressed, you are critical of yourself. A coping statement is a powerful tool to manage your depression. Come up with specific thoughts that sum up a positive point of view.

> **DEFINITION**
>
> Coping statements are short, one-sentence statements that challenge your negative self-talk.

Negative Thought	Coping Statement
I am upset about my career.	I am a smart, capable person. It takes time to build the career I want.
I am upset about money.	I can live an abundant life in many ways.
I am upset about my social life.	I am likeable, accepting, and friendly person.

Take Care of Yourself

When you become depressed, you may stop caring about yourself and your environment. You might overeat or stop eating. You might find it difficult to get showered each day or not have the energy to do the laundry. But your mind and your body are connected. You can't ignore your body and expect your mind to feel good. You must take care of your physical needs. Exercise, proper nutrition, sleep, and hygiene all play a vital role in treating depression.

Diet

There are no specific "depression" diets. Certain foods aren't going to suddenly make you feel better. However, creating and sticking to a well-balanced meal plan is important. You should be eating three meals (or five smaller meals) each day. Your diet should include fruits, vegetables, whole grains, and protein. If you are eating mostly junk food, start replacing sweets with a piece of fruit or whole grain snacks.

STOP AND THINK

When depressed, avoid caffeine, alcohol, excessive sugar, and white carbohydrates. These foods can make you feel better temporarily but generally reduce your energy in the long-term.

Exercise

Many studies have shown that exercise improves mood and feelings of well-being. For some people, exercise works as well as antidepressants in treating depression. It reduces stress and helps you sleep better at night.

Cardio exercises such as brisk walking, jogging, jumping rope, and bike riding raise your heart rate and some studies show that they improve your mood. If you are going to a gym, you can try the elliptical trainer, stationary bike, or brisk walking or jogging on the treadmill. You might also consider joining a class that will raise your heart rate, such as Zumba or aerobics. Other types of exercises, such as stretching, yoga, and Pilates, can help you to relax.

If you're not exercising now, remember to start small and check with your doctor if you have any health conditions. Begin by exercising 10 minutes a day and work your way up to 30 minutes of exercise several times per week. Exercise can also help you start socializing again. Join a gym or sign up for a fitness class. Ask a friend to join you on a walk each evening. Exercising with someone gives you motivation to keep going.

Sleep

One of the symptoms of depression is sleep disturbances. Some people have insomnia and are unable to sleep, while others sleep too much. You should be getting between seven and nine hours of sleep each night. Use your daily schedule to plan when you go to bed and what time you get up. Try not to sleep at other times. Not getting enough sleep causes symptoms of depression to worsen. Without the proper amount of sleep you can feel irritable, anxious, and depressed. You might find it hard to concentrate or have impaired memory and judgment.

You might think that there isn't anything you can do about sleep. You might believe that "I am just not a good sleeper," or "Sleep will come when it comes."

Here are number of things you can do to help you sleep better:

- Go to bed and get up at the same time each day. Even if you have nothing to do, get out of bed each morning at the same time. Plan your sleeping times into your daily schedule.

- Reduce the stimuli around you about one hour before bedtime. Lower the lights or turn them off, turn down the volume on the television, and turn off your computer.

- Spend the hour before bedtime engaged in a relaxing activity. Read a book, take a warm bath or shower, knit, or write in a journal. Get into bed only when you are ready to go to sleep.

- Write down everything you are worried about in a "worry journal." Then put the journal aside. Giving yourself a specific time each day to worry allows you to "put aside your worries" and clears your mind.

- Avoid caffeine after 1 P.M. If you find you can't sleep, eliminate caffeine altogether and then slowly add it back.

- Don't exercise right before bed as this can interfere with sleep. If you exercise in the evening, go straight to the gym after work and then relax the rest of the evening.

- Reserve the bedroom for sleep and intimacy with your partner. Don't spend time in bed eating, reading, or watching TV.

- Create a relaxing environment in your bedroom. Make it a comfortable place.

- Use white noise, such a fan or sound machine, to help you sleep.

The relaxation techniques discussed in Chapter 6 can also help you calm down and get to sleep. As you become more active during the day, learn to combat negative thoughts, and slow down or stop ruminating, you may find that sleep naturally comes easier.

The Least You Need to Know

- Sadness is a temporary reaction to a situation. Depression lasts longer and often does not go away on its own.
- Creating a daily schedule helps you fight the lack of motivation that often comes with depression.
- Engaging your mind by doing a puzzle or reading a magazine can help you stop ruminations.
- Paying attention to your diet, exercise, and sleep patterns can help reduce depression.

CHAPTER 17

Dealing with Anxiety Disorders

Everyone feels nervous from time to time, but if your anxiety becomes overwhelming and interferes with your ability to function, you may have an anxiety disorder. Usually anxious moments are intense and short-lived; once the reason for the anxiety has passed or you have escaped from the problem, you feel a sense of relief. Feelings of anxiety that last for longer periods or happen frequently can be a problem. Anxiety disorders come in different forms and have different symptoms. For example, you might worry endlessly; feel physical symptoms of anxiety; continually seek reassurance; or avoid particular situations such as flying, public speaking, or socializing. In this chapter, you will learn about the different types of anxiety and the CBT strategies to help you cope on a daily basis.

In This Chapter

- Common anxiety disorders
- Confronting your fears
- Steps to finding solutions to problems
- Learning to embrace the unknown

Types of Anxiety Disorders

The term "anxiety disorder" encompasses a number of different types of anxiety. Each has its own unique characteristics; however, there are some common symptoms:

- Trouble sleeping

- Overpowering fear

- Repeated thoughts

- Frequent worrying

- Avoiding certain places or situations

- Physical symptoms including pounding heart, shortness of breath, muscle tension, and stomachaches

> **IMAGINE THAT**
>
> There are a number of different anxiety disorders. Collectively, they are one of the most common mental disorders. According to the National Institute of Mental Health, about 18 percent of all adults in the United States have reported at least one episode of anxiety over the past 12 months.

Some of the common types of anxiety disorders:

Social Anxiety Disorder: You are often afraid of participating in any type of social interaction. You are afraid of looking foolish or stupid. You think other people are judging you and you worry about being laughed at or humiliated. You are self-conscious. It someone offers you criticism, you are devastated.

Generalized Anxiety Disorder: You worry excessively about everyday problems or what is going to happen in the future. You usually have a feeling of impending doom and are sure something terrible is going to happen. Your worry distracts you from your responsibilities and keeps you awake at night. Even though you know your worry is irrational or exaggerated, you can't stop yourself from worrying.

Panic Disorder: You have a sudden feeling of terror. Your heart starts racing; you feel like you are choking; and you are nauseous, lightheaded, dizzy, shaky, and sweaty. You feel like you are going crazy or think you are having a heart attack. The intense feelings last about 10 to 15 minutes. You avoid places or situations because you are afraid of having another panic attack.

Post-Traumatic Stress Disorder (PTSD): You went through a terrible, traumatic event. It could have been war, being a victim of or witnessing a crime, sexual assault, abuse, a serious accident, or a natural disaster. You have flashbacks, nightmares, and sometimes feel detached from life. You are often irritable, have mood swings, and are hyper-vigilant about your surroundings. You avoid places, people, and situations that remind you of the event.

Phobias: You have an excessive and irrational fear of a certain object or situation. It could be a fear of flying, dogs, heights, bridges, injections, or water—or you could be fearful of something else entirely. Your fear disrupts and limits your life because you avoid places where you might come in contact with the feared object or situation.

The Role of CBT in Treating Anxiety Disorders

As with depression, there are several treatment options for anxiety disorders. CBT is one of those options and is the most used type of therapy for treating anxiety. The strategies in this book can be used as a self-help type of program or you can use them in conjunction with other treatments, such as medication.

When using CBT to treat anxiety, the goals include…

- Learning to spot your early warning signs of anxiety.

- Lowering anxiety symptoms and managing physical sensations in the moment.

- Reducing avoidance of situations that matter to your life.

- Challenging the way you perceive problems.

- Developing a sense of internal control and a tolerance for uncertainty.

- Building tolerance for stress and discomfort.

- Accepting challenges with confidence.

You might notice certain changes when you become anxious. You might start thinking negatively or have distressing automatic images. You might realize that you are avoiding a place or situation because you don't want to feel anxious. You might notice the physical sensations of anxiety first.

GIVE IT A TRY

Start with a relaxation exercise. This calms your brain and your body so that you are more receptive to rational thoughts. If you are too anxious or stressed, chances are you won't be able to connect with rational thoughts.

Pay attention to how your body reacts in the early stages. When you "catch" it early, CBT techniques have a better chance of disarming the anxiety. A number of different strategies are explained throughout this chapter. When you first start working with CBT, you might not know where to start. That's okay. Take your time and experiment with different techniques to find what works best for you. Once you find the right combination, you will be ready to implement them as soon as you feel anxiety beginning.

Facing Fears

Right now, you might go to great lengths to avoid what causes anxiety. For example, you might go an hour out of your way to avoid driving over a bridge, or drive 20 hours to see your parents because you have a fear of flying. You might cross the street when you see a dog walking toward you. When you allow these fears to control your life, you have taken away your opportunity to confront them and overcome them.

Exposure therapy is when you face your fears, usually in small steps. Exposure can occur in person, through virtual simulation, or simply by viewing an image. Many times these methods of exposure are combined; for example, you might start exposure therapy by looking at images of the thing or situation you fear, move on to a virtual situation using videos or computer-based images, and finally confront your fears in person. While CBT often uses this type of step-by-step approach, called *graded exposure*, exposure therapy can also be done through *flooding exposure* or *systematic desensitization*.

> **DEFINITION**
>
> **Graded exposure** is a type of exposure therapy in which you are gradually exposed to your fears starting with imagery exposure, moving to virtual exposure, and then in-person exposure until you can tolerate the experience.
>
> **Flooding exposure** exposes you to the feared object or situation for a prolonged amount of time until you no longer feel anxiety. This is only used with in-person exposures.
>
> **Systematic desensitization** is similar to graded exposure except you combine it with relaxation exercises. You use a technique such as deep breathing before each step and during each step.

When you use graded exposure, you repeatedly expose yourself to the feared object or situation in steps. As you go through each step, your anxiety will be triggered. You might be tempted to stop, wanting to avoid the uncomfortable feeling. It is important to stick with it, allowing your anxiety to peak and subside. Repeat the same step until you feel your anxiety is manageable. Moving too quickly through the steps or stopping while you still feel anxious reinforces your fears. The goal is for you to tolerate a situation without feeling the need to run away.

Suppose you are afraid of dogs. You don't visit friends if you know they have a dog and have stopped taking walks after dinner because you might run into a dog in the neighborhood. Any time you see or hear a dog, you start shaking and are overcome with fear.

Your end goal might be to visit friends with a dog. Think about all the steps you need to take in order to reach your goal. Your first step might be thinking about a dog. In Chapter 5, Setting Goals, you learned how to create a ladder, with each rung representing one step. Your end goal is the top rung of your ladder, the easiest steps on the bottom.

Step	Goal
15	Visit friend with a dog.
14	Pet a dog off a leash.
13	Pet a dog on a leash.
12	Pet a small dog someone is holding.
11	Stand next to a dog off a leash.
10	Stand next to a dog on a leash.
9	Have a dog off a leash across the room.
8	Have a dog on a leash across the room.
7	Sit in a room with a dog outside in the backyard.
6	See a dog across the street.
5	Hear a dog bark.
4	Watch videos of dogs.
3	Look at pictures of big dogs.
2	Imagine a dog that scares you.
1	Imagine a dog you think is cute.

Begin with the first step until you know longer feel anxious. You might just think about a dog for several days, a week or longer. Take your time and focus on that step until you can do so comfortably. Only then should you move to the second step.

Be sure to use relaxation skills to reduce your physical feelings of anxiety. When anxiety becomes uncomfortable, you may want to take a break, but resist the urge to stop. The goal is to tolerate the anxiety. Practice deep breathing or muscle relaxation while you are completing the step. Exposure therapy teaches you that although you might feel anxious, these feelings are temporary and won't hurt you. Go through the same process for each step.

If you are working to overcome a situation that you must be in for a length of time, try starting with one minute and working your way up to ten minutes. For example, you might be working on overcoming a fear of heights and want to stand on a balcony. Your first step might be to stand inside the door, but as you go out on the balcony, set goals for yourself to stay longer each time. Exposure therapy works because with each exposure you build a sense of control over the situation; at the same time your anxiety slowly diminishes. The more you get used to something, the less fear you have.

> **CBTIDBIT**
>
> Before starting an exposure exercise, practice the relaxation skills you learned in Chapter 6. This way you can enter a relaxed state before each step.

Track your progress as you work your way up the ladder. You can give your fear a rating; for example, "On day one I was 80 percent scared looking at the pictures of dogs." If you prefer, you can use ratings such as "very," "somewhat," "a little" or "not at all." You want to see your progression and it helps when you can look back and realize that the first day you used the word "very" and now you describe your anxiety as "somewhat." This motivates you to continue.

Your Turn: Expose Yourself

Write down several situations or objects that makes you anxious. Start with the one you think will be easiest to overcome.

Create a goal. Think about what you would do if you did not have this fear to help you create your goal.

Break your goal down into steps. You can have as many steps as you want but try to create at least 5 to 10 steps. Write down which relaxation exercise you will complete before each exposure.

Focus on the easiest step.

Turn Worry into Problem Solving

One of the main symptoms of generalized anxiety disorder is constant worry. Even though you realize that your worry is irrational, you feel helpless to stop. You worry about everything. You think of every possible outcome—and usually they are all disastrous.

Worry is never helpful. Problem solving is. Whenever you find yourself worrying about something, write it down. But, write it down as a problem to be solved. For example, suppose you are worried you aren't going to have enough money to pay your bills. You imagine being evicted, living on the street; you imagine not having enough to eat, losing your job. Now, turn this around.

Problem: I need $300.00 to cover my bills.

Instead of worrying about the situation, you have reworded it so it is a problem to be solved. Look for solutions.

Possible Solutions:

- Get a second job

- Ask to borrow money

- Ask my landlord for an extra week to pay my rent

Once you have done this, choose the best possible solution and create steps to solve your problem.

If you are worrying about things or situations that can't be solved, try to redirect your attention. Find an activity for 15 minutes to change the subject in your mind. Be mindful and completely focus on the activity. This helps to bring you back to the present moment. Worry is about the future, not the present.

Accepting Uncertainty

Some people are very tolerant of uncertainty. They may relish the idea of the unexpected and look forward to finding out what life has to offer in the future. Other people feel agitated not knowing what is going to happen. It is normal to be curious about the future but they want to know all the details: what is going to happen, when it is going to happen. They become anxious not knowing.

If you have a low tolerance for uncertainty, you probably become overly worried. You probably go to great lengths to eliminate the uncertainty, but because you can't possibly know what is going to happen in the future, you will always have to live with it. If you have a low tolerance for uncertainty, you might:

- Procrastinate or avoid situations you can't control or have a high level of uncertainty.

- Always look for reassurance from others.

- Be indecisive.

- Have a hard time delegating tasks to others.

- Terminate relationships.

- Avoid challenges.

You try to control the things around you because you are trying to create the future you think should occur. You don't want to leave the future up to chance. Trying to control the future takes a lot of time and energy. It often leaves you feeling frustrated.

> **GIVE IT A TRY**
>
> To manage a fear of uncertainty, try using a backward CBT approach. Begin with your behaviors rather than your thoughts. Once you change your behavior and realize that the situation turned out okay, you learn that uncertainty is okay. Try allowing someone else to plan an activity you usually plan. Ask yourself: Did things turn out okay, even though I didn't know what was going to happen? If things didn't turn out, how did I cope with the situation? Was it as bad as I imagined?

Living with uncertainty takes practice. Those who have a high tolerance for uncertainty have learned that no matter what the outcome—good or bad—they have the ability to cope with the situation. As you practice living with uncertainty, it will get easier.

Your Turn: Create a Worry Script

A worry script is a type of exposure therapy using a scenario that hasn't occurred. It can help to relieve fears of the future. For example, you might worry about your children or significant other being in a car accident. Think about something you are worried about occurring in the future. Write down the worst case scenario. Fill in as many details as you can. Write what the scene looks like, what you hear, and how you feel. Write using all five of your senses.

Every day for two weeks, write about the same scene. Don't write exactly the same words; look at the scene from a different perspective. For example, one day you might write what the scene physically looks like, another you might write about your emotions. You might feel upset or even start to worry more about the situation. This is all normal; just continue to write about the same situation every day.

By the end of two weeks, you should find that you spend less time worrying about this and other fears. At the end of the two weeks you should feel less anxious when you rewrite the script. You might feel and think that writing about something terrible is going to make it happen. This is known as magical thinking. Rationally you know that you cannot cause something to happen simply because you think about it. You know life doesn't work that way. You are simply exposing yourself to a situation you fear so that you no longer are tied to the fear. It doesn't mean that you no longer care about your significant other or your children.

You can use this same concept to overcome flashbacks from the past. Instead of writing and reading about a future scene over and over again, write about the scene or scenes you are focused on from the past and the worst outcomes. Similar to the gradual exposure ladder, create a hierarchy of scenes to write and think about over and over again.

As you rewrite the scene from the past, your emotional reactions decrease. You should notice that you worry less or have fewer impulsive thoughts about the past after completing this exercise for two weeks.

Your Turn: Managing Big Problems

You feel anxiety when a problem outweighs your perception of your ability to cope with the situation. When you worry that you aren't going to be able to handle the anxiety, your anxiety actually increases. The following steps will help you work through your thoughts and feelings.

Step 1: Write down your perception of the problem.

Step 2: Write down your perception of your ability to cope.

Step 3: Identify your problematic thought processes using the list in Chapter 2.

Step 4: Restructure your thoughts to show a more balanced view of the situation.

Step 5: Create a more balanced attitude.

Let's look at how these steps can be applied. Imagine you are worried about your relationship. You fear getting a divorce so much that you are anxious all of the time. Every time your spouse works late, you imagine he is having an affair and will leave you. You don't think you can cope; you get an upset stomach.

Step 1: Your perception of the problem.

My husband is working late. He is spending less time at home. He is going to leave me. I don't think we are close anymore. He wants to spend less time around me.

Step 2: Your perception of your ability to cope.

I cannot cope with being alone. I need him to be home with me. My father was never home; I can't have a marriage like my parents. I accuse him and nag him, which drives him away. I always want to talk about this so he never wants to come home early.

Step 3: Problematic thought processes.

- Overgeneralizing and catastrophizing: He is never home

- Mind reading: I am making assumptions about his feelings. He has never said he doesn't love me.

- Black-and-white thinking: I assume we either have a good marriage or we are getting a divorce. I don't see any in between or recognize that problems could be temporary.

Step 4: New thoughts.

- He only has to work late once a week.

- I have no idea how he feels other than what he tells me.

- He says he wants to be home, but work is demanding.

- All relationships are not like my parents'; things are different than they were 30 years ago.

Step 5: New attitude.

If I back off and stop worrying then perhaps he will feel less stressed around me and we can start to have fun together again.

> **STOP AND THINK**
>
> Excessive worrying is the result of trying to solve problems before they happen. Make sure you are working to solve actual problems, not imagined ones. To slow down your worry, practice mindfulness, allowing your thoughts about potential problems come in your mind without searching for a solution. Instead, remind yourself that living with uncertainty is a part of life and you can find a solution if, and when, the problem occurs.

Behavior Assignments

Anxiety is driven by uncertainty, ambiguity, and discomfort. The next time you are feeling anxious, try to unravel your thoughts and feelings. Focus on figuring out when and where you are having these types of thoughts. Create a new attitude toward the situation and reword it as a behavior assignment for yourself. Use the following examples as templates for creating your own behavior assignments.

Avoiding Discomfort

Situation: If I get on the subway, I will have a panic attack. That will be awful and embarrassing. I will end up screaming.

Catching your negative thoughts: I am anxious because I am trying to avoid being uncomfortable. This is fortune-telling; I don't know for sure that I will have a panic attack. It is also mind reading because I am assuming other people will judge me.

New thoughts: If I get on the subway, my heart will start racing. I may have a panic attack but I can usually hide it so the people around me won't even know. I might not have a panic attack.

Behavior assignment: I will get on the subway and get off at the next stop. I will keep reminding myself that I can cope with this.

Uncertainty

Situation: My daughter has applied to several colleges. I am anxious about what is going to happen and am worried that she isn't going to be accepted. She is going to be devastated.

Catching your negative thoughts: I am worried about something that hasn't yet happened. I can address the problem if she doesn't get accepted, but right now there isn't a problem to solve. I am fortune-telling. I am also catastrophizing because I am assuming that she won't be accepted by any college.

New thoughts: She applied to several colleges. She has good grades and is an active student. Now that all the applications are sent, we need to sit back and wait.

Behavior assignment: I need to consider different options. If she doesn't get accepted into her first choice, there are other good schools around. She could also take a year off to do volunteering work and improve her resume.

Ambiguity

Situation: I went on a first date and enjoyed myself. He said he had a nice time. He hasn't called me since the date. Maybe he was lying and didn't like me or thinks I am unattractive. Maybe I should call him but he probably doesn't want to hear from me. Maybe it is too soon; he might still call. He is a jerk; he should have called.

Catching your negative thoughts: I am making a mountain out of a molehill; it was one date. If it doesn't work out that is okay; there are plenty of people I enjoy spending time with. I am blaming him for not acting the way I think he should act. I am mind reading, assuming he found me unattractive even though he didn't give any indication of that.

New thoughts: I can call or text him to see if he wants to meet again or sit back and wait. It was only one date; we don't have a deep emotional connection. I can take things as they come instead of rushing into something.

Behavior assignment: I will wait a few more days and then call if he hasn't called me by then. I will ask if he would like to go out again. I will keep my options open and date other people if I meet someone I like.

When you first start using this strategy, you might need to write down each step. As you continue to use this technique, you will find yourself going through the process in your mind.

The Least You Need to Know

- Using CBT techniques at the first sign of anxiety can help reduce both physical and emotional symptoms of anxiety.

- One way to combat anxiety is to use exposure therapy to gradually confront situations or objects that you fear.

- Exposure therapy works best when you break your fear into small steps and work on each one until you feel comfortable.

- Uncertainty is a part of life. Working to change your behaviors first and your thoughts second is an effective way of combating your fear of the unknown.

CHAPTER 18

Controlling Anger

Anger is a normal response to a perceived threat. Anger is energizing, and, when used in a constructive way, it helps you right a wrong. When used in destructive ways, anger eats away at your self-confidence and creates problems in your life. This chapter will help you determine if you have a problem with anger and teach you strategies to lower your anger levels.

What Is Anger?

Anger is a normal human emotion that everyone feels from time to time. It can occur when you feel stressed or when someone infringes on your rights, threatens you, disappoints you, or takes advantage of you. It can range from annoyance to uncontrolled rage. Anger can give you a burst of energy and propel you to make positive changes in your life, but it can also create problems in relationships and at work.

In This Chapter

- The roots of anger
- How to stop blame and defensiveness in your thinking
- How to know if you have a problem with anger
- Accepting frustration as a part of life

Understanding Your Anger

Every day, things happen and your anger flares—your boss asks you to stay late to finish a report, your partner doesn't take the trash out, a driver cuts you off, a cashier is rude. It's easy to assume these events caused you to become angry. However, it is not the events themselves that made you angry; your interpretation of these stressful events is what caused the anger. Each of us has core beliefs, as discussed in Chapter 3, and these beliefs create *automatic thoughts*. Those thoughts drive your reaction to the event. By identifying and changing those thoughts, you can control your reaction—and lessen your feelings of anger.

> **DEFINITION**
>
> **Automatic thoughts** are thoughts that are involuntarily generated. They are an internal reaction to situations and events and may contain errors in logic.

Your Turn: Creating an Anger Log

An anger log is a place for you to record your thoughts and feelings about specific situations. As you look over your log, you should start to see the relationship between them. This gives you information to better manage similar situations in the future.

Divide a paper into three columns (we'll add additional columns later as we continue through the process). Label your columns:

- My Pain/Stressors

- What Happened

- What I Thought

You may not be aware of your automatic thoughts at first, but as you continue to do this exercise, these thoughts will become more apparent. Start by completing as much as you can each time you feel annoyed, irritated, or angry.

Here's a sample scenario: You came home from a long day at work. Your partner, Justin, had the day off from work and had planned to be home all day. As you walked in the door, you saw a complete mess. There were dishes in the sink and clothes on floor. Justin was sitting on the couch watching television. Your temper immediately flared.

Your anger log would look like this:

My Pain/Stressors	What Happened	What I Thought
Tired from long day at work	Walked in the house to a complete mess; noticed dishes from breakfast in sink and clothes on floor. Justin was sitting and doing nothing.	Justin should have cleaned up before I got home.
		If he cared about me, he would have.
		Justin is so inconsiderate and doesn't care about how tired I am.
		I need to do everything around here.
		I can't count on anyone.

Rather than reacting immediately, try to take a few minutes to complete your anger log as soon as you feel irritated or angry. Many times your emotions change as the situation changes and you want to be sure to capture the thoughts that first pop in your head. As you go through the different exercises in this chapter, we will refer to your log and ask you to add to it.

Completing the anger log helps you focus on the thoughts behind your emotions. You can then look for distortions in your thinking and challenge your thoughts.

CBTIDBIT

Review your anger diary after completing it for at least a week; look for automatic thoughts that resemble the types of thought processes and try to put each into one category. Then use the strategies to counterattack the past situation.

Causes of Anger

In Chapter 2, we talked about different types of problematic thought processes. A few of these—intention, blame, and defensiveness—usually cause anger.

Problematic Thought Process: Intention; you assume a purposeful and harmful intent behind an action.

- Your friend is late for lunch and you assume your friendship isn't important.

- Your husband doesn't take out the trash and you assume he is being inconsiderate.

- Your boss is in a bad mood and you assume he isn't happy with your work.

Counterstrategy: Depersonalize the act.

Ask yourself, "What are some other reasons that explain the actions of others?"

New thoughts:

- Maybe he got caught in traffic.

- Maybe he has an important meeting that he is worried about and forgot to take out the trash.

- Maybe he is upset because he didn't sleep well the night before.

Problematic Thought Process: Blame; you place the blame on someone else instead of accepting responsibility.

- You blame the taxi driver when you are late for a meeting.

- You blame your co-worker for a report being late.

- You blame your husband for spending too much money.

Counterstrategy: Take responsibility.

Ask yourself, "What about this situation is my responsibility?"

New thoughts:

- I didn't allow enough time to get across town.

- I need to give my co-worker at least four days to complete the report or clear her plate of other tasks.

- I need to look at my own spending habits first.

Problematic Thought Process: Defensiveness; you believe everything should be done your way and are not able to accept that there are different ways of doing things.

- Your boss wants you to redo a report to make it more comprehensive. You think, "What a tyrant!"

- Your friend suggests a different route to drive when going out to dinner. You think, "She's wrong; my way would be much faster."

- Your husband comments on how he thinks the house could be cleaner. You think, "He is telling me I am not a good wife."

Counterstrategy: Practice empathy.

Ask yourself, "What ideas and experiences does the other person bring to this situation? Why is this person expressing themselves?"

New thoughts:

- My boss has more experience than I do in completing these reports. His changes will improve the report and help me improve my work performance.

- I always take the same route; it will be good to know more than one way to the restaurant.

- I can see that the house could be tidier. I'll talk to my husband about setting up a regular cleaning schedule that we work on together.

STOP AND THINK

When someone criticizes you or makes a complaint, you can choose how to respond. Although you may want to get defensive, try thinking about what the other person has said. Identify the information in the request and repeat it back to them. This acknowledges the complaint and forces you to consider the other person's point of view.

There might be times that you feel your anger is justified; someone did something wrong and you have every right to be angry. Imagine you came home from work to find your son playing video games. You had specifically left instructions for him to mow the lawn, take out the trash, and clean up his room. None of this was done, and even worse, the kitchen is now a mess with his dishes from breakfast and lunch. He has obviously spent the entire day eating, watching television, and playing video games. You are fuming.

When a situation such as this happens, it is important to remember that while you can't control the other person's actions, you can control your response. Sometimes anger boils up so quickly you feel as if you have no control over it. Remember that you can control your reaction. Before blowing up at your son, take a few minutes to cool down and review the situation. Ask yourself these questions:

- How important will this be in an hour, tomorrow, next week, or next year?

- Is this worth being angry and ruining my entire evening?

- What steps can I take to resolve the situation?

You might decide that the television and video games are turned off until the chores are completed. You might decide that you will give your son another chance tomorrow to complete the chores, but make it clear that the television and video games are off-limits until the work is done. You might take other privileges, such as his cell phone, away until he proves he can follow your instructions. You might decide in the future he needs to text you pictures of the completed chores before he is allowed to watch television or play video games.

Listing the steps you can take helps you feel back in control and can reduce the overwhelming feelings of anger. If this doesn't work, remove yourself from the situation by going for a walk, doing some exercise, listening to some music, or enjoying some activity you find relaxing. Once you have calmed down, look at the situation again and come up with steps to resolve it.

Your Turn: Criticism, Complaint, or Request?

When someone makes a complaint or request, do you jump to conclusions, sure he or she is criticizing what you have done or haven't done? The following exercise helps you look at complaints and requests from both sides—yours and theirs.

Let's practice dealing with criticisms and complaints as requests and information. Divide a paper into two columns. In the first column are your automatic thoughts and in the second are different ways of looking at the situation. Imagine you come home from work and your wife wants you to cut the grass.

Automatic Thoughts: Criticisms and Complaints	Request and Information Perspective
She is always telling me what to do.	She is making a request, not ordering me.
I just got home; can't she give me time to relax?	We are having people over tomorrow; the lawn should look nice.
She's always complaining about what I haven't done.	The grass is looking pretty long.
She never sees everything I do around here.	I can say I will cut the lawn later.
	I can negotiate cutting the lawn at a different time.
	I can explain why I don't want to cut the grass right now.

Or, imagine that your boss hands you a report to complete at 4 P.M. on a Friday afternoon.

Automatic Thoughts: Criticisms and Complaints	Request and Information Perspective
He is so demanding.	He is under a lot of pressure; the client meeting is on Monday.
He just wants to ruin my weekend.	He must think highly of me to ask me to complete this for him.
He isn't happy with my work and wants to punish me.	I do have plans for this evening, maybe I could offer to come in early on Monday to finish this.
He is saying the first draft wasn't good.	He is just telling me the report needs to be completed.

Instead of jumping to conclusions based on your automatic thoughts, this exercise gives you time to sit down, look at the situation from a different perspective, and find a solution. It helps you to move from anger to problem solving.

Healthy vs. Unhealthy Anger

Anger itself is neither healthy nor unhealthy. The frequency, intensity, and expression of your anger determine whether it is constructive or destructive. Healthy anger is milder, occurs less often, and is used to solve problems and set boundaries for yourself. It is expressed, discussed, worked through, and then let go.

Some people have trouble controlling their anger, letting it boil over and explode. They use their anger to control, intimidate, manipulate, or punish others. Unhealthy anger is out of proportion to the situation and usually lasts longer than necessary for the problem. Unhealthy anger occurs more frequently than healthy anger. Frequent or intense anger is not healthy because it hurts your immune systems, increases blood pressure, and sets you up to be angry repeatedly.

Look for some of these ways that unhealthy anger is communicated.

- Yelling
- Screaming
- Fighting
- Blaming
- Threats

- Violence
- Retaliating
- Holding grudges
- Ending relationships
- Punishing others

When you express your anger in these ways, your needs might be met in the short term but you usually end up alienating those around you or causing conflict in your relationships. You might have legal problems because of fights or property destruction. Once you calm down, you might regret what you did or said; even so, when anger strikes again, you react the same way.

Not expressing your anger is also unhealthy. You bottle it up inside, never telling anyone how you feel. Suppressed anger has been associated with high blood pressure, heart disease, and cancer.

When you manage your anger in healthy ways, you use it as a guide to tell you something is wrong. It is your way of noticing disappointment or injustice. Suppose your children are playing outside. A car speeds down the street. You get angry. "What is that car doing? What a jerk! Don't they know there are children playing? That is so dangerous!" You have a choice. You can react by running after the car, yelling and waving your arms although this probably isn't going to solve anything. You can take positive action, getting involved in your community and working with the police to have signs and speed bumps placed on the street. You can use your anger to create change. Expressing anger in this way helps you feel more in control of your life.

Your Turn: How Angry Are You?

Review the behaviors on the chart, and rate the frequency and the intensity of each on a scale of 0 to 5, with 5 being very frequent or very intense. Add up your score for each column.

Behavior	Frequency	Intensity
Yelling		
Screaming		
Verbal fighting		
Physical fighting		
Blaming others		
Making threats		
Acting violently		
Retaliating		
Holding grudges		
Ending relationships		
Punishing others		
Totals		

Total score of 0–22: You are probably able to manage your anger within reasonable limits. You might still benefit from the skills in this chapter and learn helpful ways of handling frustrating situations.

Total score of 23–44: You probably have some anger management problems and need to learn how to manage your reactions differently.

Total score of 45–55: It is most likely you have an anger management problem and need to use the skills in this chapter to help you manage your reactions.

Common Hot Buttons

Hot buttons are situations that trigger certain attitudes, which, in turn, cause anger. While each person has hot buttons specific to his or her life and past experiences, there are some common themes that underlie most people's triggers. You can combat hot button triggers by using *coping statements*, short declarations that help you manage difficult situations.

> **DEFINITION**
>
> **Coping statements** are short statements that provide help for attitudes and problematic thinking processes. They are used to counterattack triggers. When you practice using these statements, your brain automatically remembers them and creates new mental habits and reflexes.

Let's look at some examples of hot button triggers along with the associated attitudes and some suggested coping statements to help deal with the situation.

Situation 1: Things don't go your way.

Attitude: You feel entitled to your desires and become annoyed when other people prevent you from getting what you want.

Coping statements: "I have my wants and needs but others are entitled to disagree or say no. I need to respect their right to do that." "I have my needs but others have needs, too."

Example: You're passed over for a promotion at work. Instead of thinking, "How dare they; they backstabbed me," practice acceptance. "Everyone at work wants to get ahead. The person who got the promotion deserves it as much as I do."

Situation 2: Something is unfair or you are being taken advantage of.

Attitude: You believe everything should be fair, and if things are not just you feel the need to correct it.

Coping Statements: "I see fairness based on my perspective; other people are entitled to their perspective." "Fairness is subjective. Others have a right to see things according to their own ideas, principles, and expectations." "Life is not always fair; that is something I need to accept." "Not every battle is worth fighting."

Example: Your friend purchases an expensive necklace. You feel angry and jealous and think, "It's so unfair; I can barely pay my rent." Instead, practice acceptance. "Not everything in life is fair; I'm sure she has her battles, too. It isn't for me to say how she should spend her money."

Situation 3: Someone lets you down or doesn't do what you expected.

Attitude: You assume others are intentionally trying to harm you or don't care about your needs.

Coping statements: "No one is perfect; not everyone behaves the way I would." "When someone doesn't do something that I expect, it doesn't mean they don't care about my needs. Others have their own needs and at times they might compete with my needs."

Example: Your partner forgets your birthday and you assume it means he doesn't love you and is trying to hurt your feelings. Instead, think: "I know he is not good about remembering social events. I can help him out and remind him my birthday is approaching rather than setting him up to feel guilty."

Situation 4: Others around you make the same mistakes over and over.

Attitude: You believe that you need to change them. You think if you try hard enough, yell at them, or complain enough, you will eventually whip them into shape.

Coping statement: "Other people have their own methods and limits. Demanding they change without understanding their motivation and limitations only leads to dead ends."

Example: Your employee keeps handing in his reports in an incoherent manner. You think, "What an incompetent idiot; why he is so defiant?" Instead, try thinking, "Apparently he does not understand what I want in this report. I will set up a time for us to go over exactly how to complete these reports."

GIVE IT A TRY

Think about a recent situation that made you upset. Write down a short description of the situation. Ask yourself: What can I do to change my perception of the situation? Then write a coping statement.

Reframe Your Emotion

Some of the most common problematic thinking processes in anger are personalization and labeling. When you label situations, others, or yourself using extreme language, you can escalate your anger and mood. Behaviors such as cursing, calling others names, or exaggerating the negativity ("This is awful!" "I have never been treated so poorly!") make the situation worse rather than better. Instead of living in disbelief, try to accept the situation.

When going through a difficult situation, write down the descriptive words you use. Replace the words with more objective or moderate descriptions. Repeat your original statement using the new words and see if the level of intensity of your emotion decreases.

Original statement: "I can't believe he forgot my birthday! What a jerk! I am furious!"

New statement: "He forgot my birthday. This is disappointing. I'm annoyed."

Original statement: "I can't believe my doorman lost my package; what an idiot! What a disaster. I am so upset. I need to report him."

New statement: "My doorman lost my package. The delivery system is not perfect at my office. This is frustrating. I need to call and file a claim."

Accept Fallibility in Yourself and Others

You know you are not a perfect person. You know you make mistakes and you know you have faults—you just prefer not to think about them. You prefer to push them to the back of your mind. After all, when you think about your faults you must either think you are a terrible person or you must commit to change. Ignoring your faults is much easier. Even so, you expect others to see and own their faults. You expect them to take responsibility for their mistakes and when they don't, you get angry.

Disarming your anger starts with accepting that you are fallible, along with everyone else. Once you do this, you can see the triggers listed in the previous section from a different perspective. Suppose your partner forgets your birthday. You are angry because he hasn't lived up to your expectation. You assume that he is an inconsiderate person and does not deserve you. However, if you see your partner as fallible, then the situation and your perception of it changes. "He is forgetful but he shows me how much he loves me in other ways. I have forgotten things before and wanted people to understand. I should understand when he is forgetful."

CBTIDBIT

When you catch yourself judging other people, stop and immediately find one thing you like about the other person. Praise them for that quality. This makes you stop and look at the person differently and changes your perception.

When you are angry, you judge others. You perceive them as inconsiderate, rude, unfeeling, or unfair. You become angry because they are not behaving the way you think is appropriate. For example, suppose you are talking to a co-worker when another co-worker comes along and interrupts the conversation. You think he is being rude. What your attitude really implies is, "He should behave the way I would." If you judge yourself first, and remember that you interrupt sometimes or do other things people may not like, then you are more apt to see his behavior differently. Remember, you can't force anyone to change. You must change your behavior and your reaction.

Your Turn: Judge Yourself First

Try to catch yourself placing a label on someone. You probably do this many times throughout the day without even thinking about it. Pay attention and listen to how often you judge others. Stop and judge yourself instead. Place a label on your reaction. For example, when a co-worker interrupts your conversation, you might write that you are being impatient. Maybe he has an emergency or something important that needs to be discussed immediately. This exercise helps you focus on your own behavior rather than on other people's behaviors.

Increase Your Frustration Tolerance

Do you get annoyed over the small details? Do you find yourself irritated every time something goes wrong? You might have what is called a low frustration tolerance. This is usually caused because you catastrophize or overgeneralize about being frustrated. You think being frustrated is going to be terrible. You try to avoid any type of frustration.

When you have a low frustration tolerance you demand that everything is the way you want it to be. You don't see problems as inconvenient or see levels of problems, such as "this is a small problem; it shouldn't take much to get it cleared up." Instead, every problem is a catastrophe. When you have a low frustration tolerance, you...

- Seek activities that give you immediate pleasure.

- Spend your time trying to avoid pain.

- Complain.

- Become distressed over small setbacks.

- Are overly concerned about fairness.

- Tend to compare your circumstances to other people's circumstances.

People with low frustration tolerance have a higher risk of addiction or other impulsive behaviors such as unsafe sex or overspending. They tend to have a "short fuse," becoming angry quickly when things go wrong.

When frustrated about a specific problem, write about it. Use one of the following viewpoints to see the situation from different perspectives.

- Write a letter to your best friend describing the situation and the steps you plan to take to improve it.

- Imagine you are alone on a desert island. Write a letter describing the situation and how your life improved once you solved it. You are going to put into a bottle and throw into the sea for a potential rescuer to read.

- Write a letter to yourself from the future. View the situation from one month, one year, and three years from now. Describe the situation and how you resolved it.

- Write a worst case scenario describing the absolute worst that could happen. Think about the physical and emotional problems that might ensue if the problem continues. Imagine what life will be like after the worst possible solution occurs.

Once you look at the problem from a different perspective, it probably doesn't seem as bad as it originally did.

Your Turn: Raise Your Frustration Tolerance

You can use the ABCDEF chart to analyze your frustration and come up with ways to change your reaction.

A: Activating Event

B: Beliefs

C: Consequences

D: Problematic Thinking Processes

E: New Thoughts

F: Coping Statement

Let's look at an example.

A: My supervisor criticized me in front of my co-workers.

B: It was very unfair. She should have talked to me in private instead of treating me like a child. It was so embarrassing; everyone was looking at me. I can't deal with someone treating me without respect.

C: I was angry the rest of day. I couldn't concentrate and didn't get much work done. I want to quit.

D: Personalization and blame, "should" and "must," emotional reasoning

E: I would have preferred she talked to me in private, but she doesn't have to do things the way I want. I would prefer to be treated with respect, but sometimes that isn't going to happen. I was uncomfortable and embarrassed, but it was not the worst thing that has ever happened to me. I am sure no one is judging me; after all, other people get reprimanded at work and I don't judge them.

F: I would prefer not to be annoyed but be able to let it go and not carry anger with me all day. If I get in trouble at work, it isn't the end of the world.

When thinking about your desired behavior or reaction, avoid replacing an intensely negative emotion with an intensely positive emotion. Instead, work on moving to a more moderate reaction. Use the emotion levels and alternate words described in Chapter 4. For example, instead of "furious," try "annoyed."

The Least You Need to Know

- Anger is neither good nor bad; it is the frequency, the intensity, and your expression of your anger that is either positive or destructive in your life.
- When someone criticizes or complains about your behavior, reword it to think of it as a request rather than a demand.
- Unhealthy anger might give you short-term relief but often causes problems in the long term.
- Low frustration tolerance comes from catastrophizing and overgeneralizing situations.

CHAPTER 19

Overcoming Addictions or Substance Abuse

When you're struggling with addiction, ending it may seem impossible. There is hope. You can change your life. Battling an addiction takes courage and determination. The exercises in this chapter will help you find your personal motivation for quitting, identify triggers to prevent relapse, and discover the emotions fueling your addiction.

The Many Sizes and Shapes of Addiction

An *addiction* is a dependency on a substance or a compulsive behavior. You rarely go through a day without thinking about or participating in your addiction in some way. You feel a need for the substance or behavior to get you through stressful situations and you find that you need more of it to feel the same result.

In This Chapter

- Signs of addiction
- The pros and cons of ending your addiction
- Finding alternative activities
- Managing cravings

DEFINITION

An **addiction** is the physical or psychological dependence on a substance or activity. The addiction is usually pleasurable in the beginning, but with continued use it becomes compulsive. It often interferes with personal responsibilities, such as work and relationships.

Some of the most common addictions include the following:

- Alcohol

- Nicotine

- Cocaine or other illegal drugs

- Prescription painkillers

- Pornography

- Sex

- Shopping

- Gambling

- Food

Some people have binge dependencies. This is when they don't engage in a behavior or use a substance for days, weeks, or months and then binge, indulging to excess for a short period of time.

Addictions often begin as a way of feeling better or dealing with a difficult situation. The addiction relaxes you but every time you use it, you become more hooked, until you rely on the substance or behavior to get you through life. Addictions are often destructive to your relationships, your job, and your finances. They frequently lead to legal problems.

Some of the signs of addiction include the following:

- You need more of the substance or behavior to get the same result.

- Going without the addictive substance leads to effects of withdrawal, such as irritability, headache, sweating, shaking, nausea, or an inability to concentrate.

- You miss time at work because of obtaining, engaging in, or recovering from your addiction.

- You engage in your addiction despite your resolve not to.

- You engage in your addiction at times of the day others would find inappropriate.

- You find it difficult to go an entire day without your addiction.

- You make efforts to hide your addiction.

- You feel irritable when not using or deprived of using.

- You neglect responsibilities, tasks, or activities so you can obtain, engage in, or recover from your addiction.

- Your relationship is in trouble.

- You have health, legal, or financial problems as a result of your dependency.

IMAGINE THAT

Substance abuse is a milder form of addiction. Substance abuse is a psychological dependency rather than a physical dependency. It has many of the same symptoms except there is no physical tolerance and withdrawal. It can still interfere with your job, relationships, and health.

You might find it difficult to imagine your life without your dependency of choice. It has become a part of your life. You don't think you can manage stressful situations without having the relief of turning to your addiction.

Accept Your Addiction

Accepting your addiction doesn't mean to give in and give up. You have to accept that you have an addiction before you can take steps to improve your life. You might hide behind statements such as:

"Both my parents were alcoholics; it is hereditary."

"I had a hard day, I need to…"

"I wouldn't be in this situation if my friend hadn't started me down this road."

"It's not like I don't go to work every day."

Blame and denial are an escape. They stop you from accepting responsibility for the addiction and your behaviors. For example, while it is true that alcoholism runs in families, not everyone with an alcoholic parent turns into an alcoholic himself. There are factors, heredity and environmental, that contribute to your tendency toward addiction, but it is up to you to determine your path. You must claim ownership of the fact that you are an addict.

Your Turn: Identify Blame Statements

How often do you blame someone else in order to avoid taking personal responsibility? You might do this in different areas of your life, not just your addiction. For example, you might say:

"Nobody understands."

"Why does this always happen to me?"

"No one ever tells me what is going on."

"You always criticize me."

Spend the next week listening to how you talk and think. Write down every blame statement. Then write down a statement that conveys the same thought without blaming someone.

> 👉 **CBTIDBIT**
>
> There are a few speech patterns that signal blame even when you think you are making a statement. One is using the words "it" and "that" to signal something is wrong, such as, "It makes me mad…" Another is using "I feel…because…" such as "I feel angry because my boss didn't like my report." The third one is when you make a statement mentioning only the other person's actions, such as "When you come home late, I get worried."

The Personal Costs of Addiction

Addiction of any kind has its costs, financially and emotionally. For some people, these costs are immense: financial ruin, inability to pay rent or buy food, irreparable relationship damage, job loss, or serious health issues. The very nature of an addiction is that there are negative consequences and yet, despite that, you continue your behavior.

Taking an inventory of the personal costs of your addiction helps motivate you to change and to remain away from the substance or behavior. Review the following categories. For each one, write down ways that your life has suffered from your addiction.

- Self-esteem

- Relationships

- Job

- Finances

- Physical health

- Emotional health

If you are having a hard time accepting your addiction, remember that if something doesn't change, these costs are only going to continue and worsen. You don't need to wait until your life crashes around you to stop. You can decide now that the costs outweigh the benefits.

GIVE IT A TRY

Write down three to five things that are important to you, such as significant other, kids, career, or parents. Write down three ways your addiction impacts each one.

Your Turn: Cost Analysis

Divide a paper into four sections.

In the top two sections write:

- Benefits

- What I don't like

In the bottom two sections write:

- Benefits of quitting

- Disadvantages of quitting

Fill in as many thoughts as you can in each section.

Suppose you have an alcohol addiction; you might write:

Benefits

- It helps me relax.

- It gives me confidence in social situations.

- It allows me to forget my problems for a little while.

What I don't like

- Hangovers

- I spend too much money.

- I only go places where alcohol is served.

- I miss work too often.

- My partner thinks I drink too much.

Benefits of quitting

- I won't have hangovers any more

- I can save the money I spend on alcohol

- My work performance will improve.

- My relationship will improve.

- I can go out to dinner or to a friend's house without thinking of whether there will be alcohol

Disadvantages of quitting

- I'll lose some friends because drinking is our activity.

- Life won't be as fun.

- I'll be nervous in social settings.

Your cost-benefit analysis should give you clear evidence that the consequences of your addiction interfere with your life and list specific ways that quitting your addiction can improve your life.

Identifying Your Triggers

Your addiction serves a purpose. It fills a need or want, or maybe it helps you avoid thinking or feeling about negative emotions. In order to quit your addiction, you must be able to fill that need in a different way. First, you have to find your triggers; you need to know why you need your addiction.

Use a notebook to keep a log of each time you engage in your addiction. Write down:

- When and where did this happen?

- Who was with you?

- What events or situation took place right before?

- Were you using your addiction to avoid something? If so, what?

- Were you using your addiction to gain access to something or someone? If so what, who?

- What were you thinking?

- What were you feeling?

- What is your justification?

- When did you make the decision to engage in your addiction?

As you keep track, you should notice some patterns. For example, your answers to the questions about what you were doing, thinking, and feeling might have similar answers. You might see the same social situation occurring, such as trying to fit in a group and the same thoughts: "I am being judged," "This is unfair." The emotions of anger, loneliness, boredom, or physical pain might be written down more often than other reasons. Start quitting your addiction by tackling the easiest part first. This is usually avoiding the social setup or what you are doing that triggers the cravings or behaviors. Check out these following examples:

- If you are a compulsive gambler, block gambling sites or put yourself on the "do not collect" gambling winning list.

- If you are addicted to food, change the way you shop or keep only enough food to last you for one day.

- If you are an alcoholic or abuse alcohol, remove alcohol from your house and avoid bars.

- If you are addicted to cigarettes and find that you usually smoke during breaks at work, find something different to do during breaks.

STOP AND THINK

Most addictions are driven by psychological or behavioral habits. This means you are more likely to crave a drink in a bar, grab a cigarette during a work break, binge eat when home alone with a refrigerator full of food, gamble when near a casino, or do drugs when hanging out with other drug users. Changing or avoiding these habits is the first step in quitting your addiction.

Your Turn: New Behavior Plan

Look over your log, paying attention to any patterns. Write these down.

For example, you might write: I am addicted to alcohol. From my log I noticed several common situations in which I find it hard not to drink.

Situation: I often stop on my way home from work to buy a bottle of wine. I start by having one glass of wine, but it usually leads to at least three.

Thoughts: I need to unwind.

Feelings: stressed, lonely, bored

Situation: When I go out in the evening with certain friends, we start off at someone's apartment and pre-drink with shots to save money.

Thoughts: need to fit in, save money.

Feelings: anxiousness

GIVE IT A TRY

Quitting an addiction and entering recovery require lifestyle changes. Here are a few changes you can make:

Surround yourself with people who support your choice to quit, even if that means giving up friends who still participate in drinking, drugs, gambling, or your addiction of choice.

Avoid drinking even if you aren't addicted to alcohol. Drinking lowers your inhibitions and having a few drinks can lead to a relapse.

Add healthy choices to your day including eating right, getting enough sleep, and exercising.

Situation: When I go on a date with someone new, I usually have several drinks.

Thoughts: Having a few drinks makes me more social and interesting.

Feeling: anxiousness

Write a plan listing alternative behaviors and activities to help you warm up to quitting. Use the following example as a template.

Instead of buying wine on my way home, I will walk a different route. I will keep a fruit juice in my refrigerator. I will do a relaxation exercise when I get home. I will put the money I don't spend in a jar toward a vacation to reward myself.

I will meet my friends at the restaurant until I can resist doing shots before we go out. I will try to make plans that don't involve drinking, such as a yoga class, going to the movies, or bike riding.

When I go on a date, I will suggest an activity like mini golf or watching a movie. I should be able to feel comfortable with someone without getting drunk.

IMAGINE THAT

Most people think of addiction as a lifelong burden where they will always "crave" their substance or behavior of choice, but that isn't necessarily the case. Addiction is a spectrum disorder, which means that every person reacts differently to addiction and to overcoming addiction. Many people are able to put their addiction behind them to lead normal, productive lives.

The second step is dealing with the emotion driving your addiction. Once you reduce your behavior situations, it is easier to deal with the underlying emotions and to make deeper, long-lasting changes. In the previous example, the underlying emotions were anxiety and stress. You would list alternative ways of dealing with these emotions. You might list exercising, calling a friend, taking a walk, or using a relaxation technique. Turn to this list to find something to do whenever you feel anxious. Create alternative activities for each reason you engaged in your addiction. Look for the chapter in this book relating to your underlying emotions for ways to challenge the unhelpful thoughts.

Turn Intention into Action

It's easy to want to quit but much harder to actually go through with it. Whatever your addiction is, it has given you some positive benefits, as you listed in your cost-benefit analysis. The addiction is a powerful motivator to keep engaging in the behavior. CBT helps you to increase the positive reaction of not engaging in the addiction. It builds skills to help you end the addiction and to help you stay away.

Set a quit date. This date should be within few days up to a week from when you decide to quit. Be careful not to overindulge before the quit date; this just makes quitting harder. Instead warm yourself up by doing the exercise in the section above. Ask for support from close friends and family. Let them know you are trying to change your addictive habits and ask them to help you.

Restructure Your Thoughts

Throughout this book, you have learned to recognize and change negative and problematic thought patterns. You probably have some thoughts specific to your addiction, such as "I will always be an addict," or "I just need one," or "It will help me relax." Listen to what you tell yourself about your addiction. Use the ABCD chart to determine whether these thoughts are true and to create alternative thoughts.

You can also use behavioral experiments to determine the validity of your beliefs. For example, you may believe you need a few drinks to relax and be able to talk to other people at a party. Your behavioral experiment is to test whether you can talk to others without having a drink.

Deal with Cravings

You should expect to have intense cravings. Sometimes these cravings will go away; other times it will be difficult to say "no" to the craving. Use the following techniques to help manage cravings:

- Challenge them—what is going to happen if you don't give in to the craving?

- Recall unpleasant memories from times you engaged in your addiction.

- Use imagery to focus on possible negative consequences, such as getting caught by your spouse or boss, getting fired, losing all of your money, gaining weight, losing custody your children, becoming ill, or aging quickly.

- Review your list of the benefits of stopping your addiction.

- Choose to delay your decision. Instead of giving in to your craving, give yourself time to decide.

- Distract yourself. Choose something from your list of alternative activities and do it.

> **GIVE IT A TRY**
>
> Most cravings last only 15 minutes. When you have a craving that is too strong to ignore, try urge surfing. This is when you stay with the urge until it passes. Imagine you are a surfer riding a wave as it crests, breaks, and then turns into the foamy, less dangerous, surf.

Coping cards might also help. On an index card, list positive statements, the unpleasant affects of engaging in your addiction, and the benefits of not using. Keep the cards with you to review when you are having a craving. Some positive self statements to help give you a boost might look like this:

- I am a strong person.

- I am not my addition.

- I am not owned by food (or drugs, alcohol, gambling, cigarettes, etc.)

- Giving in to my addiction only makes me feel better temporarily.

- I have gone X number of days; each day it will get easier. Giving in will only make it harder tomorrow.

- Others are dependent on me.

- I think I can hide behind my addiction but people see through my lies.

Additions are a great time to use positive affirmations, imagery, and relaxation exercises. Refer to Chapter 6 to review visualization and imagery, Chapter 7 for relaxation techniques, and Chapter 9 for positive self-talk. These tools help you feel calmer and relaxed and tap into your inner strength.

The Least You Need to Know

- An addiction can be a dependency on a substance or a behavior, such as gambling or shopping.
- Your addiction serves a purpose in your life but also causes destruction. Adding up the pros and cons of your addiction helps you find reasons to quit.
- Your emotions and behaviors drive your addiction. Having a behavior plan helps you say "no."
- Make coping cards with positive statements, the unpleasant affects of your addiction, and the reasons you want to quit. Keep them with you to help stave off cravings.

CHAPTER 20

Managing OCD

You think you forgot to turn off the stove and go back and check. You can't leave the house without systematically checking that every window and door is locked. You spend hours organizing and reorganizing your bookshelves. Everyone has daily routines and double-checks things sometimes, but if you have obsessive compulsive disorder (OCD), these behaviors become obsessions and compulsions that take up time and interfere with your daily life. This chapter will help you understand the relationship between obsessions and compulsions and provide you with strategies to help lessen your dependence on rituals.

Understanding Obsessive Compulsive Disorder

Obsessive compulsive disorder (OCD) is an anxiety disorder characterized by obsessions and compulsions. Obsessions are intrusive and upsetting thoughts, images, or impulses that occur repeatedly in your mind. You feel powerless to control these thoughts. Compulsions are behaviors and rituals you feel you must complete. Compulsions are often repeated and done in an effort to relieve the obsessive thoughts.

For example, suppose you worry about germs; you are afraid you might touch someone or something and become ill. These thoughts overtake you and you must wash your hands. Until you are able to wash your hands, you don't feel relief. In more severe cases of OCD you have a ritual, such as washing your hands five times. You perform this ritual to try to diminish the thoughts about germs; however, it probably only provides short-term relief.

> **IMAGINE THAT**
>
> Not all obsessions are accompanied by rituals. Some forms of OCD are known as "Pure O." You may just experience the obsession part and hold on to the obsessions in your mind until you are exhausted or an external event resolves the problem.

Common obsessions include the following:

- Distressing religious or sacrilegious thoughts; for example, thoughts about joining a cult or worrying about religious prosecution for your sins.

- Intrusive thoughts of violent acts, such as having hurt someone in the past or thoughts about hurting someone in the future.

- Sexual thoughts or images; for example, worrying you are homosexual, have a sexually transmitted disease, or that you did something inappropriate.

- Constant worry about contamination from dirt, germs, bodily fluids, and other materials.

- Worry about throwing away something important or needing something you threw away; for example, hoarding newspapers, communications, tax papers, or clothing.

- Constantly worrying that you made a mistake.

- Worry that you have a disease.

Common rituals:

- Spending excessive time putting things in order to make them "right," such as lining things up, making lists, or reorganizing files.

- Washing hands, kitchen counters, and bathrooms excessively.

- Repeated checking to make sure you completed a task; for example, turning off the oven, locking the door, or rereading communication.

- Mental rituals such as repeating words or phrases.

- Seeking reassurance or medical advice; for example, surfing the internet for medical diagnoses or repeatedly checking with friends and family to make sure things will turn out okay.

When you suffer from OCD, you become irritated or distressed when interrupted or prevented from performing your rituals. You might need to seek constant reassurance from your partner, friends, or family, wanting to be assured that nothing bad is going to happen, you don't have a disease, and how you look is acceptable. If your obsessive thoughts are about violence, you might believe you are a terrible, evil person and your obsessions are causing others pain.

When you try to avoid your obsessive thoughts or resist completing compulsions, you end up giving in because it seems unbearable when you don't. Your obsessions and compulsions take time out of your day; often several hours per day is spent on dealing with obsessive thoughts or carrying out rituals. OCD is a spectrum disorder, which means it ranges from mild to severe.

STOP AND THINK

Rituals do not need to be external or physical acts. Rituals are sometimes internalized, such as counting, going through a checklist in your mind, or creating an elaborate plan to overcome a disaster.

Some people who experience obsessions recognize that their beliefs are false and the need to complete their ritual is simply a way to alleviate their anxiety. This is the first goal in overcoming OCD.

Your Turn: Identify Your Triggers

Keep a log for several days to find if there are certain places or situations that trigger your obsessive thoughts. If you have many obsessive thoughts per day, write down between three and five each day rather than writing each individual obsession.

Trigger	Obsession	Compulsion
Took out trash	Germs on trash	Washed hands with soap five times
Loaned someone a pen	Germs from the other person on the pen	Threw out pen
Used a shopping cart	Germs on the cart from other people	Wore latex gloves while shopping

GIVE IT A TRY

Use the ladder technique described in Chapter 5. List your triggers in order from easiest to hardest. Start with working on overcoming the easiest trigger first and work your way up the ladder. If you try to face fears too quickly, you decrease the effectiveness of exposure exercises. Be sure to write a specific goal, such as using the shopping cart without antiseptic, as the top rung of your ladder.

This example includes obsessions about germs, but you might find you have several different obsessions, such as contamination, the need for exactness or evenness, or the fear of harming others because you aren't careful enough. When you go through the other exercises in the chapter, choose one of your obsessions first. Once you have learned to manage that obsession, move on to another.

Thoughts Are Just Thoughts

It is impossible to avoid your thoughts. In CBT therapy for OCD, the goal is not necessarily to challenge your thoughts but rather learn to accept that the thoughts are there without attaching any validity and meaning to the thoughts. A thought is just a thought; it is when you attach a meaning that you react to it and likely to keep having the thought.

Your Turn: Thought Exposure

When you have OCD, your fear isn't necessarily something physical; instead, you have obsessive thoughts. As with anxiety, exposure therapy works to lessen your obsessions. However, you can't physically face your thoughts. Thought exposure involves writing down your obsessive thoughts, in detail.

Start by writing down your obsessive thoughts. Fill in as many details as you can. Write down how you feel and what you want to do.

For the next two weeks, write down the same obsessive thoughts. Your obsession might change slightly or it might remain relatively the same. Try not to use the same words every day.

Writing your obsessions might trigger additional obsessions or cause you to create more scenarios revolving around the same obsession. Don't worry; this is normal. Keep writing about it every day. This exercise should desensitize you to your obsession. Over several weeks, you should notice the frequency of your obsession decrease.

Overcoming Magical Thinking

Many people with OCD have what is called the *magical thinking* phenomenon. This is when you believe that if you don't complete your compulsions, something bad will happen and it will be your fault. You think that what you do, or don't do, has a negative impact in your environment or the world. For example, your obsessive thoughts are about causing harm to another. You worry that if you don't count and tap your hand on the wall 10 times, your grandparent will become ill.

> **DEFINITION**
>
> **Magical thinking** is when you believe that if you do something, or don't do something, that it has an effect on your environment or on the world. For example, you might believe going through a certain good-bye ritual with your children each morning will keep them safe through the day.

Gathering evidence to disprove your obsession is a good way to combat magical thinking. The following is an example of how this works.

Obsession: I am contaminated. Germs make me sick or cause me to get a disease.

Compulsion: I need to wash my hands immediately after riding the subway.

Magical thinking: I will get a disease and spread germs to my children if I do not wash my hands as soon as I get off the subway.

Gathering evidence: Think back to a time you rode the subway but did not wash your hands for at least 15 minutes. Did you get sick? Did your children get sick? Did your prediction come true?

Practice by delaying completing your ritual. This challenges your belief that something is going to happen, or not happen, as a direct result of your compulsions.

As you continue working with your OCD, it is important to postpone completing your ritual without looking for evidence or challenging the thought. Doing this is considered a mental form of seeking reassurance.

Response Prevention

As you begin to accept that your obsessions cannot cause someone harm and are not a sign of what is going to happen in the future, you need to work on accepting the discomfort that comes from not carrying out your rituals. Rituals are often carried out in order to avoid a feeling of discomfort. You want it to relieve your anxiety. Lessening your dependence on completing rituals is called response prevention. It means to delay or ignore your need to complete the ritual.

Imagine you have a cold. You start obsessing that it is much more serious, that you have a serious disease. Your first thought is to surf the internet for reassurance that this is not a serious disease. This is your ritual. Start by waiting 15 minutes before giving in to your desire to search the web. When 15 minutes has passed, if you still have the urge to carry out the ritual, ask yourself, "Can I handle the discomfort for another 15 minutes?" Try to delay the ritual another 15 minutes. Keep doing this until you no longer have the urge or anxiety. In the beginning, it will be harder to not give in to the ritual, but eventually you will find that it's easier to ignore the ritual. The more you resist your compulsion, the more your obsession will subside.

Behavioral Experiments

In Chapter 10 you learned how to create a new belief and then test its validity. This technique is helpful when trying to change obsessive thoughts.

Situation: You constantly seek reassurance from your partner about what you are wearing. You want to make sure your clothes are appropriate for work or an evening event. You don't like to leave the house without first checking with him; when you do you spend the entire day self-conscious of your appearance.

Belief: I must check with my husband on my appearance before I leave the house.

Experiment: I will plan to get dressed and purposely leave for the store without asking him.

You get dressed, go to the store, and come back. Nothing terrible has happened. No one pointed at you and laughed. No one seemed to notice that you didn't look perfect. No one seemed to care what you were wearing. You complete this experiment several times and have similar results. Sometimes people comment on how nice you look. Your experiment shows that you can get dressed and leave the house without first asking for reassurance on your appearance.

Do the same experiment when getting dressed for work or going out for the evening.

Let's look at another example.

Situation: You have a fear of getting sick from drinking from a public water fountain. You always carry water with you so you don't have to use a water fountain. You become agitated if your children ask to get a drink from the water fountain when you are at the mall.

Belief: My children or I will get sick if we use a water fountain.

Experiment: Drink from the water fountain.

You go to the mall and take a drink from the water fountain. You watch over the next several days but you don't get sick. You repeat the experiment several times over the next couple weeks, using different water fountains. You still don't get sick. Your obsession slowly starts to disappear.

> **STOP AND THINK**
>
> When creating a behavior experiment, decide how you are going to know whether your prediction comes true. Vague statements such as "to see what happens" aren't going to give you the information to disprove your original belief. Use specific statements, such as "If no one gets sick within three days of drinking a water fountain," or "If no one at work states something critical about my outfit."

You can also use the opposite technique when completing experiments by increasing the frequency of completing rituals. This helps in associating the ritual with the unpleasant obsessions. For example, suppose you are worried that your house is going to burn down. You repeatedly check to make sure the stove is turned off. You believe that checking the stove helps relieve the anxiety. Try the following experiment.

Day 1: Keep a log and mark down each time you check the stove. Rate the intensity and duration of your anxiety before and after you check the stove.

Day 2: Increase how often you check the stove. If you did so 15 times the day before, check it 25 times today. Continue to rate your level and duration of anxiety.

If you notice an increase in your anxiety on Day 2, checking the stove is not helping your anxiety; in fact, it is making your anxiety worse. From this experiment you can tell your ritual is part of the problem, not part of the solution. Eliminating the ritual will reduce your anxiety.

In order to reap the benefits of behavior experiments, the same experiment needs to be repeated several times. Each time you repeat it you reinforce your new belief. Once you have mastered an experiment where you feel no anxiety, move on to another experiment.

Exposure Therapy

You learned a CBT technique involving exposure to your fears in Chapter 17. You can use this same technique to help relieve your fear of certain situations when you have OCD.

Start by making a list of situations that provoke your intrusive thoughts or compulsions, such as shaking someone's hand. The more you confront the fear and learn nothing happens, the less control your fear has over you. The anxiety surrounding shaking someone's hand will slowly diminish.

GIVE IT A TRY

Sometimes you are not able to face your perceived fears because they are not an object or situation. Suppose you check your stove repeatedly because you are afraid your house is going to burn down. You can't face the fear of your house burning down. Instead you can use imagery. Create detailed images of the disaster you fear will happen. In this example, you would imagine your house burning down and resist the urge to check the stove.

Rank the situations on your list from mild to severe, with those that cause only mild anxiety on the top of your list. Begin your exposure exercises with these and work your way down your list to those that cause greater anxiety. Stay with each situation until you feel comfortable and don't need to perform any rituals to lessen your anxiety.

Begin your exposure gradually. For example, if you are anxious about shaking someone's hand, start by shaking the hands of friends or relatives without washing your hands after. Work your way up to shaking the hand of a stranger. It is important to resist your urge to perform any rituals after exposure. Your rituals reinforce your fears; therefore, you can't move past those fears without ending the ritual.

Each time you shake someone's hand, rate your anxiety level. In the beginning, you might rate it at 100 percent, but as you practice, you find your anxiety levels decrease. Use this technique in conjunction with your behavioral experiments, noting in your log that you did not get sick after shaking someone's hand. This helps you reevaluate your beliefs and challenge their validity.

Tips for Reducing Rituals

There are some thinking styles that contribute to OCD. By working on changing your thinking, you can help to reduce the obsessions and your need for rituals.

Manage stress. Managing OCD is not easy. You might have some days when you face your fears and feel you made progress, and then the next day your fears resurface, causing you to feel hopeless. Stress often causes symptoms of OCD to increase. Create a plan to help you deal with stress. Chapter 15 goes over strategies you can employ in your everyday life to manage your stress. You can also go over the relaxation techniques described in Chapter 7. Using deep breathing during stressful moments helps you calm your anxiety.

Be flexible. When you have obsessions, you usually catastrophize events and situations. You believe disasters will occur if you don't do a certain ritual. When you think of your health, you worry about major illnesses and diseases. When you worry about your children, you think about horrible accidents or illnesses. When you worry about your house, you imagine it burning down. This type of thinking often boils over to other parts of your life. You try hard to keep your children safe, to be the perfect wife, or to never make a mistake at work. Reread Chapter 12 to learn strategies to lower your inner criticism and eliminate your need to have everything in your life turn out perfectly.

Live with uncertainty. Uncertainty is a part of life. If you have OCD, not knowing what to expect or not being able to control your environment is probably difficult. Stopping your rituals doesn't guarantee that nothing bad is going to happen. But there isn't any guarantee that it isn't going to happen even when you do complete your rituals. In Chapter 17, you learn strategies for accepting that life is full of uncertainty and managing the fears that come with the unknown future.

Let go of internal measurement. If you have OCD, you might measure when to stop checking the stove when you feel "comfortable." You might stop washing your hands when it feels "right." These measurements are based on your internal feelings, not on facts or external measures. Those without OCD usually use more external and practical measurements. Try to come up with practical measurements for your obsessions, such as "washing my hands with soap and water for three minutes is enough."

Don't give your thoughts too much weight. If you have OCD, you probably disregard facts, giving your thoughts much more weight. For example, if you have a cold, you ignore the fact that your symptoms indicate you have a cold. Instead you focus on your thoughts, which tell you that this is the beginning of a serious illness. Remind yourself that thoughts are just thoughts. Work to pay attention to the facts of the situation.

Build on Successes

Each time you go through a feared situation without performing your ritual is progress. Give yourself credit for having faced your fear. Some days you might not feel like you are making any progress. Keeping a log of your fears and the exercises you complete helps. You can look through it to see if you are improving; for example, if you began with an anxiety level of 80 percent and you now have an anxiety level of 60 percent, that is progress.

Managing your OCD takes practice. Commit to using the skills in this chapter every day. Over time you will find that your fears and anxieties no longer have the same control over you they did before. Consistency is the key to learning how to manage your OCD.

There may be times when a fear resurfaces; one you thought you had conquered suddenly reappears. Don't worry. Look back over your exercises and practice the strategies again. This time it isn't going to take as long as it did the first time. Try to expose yourself or follow the exercises for changing your thought process as soon as possible. For example, suppose you worked on not washing your hands after touching something and a few weeks later this fear returned. You find yourself washing your hands repeatedly. Immediately refocus your attention to exposure, touching the object and not washing your hands for five minutes. Keep doing it until your anxiety level decreases.

Remember, anxiety usually lessens on its own. Anxiety rises in intensity, peaks, and then decreases. Sometimes you simply need to wait it out and give your anxiety a chance to subside.

The Least You Need to Know

- Obsessions are intrusive and upsetting thoughts. Compulsions are rituals you complete in order to alleviate the anxiety caused by your obsessions.

- Magical thinking is when you believe your rituals are linked to external events in your environment or in the world.

- Lessening your dependence on rituals will cause some discomfort in the short term, but will benefit you in the long term.

- Behavior experiments are used to test the validity and need for your rituals.

Developing a Positive Body Image

You diet, forego the dessert, and spend time looking in the mirror wishing you could change your nose, lower your forehead, or grow more hair. You see all the problems and focus on everything you perceive as wrong. Many people are unhappy with their appearance, but some people believe that their looks define who they are. In this chapter, you will learn what it means to have a poor body image and how problematic thought processes contribute to it. The exercises help you define yourself through your character traits rather than your appearance.

In This Chapter

- Accepting your flaws
- How your thinking influences your body image
- Recognizing that body flaws don't define who you are
- The similarities and differences between poor body image and eating disorders

What Is Body Image?

Body image is how you think and feel about your body. It is the combination of the picture you have in your mind, what you see in the mirror, how you feel about those images, and how you think you compare to others. Everyone has parts of their body they would like to change. You might think your nose is too big or your chin too pointy. You might wish your hips were a little smaller or your thighs thinner. When you focus too much on these perceived faults and use them as a reflection of your self-worth, you probably have a body image problem.

> **IMAGINE THAT**
>
> Adolescents with body image problems are more likely to suffer from depression, anxiety, and suicidal thoughts than those without body image concerns.

Healthy vs. Unhealthy Body Image

When you have a healthy body image, you accept how you look. While you might not believe yourself to be perfect, you accept your positive traits as well as your flaws. While you might work to change those flaws, in general you accept your appearance and don't allow it to color your opinion of yourself. You don't dwell on those who might not see you as attractive. You believe that someone could be or is attracted to you physically. You understand your appearance is only one part of your whole self.

An unhealthy body image places too much emphasis on appearance. You equate a large part of your value as a person to your looks. You are so unhappy with your weight, your size, your shape, or other attributes that it keeps you from enjoying social encounters or accepting compliments. You are embarrassed in public and often spend hours hiding or disguising your body or avoiding going outside at all.

Your Turn: Do You Have a Body Image Problem?

Check off any of the following statements that are relevant to you:

- ❑ I am unhappy with my looks or how a particular body part looks despite reassurance from others.

- ❑ Sometimes I don't go out socially because of my appearance.

- ❑ I spend a considerable amount of time daily thinking about or worrying about my appearance.

- ❑ I spend considerable time trying to find clothing that hides my imperfections.

- ❑ I avoid clothes shopping because I am not happy with how I look.

- ❑ At times I avoid looking at myself in the mirror or over check my appearance in any reflection I pass.

- ❑ I make excuses to avoid situations, such as going to the beach or the pool, where I need to have my body exposed.

- ❑ I believe physical appearance is the most important thing. I believe others judge me solely based on physical appearance.

- ❑ I often compare my looks with others. If I don't feel as attractive as someone else, I get upset.

- ❑ I avoid intimate relationships or sexual situations because I don't feel comfortable with someone seeing or touching my body.

- ❑ I diet constantly to lose weight or look for ways to improve my physical appearance.

- ❑ I feel driven to work out, to lose weight, or improve my body shape. I feel guilty if I skip one exercise routine or miss a day of exercise.

- ❑ I don't believe other people when they say I look nice.

- ❑ If someone doesn't like me, I think it's because I'm ugly.

- ❑ I use or research cosmetic surgery or other dermatological treatments to correct flaws in my appearance.

If you have checked five or more items, you probably have a problem with body image. The exercises in this chapter can help you resolve your issues; however, if your body image problem is severe, you might consider working with a therapist.

> **GIVE IT A TRY**
>
> To combat an unhealthy body image, write a list of 10 things you like about yourself that don't have anything to do with your weight or appearance. Your list could include, "good friend," "hard worker," or "good at decorating." Keep this list in a place where you see it regularly.

Problematic Thinking Processes

In Chapter 2, you learned about problematic thinking processes. Some of those that are common with a poor body image are:

Overgeneralizing: You see flaws in your appearance as proof "I am not worthy; I cannot change" and assume "Others will think I am unattractive because of this flaw." For example, if you gain weight, you assume you will continue to gain weight rather than trying to lose weight. If someone does not find you attractive, you assume no one will ever think you are attractive enough.

Magnification: You obsess and magnify the importance of one part of your body. For example, if you have a pimple, you think it has ruined your appearance and that no one can see past this. You see yourself as this flaw. If you gain weight you see yourself as "fat" rather than think in terms of "I gained a few pounds; I still have a nice figure."

Black-and-white thinking: You compare yourself to everyone and categorize yourself and others as either "attractive" or "not attractive." You don't consider the grey areas in your own attractiveness or your behaviors. For example, you categorize your eating as either "I am on diet" or "I am indulging" rather than focusing on trying your best to eat healthy. You see yourself as either a "slob" or "perfectly put together."

Ignoring the positive: You discount compliments or positive attention you receive based on your appearance. You don't believe it when others say you look nice; you assume they are just being nice or devalue their importance. For example, if someone says, "You look great; you've lost weight!" you think they are pointing out that you have more weight to lose.

Mind reading: You assume that others judge you because of your looks. You assume everyone thinks you are fat, ugly, have a big nose, etc.

Personalization and blame: You avoid taking responsibility for your interactions. For example, you might think, "They didn't like me because I am ugly," rather than, "We didn't have a lot in common" and blame any rejection solely on your looks. You call yourself names like "fat," "ugly," and "disgusting" instead of thinking objectively: "I am 20 pounds heavier than I would like to be."

Fortune-telling: You decide how the future is going to turn out and think things like, "No one will ever want to go out with me because I am ugly or fat," or "I will never stay on a diet." You don't try hard and when you are rejected or go off the diet, you feel validated in your predictions.

> **STOP AND THINK**
>
> "Fat talk," the banter among women about their bodies, such as "My thighs look so big in these jeans," "I feel fat today," or "This ice cream is going straight to my hips," is often considered harmless. But one study found that women who use this type of talk on a regular basis are more unhappy with their bodies than those who don't and may have a higher risk of eating disorders.

Your Turn: Changing the Image

Use the chart to record your negative thoughts about your body in different situations. Then restructure your thoughts about yourself and your body.

Negative Statements	Problematic Thought Processes	New Thoughts
I am fat. She is skinny.	Black-and-white thinking	I weigh about 15 pounds more than she does, this does not mean I am obese or that no one thinks I am attractive.
I had a bite of my husband's burger and fries so I am off my diet. I should have a sundae and start again tomorrow.	Black-and-white thinking	I had a bite of my husband's burger and a few French fries. I should skip dessert to keep within my calorie limit.
I am not tall. Women like tall men.	Magnification	I cannot change my height, but I am a good person and am loyal and loving. I will find the right person.
I am not as pretty as the models. I should just keep to myself.	Overgeneralization	I might not be as tall as I would like but men have paid attention to me before. I should be charming and friendly.
I look horrible.	Personalization/blame	I am not dressed my best today. I can spend a little more time in the morning on my appearance since it is important to me.

How Body Image Effects Your Life

People with body image problems magnify the significance of their flaws and ignore how much their flaws limit, or don't limit, their life. For example, you might have a big nose. You might be self-conscious about your nose. But, you are married and have a good job. Despite the fact that you don't like your nose, it hasn't interfered with your life. Instead of worrying excessively about your body, or a certain part of it, accept it and then look at how much it limits your life. Let's look at some examples.

Scenario 1: You see someone thinner than you walking down the street.

Unhealthy thought: "I am so fat; why can't I lose weight and look like her? I am going to skip dinner tonight."

Acceptance thought: "She is thinner than me but I am attractive enough. I don't need to be a size 6 in order to have a nice figure. I do not need to be that thin to be happy."

Scenario 2: While getting dressed in the morning, you look in the mirror and notice your hair is thinning.

Unhealthy thought: "I am going bald. I cannot be bald! Everyone will notice."

Acceptance thought: "I don't have as much hair as I used to, but plenty of men my age have thinning hair. They are still married and working. Even movie stars have thinning hair."

> ☞ **CBTIDBIT**
>
> Make a goal to look healthy rather than look thin or perfect. Looking healthy means you get enough sleep, eat properly, and take care of your skin. When you look in the mirror, focus on whether you look healthy instead of focusing on your body. You can take steps to be healthy; you can't take steps to change attributes of your body.

Scenario 3: You are putting on makeup in the mirror and notice a pimple.

Unhealthy thought: "I am so ugly. Everyone is going to notice this. No one will want to talk to me."

Acceptance thought: "I may have bad skin, but it does not mean I am not a good person. I can still dress nicely and have a fun time. I'll cover it up with concealer."

Scenario 4: You think your nose is too big.

Unhealthy thought: "My nose is too big. I can't stop thinking about how ugly it is. No one will take me seriously because of my nose."

Acceptance thought: "I wish my nose was smaller, but I have other positive physical traits. I get asked out on plenty of dates and I have been asked at work to give several presentations."

Everyone has flaws, some minor and some major. Everyone also has strengths and positive qualities. When you accept your flaws, you can then move past them. But that doesn't mean you give up on improving yourself. For example, if you are considerably overweight, you can accept where you are right now and take steps to make healthy changes. You can also accept that being overweight doesn't define who you are as a person. Instead, focus on your positive qualities and understand that flaws in your appearance shouldn't limit your life.

Your Turn: The Real Impact

This exercise will help you to accept your flaws and evaluate how much they actually influence your life.

Step 1: Write down what you believe to be the flaw with your appearance.

Step 2: Write down how this flaw limits your life. Make a list of all your concerns.

Step 3: Find evidence to counter how it really limits your life and create a coping statement.

Let's look at an example.

Step 1: I am overweight.

Step 2: Being overweight limits me in these ways:

- No one will think I am attractive.

- People will make fun of me; no one will like me.

- People will stare at me so I need to avoid talking to them.

Step 3: Counter evidence and coping statement

Counter evidence: The last time I went to a social outing and talked to people I did okay. I met some new people and even got a friend of it.

Coping statement: When I put myself out there I can connect with others in a positive way.

Counter evidence: I have friends.

Coping statement: I can connect with others. Not everyone wants to avoid me.

Counter evidence: No one has laughed at me or pointed out my weight since I was a teenager. People usually act like respectful adults.

Coping statement: This social event will be a safe place. The people who invited me want me to be there.

Make a list of 10 people you admire. Your list might include musicians, artists, a person in your community, a teacher at your child's school, or a neighbor who is always willing to help others. Chances are the people on your list have different shapes. Some might wear glasses, some might be bald, others might have big noses. You probably didn't list these people for their appearances; you admire them because of their behaviors and personalities. Remember that just as you don't judge people by their appearance, they don't judge you by yours.

Standing in Your Own Way

Your own behavior can perpetuate your fears and reinforce your belief that you should hide your body, or specific parts of your body, from others. Look through the following behaviors and determine which ones you use. There are suggestions to help you change your behaviors listed.

Avoidance: You might avoid going clothes shopping, to the beach, to the pool, or other places where you expose your body. You might avoid intimate relationships. You might avoid social situations because you are afraid others judge you. You might avoid going out of your house unless absolutely necessary. Avoidance works in the short term. You feel better because you avoided being uncomfortable. In the long term, however, avoidance can cause loneliness and depression. You don't give yourself the chance to learn that others aren't judging you by your appearance. You don't give yourself the opportunity to learn that you can handle the situation and that appearance doesn't matter as much as you think it does.

Use exposure strategies as described in Chapter 17 to expose yourself to your fears. For example, if you are convinced you must only go out in public with a full face of makeup, then put on makeup on each day to see if other people notice.

Intentionally act in ways that disprove your beliefs, such as not wearing a hat to cover your bald spot, going out with flats instead of heels if you are self-conscious about your height, or wearing clothes to show off your figure if you usually wear baggy clothes. Pay attention to whether other people react by pointing, staring, or treating you disrespectfully. If they don't, it reinforces that your appearance doesn't influence how you are treated.

Body Checking: You need to weigh yourself several times a day. You need to look at yourself in the mirror for extended periods to see how you look or check to see if your camouflage worked. You must keep an eye on your body and your weight. You need to know what other people are seeing. When you body check, you usually focus on the worst parts of your appearance. You are preoccupied with not being good enough. You focus on how you feel about your body, not on your appearance.

Stand in front of a full-length mirror. Describe your body as if you were describing it to someone over the phone. Don't add in any judgments; just the facts. Don't skip over parts you don't like. This exercise helps you see your body in a more objective way, without evaluating it. Repeat this exercise every hour on the hour until you no longer feel anxious and actually start to feel annoyed with the exercise.

Or, avoid checking your appearance all together. Initially the anxiety will build but eventually it will subside. Each day the anxiety and urge to check will lessen. Then slowly introduce looking in the mirror or weighing yourself on a scheduled basis. You might weigh yourself once a week or look in the mirror only when you get dressed in the morning.

Misinterpreting external signals: You interpret everyday events or things as evidence that you are ugly or fat. For example, when someone does not ask you out on a second date, you think it's because you are not attractive and personalize the rejections.

Try creating a list of alternative reasons why you were not asked out again. For example, you might write: we did not have a lot to talk about; we seemed more like friends than romantic connection; I may not be her type. Everyone has a type; some people like fuller bodies, some people prefer thinner types; some people like blondes, others brunettes. I cannot be everyone's type.

IMAGINE THAT

According to the National Association of Anorexia Nervosa and Associated Disorders, approximately 90 percent of women are unhappy with their bodies, almost 60 percent of college students feel pressured to be a certain weight, and about 30 percent of women and 20 percent of men would consider cosmetic surgery in the future.

See Yourself as a Whole Person

When you receive a gift, you notice the packaging. It could be small or big. It could be wrapped in colorful paper or in a single color. It might have a bow. The wrapping might look beautiful or look hastily wrapped. But what is important is the gift inside. Your body is the same. Your body is the packaging; it is what contains who you are. When you focus on your body, you tend to lose sight of the important things. You view the package as more important than the gift inside.

Complete a whole person review to remind yourself about all of your traits. Write down as many points as you can in each of the following categories:

- Values—What are the philosophies you try to live by?

- Hobbies and interests

- Talents and skills

- Personality traits

- Spiritual beliefs

- Humor—What makes you laugh?

- Future goals

Write down everything, no matter how small—but don't write down anything that has to do with your appearance. Think about what qualities you see as most important in other people. Is your opinion about other people based on their appearance or is it based on more internal traits?

GIVE IT A TRY

Create a pie chart of your "whole self." Place all the things you think make up your personality, such as being a good friend, being creative, and being a good listener. How much of the pie did you attribute to appearance? Remind yourself each day that appearance is only one part of who you are. Focus on the other areas by spending more time and energy in the next two weeks on these traits. For example, if you put being a good friend at 10 percent, instead of spending 20 minutes in the morning applying your makeup, spend 20 minutes calling or emailing your friends and wishing them a great day.

A Word About Eating Disorders

A poor body image doesn't mean you have an *eating disorder*; however, there are some features common to both—for example, a preoccupation with appearance. If you have an eating disorder, you worry about your weight and body shape and are preoccupied with food. When you have a body image problem, you might worry about these things, but you obsess about your overall appearance or one particular face or body part.

> **DEFINITION**
>
> An **eating disorder** is a mental illness that causes disturbances in eating patterns. It can involve undereating or eating excessively. Obsessions about food take over your life. You are overly concerned about body weight and body shape.

There are three main types of eating disorders:

Anorexia nervosa This disorder is characterized by an unhealthy effort to maintain a weight far below the normal for your age and height. People who suffer from anorexia starve themselves or eat very little in order to prevent weight gain or to continue losing weight. They may also feel driven to exercise excessively.

Bulimia nervosa This disorder is characterized by a cycle of overeating and then purging to alleviate feelings of guilt and shame from the overeating. The purging can be achieved through self-induced vomiting, over-exercise, or the use of laxatives.

Binge-eating disorder This disorder is characterized by a compulsive need to eat large amounts of food in a short period. People who binge eat often feel they have no control over their eating and are commonly overweight.

Eating disorders cause serious health issues. If you or someone you know shows the signs of an eating disorder, you should contact a medical professional. While CBT might be a part of the treatment for eating disorders, it is important to have a medical professional involved.

The Least You Need to Know

- If you have a healthy body image, you understand you have flaws but these do not define who you are. You accept your positive traits as well as your flaws.
- Problematic thinking processes, such as overgeneralization and mind reading, can contribute to a poor body image.
- Perceived flaws in your body don't limit your life; it is the excessive worry about the flaws that creates limitations.
- Having a poor body image is not the same as having an eating disorder, although some of the characteristics are the same.

PART 5

Moving Forward

CBT is not a "quick fix." CBT is a lifelong process; it is a lifestyle change. It takes commitment and practice. You might experience setbacks along the way, times when you find yourself reverting to your old way of thinking and your old habits. This is normal and to be expected. In this section, we give you the tools you need to maintain the goals and pull yourself back from any temporary setbacks. We help you make CBT part of your daily life.

Should you decide that this book isn't enough and want to work with a therapist, we provide information on where to find a therapist and what to look for. We explain the different types of therapy and give you an idea of what to expect during a typical CBT therapy session. You might want to bring this book to your therapy session. You and your therapist can work through the sections that are most relevant to your life. You can work together to choose which of the exercises are most appropriate for your homework.

Knocking Down Obstacles to Progress

Maybe you aren't making the progress you expected. You wanted to feel better, but you feel worse than when you started. Before giving up, try to find the reasons CBT may not be working as well as you imagined. In this chapter, you will learn about some of the common reasons CBT doesn't work and what steps you can take to overcome the obstacles and keep moving forward.

Uncovering More Problems and Feeling Overwhelmed

CBT requires you to pay attention to your negative thoughts, bad feelings, and the behaviors you want to avoid. Sometimes, when you start doing this, you become overwhelmed. It seems as if you "opened a can of worms," and you wonder if it would be better if you weren't aware of all the negative thoughts and feelings running through your mind. Instead of feeling better, you feel worse. You don't like yourself as much. Once you start focusing on your negative thoughts, you realize how often you they pop into your mind. You feel more self-conscious, more hopeless.

You might be waging a war inside your mind. On one side you are making a conscious effort to improve. You notice your thoughts, challenge them, and come up with a more balanced view of the situation. On the other side, you don't believe you will ever change. You berate yourself for even trying. Part of you wants to keep trying and part of you doesn't believe it is going to do any good.

> **STOP AND THINK**
>
> CBT, like any therapy, works better when you make positive and healthy choices in your life. You can increase the benefits of CBT by making conscious decisions to live a healthy life by...
>
> - Exercising, eating right, and getting enough sleep.
> - Connecting with other people on a regular basis.
> - Scheduling time for relaxation and enjoyable activities every day.
>
> Instead of seeing CBT as a "stand-alone" therapy, see it as one of your lifestyle changes.

CBT has been shown in numerous studies to be effective at treating a number of different mental disorders, such as depression and anxiety. It works in reducing stress and improving self-image. However, CBT takes commitment and hard work. It isn't a miracle cure and doesn't work overnight. For a short time, you might feel worse. In the beginning, you might not believe or feel connected to your new thoughts. However, it's important to keep at the assignments and give your brain the opportunity to adjust to the new thoughts and behaviors. The important thing is to keep going, to work through the exercises in this book, and commit to spending time every day looking at your thought processes and finding ways to change perspectives. There is no easy answer to overcoming depression, anxiety, or anger. There is no easy way to improve your self-image or your relationship. It takes dedication and hard work.

Common Reasons CBT Doesn't Work

If you use the information and exercises in this book and find that you don't see or feel any improvements in your life, don't despair. CBT is a new skill you are learning. It is a new way of thinking. Just as with learning any new skill, you are going to make mistakes and have setbacks along the way. The following sections outline some of the common reasons CBT doesn't work as effectively as it could. Look through these to see if any relate to your situation.

You Lack Repetition

It has taken you years of thinking negatively to get where you are today. It doesn't need to take years to undo these thought processes, but it does take a lot of repetition. When you challenge a negative thought, stating or reading your new thought doesn't make you believe it. But if you repeat it again and again, you learn to accept it. Think back to when you learned to ride a two-wheel bicycle. You didn't get on it and start riding. You had to practice. You had to fall, get up, and do it again. Some people learn to ride a bicycle more quickly than others. Others take many attempts to keep the bike upright and ride down the street. CBT is the same. You have to repeat the new thoughts in your mind, many times each day.

> **CBTIDBIT**
>
> As you work through the different techniques in this book, don't forget to practice the skills you already learned. Set aside a few hours each week to review strategies you have already learned. Review the exercises you completed; think about times you used the strategies in real-life situations during the past week. Congratulate yourself on your progress. This helps reinforce your gains.

Imagine you are completing a project at work. Your boss gave you a deadline you think is unreasonable. You tell yourself, "I am never going to get this done on time." Your body sags. You can't muster up the motivation to work on the project. You realize your negative thought is affecting your behavior. You challenge it, remembering other times you have completed projects within short time frames. You rephrase your thought to, "This is going to be difficult but I can get this done." You repeat this thought, emphasizing the "I can get this done." The more you repeat the phrase in your mind, the more you become motivated and the more intensely you work on the project.

When you challenge a thought and create a new thought or attitude that is beneficial in your life, write it down. Post it on your mirror, refrigerator, or the dashboard of your car. Keep a copy with you and read it aloud throughout the day. For CBT to work, you must use repetition.

You Believe Self-Acceptance Means Not Changing

In CBT, you learn to accept who you are. You learn to appreciate all of you and to understand that, as a human being, you might make mistakes. You learn not to define yourself by those mistakes but to accept them and move on. Some people see this as a reason not to change. When challenging thoughts, they move from, "I am a loser," to "I made a mistake; that is okay," but don't continue to move forward to make positive changes in their lives. It is the difference between "I made a mistake. I am human," and "I made a mistake. What can I learn from this experience and how can I improve next time?"

CBT is meant to help you examine your thoughts and make healthier choices in your life. When used in this way, it improves your satisfaction with life. It is not meant to be used as an excuse for remaining stuck in unhealthy thinking patterns.

You Try to Eliminate Emotions

In many of the exercises in this book, you are told to look at the facts of a situation, take your emotion out of the equation, and react according to the facts. This doesn't mean you should try to be emotionless. As explained in Chapter 4, emotions are neither good nor bad; they reflect how you feel and think. It is not your emotion that is positive or negative; it is your reaction to the situation at hand. Suppose you are angry because cars often speed on your street, even when there are children playing. You want the cars to slow down. You could use your anger to take constructive action by attending local government meetings and talking to the police department. Together you work on finding solutions, such as having speed bumps installed on your street.

You can't eliminate your emotions. You need your emotions to help interpret the world around you. Your emotions raise a flag to let you know that something is amiss. CBT doesn't teach you to ignore your emotions, it teaches you to reflect on your emotion and then intellectually choose the best response.

You Assume Learning CBT Is Enough

You have read through the information. It makes sense to you. You can even name a few negative thoughts you have had over the past day. And that, you believe, is that. Now you will start thinking in a more positive way. You will focus on the problem; restructure your thoughts; and improve your anxiety, depression, relationships, or self-image.

Learning CBT, however, is just the first step. Now it is up to you to put into practice the new skills and put the concepts into action. Imagine you are trying to learn how to bowl. You have never done it before. You watch some videos and read a book on how to bowl. You go to the bowling alley and completely bomb. Why? Because learning how to do something is not the same as doing it. It might take you 100 or 1,000 practice games of bowling for you to be satisfied with your score.

IMAGINE THAT

A number of studies have shown that completing homework or practicing skills has a direct correlation to both the effectiveness of CBT and how quickly it works. When deciding how much time should be spent on completing the exercises and practicing strategies in real-life situations, consider that it has been shown the more, the better. Studies show that clients who did the most homework had the best outcomes.

Certainly, it is important to learn and understand the concepts behind CBT. But creating change in your life takes practice. Suppose you often assume you know what another person is thinking. You completed an ABCD chart and now know where the errors in your thinking were. You are now one step closer to completing this process automatically but you aren't there yet. It isn't going to happen automatically unless you go through this process repeatedly.

As you practice each exercise, you will find there is a pattern. First, you stumble through the exercise, thinking about each answer. Then, it begins to get easier and you can quickly write down the process on paper. Soon, you can go through the process in your mind, without writing anything down. Finally, you might find that you move from the first to last steps without thinking about the steps in between. It has become automatic.

There is no right or wrong length of time between beginning an exercise and it becoming automatic. Everyone is different. Keep practicing and putting the concepts into practice every day. It will become automatic.

You Analyze Everything You Think

Sometimes CBT doesn't work because you use it too much. You don't say or react to anything without first analyzing your thoughts. You make everything a rational, emotionless decision. While it is important to be on the lookout for negative thought processes, you don't need to analyze every thought. Imagine you are driving on a road you have never been on before. You have a passing thought of having a car accident. You quickly dismissed the thought and continued on your trip. Although it could be classified as worry about a future event, it doesn't need to be analyzed. It is a passing thought.

> **STOP AND THINK**
>
> When you have a negative thought or emotion, stop and determine if it is one that needs to be challenged. For example, suppose you feel sad because a friend is moving out of the area and you aren't going to spend time together each week. This is a normal feeling of sadness and you don't need to challenge it. On the other hand, if your friend calls and has to cancel lunch this week but still plans to meet you next week and you become angry or depressed, these thoughts can be challenged because your emotion doesn't match the situation. Remember, not all negative emotions are wrong. You choose which thoughts and emotions to challenge.

CBT is about finding the negative thoughts that are interfering with your ability to function or enjoy life. Many of the exercises in the first section of this book work on narrowing down areas you are experiencing problems. Other chapters focus on specific areas, such as relationships, stress, self-esteem, depression, or anxiety. While it can help in all these areas, it is not productive if you use it to catch and analyze every thought.

You Expect an Instant Cure

CBT doesn't work overnight. You can't use one technique or challenge one thought and suddenly think in healthy ways and feel great all of the time. CBT takes work, commitment, repetition, and practice. The average number of CBT sessions with a therapist is 16. When using this book for self-directed CBT you might take a shorter or longer time, depending on your commitment to completing the exercises and practicing each day. Even so, you aren't going to see changes overnight.

Getting in Your Own Way

Years ago there was a very negative stigma attached to seeing a therapist or having emotional problems. People were labeled "crazy" or "loony." Today, more is understood about mental illness and going to a therapist is more accepted. The stigma has decreased but it is still there. You might be ashamed or embarrassed that you "need help." You feel it means you are defective in some way.

Shame, Guilt, and Pride

Hiding your problems usually causes them to grow. You might think reaching out for help is embarrassing, but keeping your problems to yourself creates even more problems. Having someone who understands what you are going through can help immensely. Think about the people in your life. Is there one person you trust? Reach out and let him know what you are going through.

You might also feel guilty. Who are you to need help? You might think there are so many people in this world in much worse shape. You might think your family will find your needs to be a burden—emotionally and financially. Because of these beliefs, you might stop yourself from seeking the help and support you need. Remember, you are important. Your well-being is important. Chances are there are people in your life that want you to be happy and will be more understanding of your situation than you think. Open up and let others know how you are feeling.

Pride also gets in the way. You might think the following:

- I am a strong person; self-help and therapy are for weak people.

- I can work this out on my own; I don't need anyone to help me.

- I don't go to doctors.

Pride sometimes masks the shame you feel. You think only weak people need help, and because you need help, you feel ashamed for being weak. You might think it is therefore better to suffer through than to ask for help. Remember, reaching out for help is a sign of strength, not weakness. Everyone needs help sometime in their life.

The Fear of Being Uncomfortable

Wouldn't it be nice if everything in life was pleasant? If you never needed to feel pain, sadness, or fear? Unfortunately, life isn't like that. Feelings of discomfort are a normal part of life. As much as you try, you can't avoid them. In CBT you face your fears in order to understand that feeling the discomfort is okay. You confront problems and work through the feelings of pain to come up with solutions.

> **GIVE IT A TRY**
>
> When you are worried about feeling fear or discomfort, it can be paralyzing and overwhelming. You move into the "all or nothing" thinking pattern, believing if you can't face the entire exercise, there is no reason to try. Instead of focusing on the complete exercise or skill, break it down into steps. Commit to doing just the first step. Commit to taking one action. Each journey begins with a single step. Once you take that step, the second step is a little easier.

One of the ways you might sabotage your progress is by avoiding any exercises that make you think or feel things that cause discomfort. This type of thinking reinforces your feelings of depression, anxiety, or self-loathing. By avoiding them, you tell yourself there is a good reason to avoid them. You reinforce the idea that these thoughts and feelings are a threat to your well-being and instead of facing them, you run away. In order to work through your feelings and start feeling better, you must go through some discomfort. Accepting and learning to tolerate discomfort helps you better manage difficult situations throughout your life.

The Fear of Failure

Some people don't want to put too much effort into getting better. They worry that if they try, and it doesn't work, it will prove they are hopeless. It is easier to simply not try. You might read the information in this book but neglect to do any of the exercises. Feelings of hopelessness are a sign of depression. If you feel hopeless and don't believe that any help will ever make you feel better, try to reach out to talk to someone. Take a chance; look through the chapter on depression and work through the exercises.

Your Turn: Find Your Motivation

Often, when you sabotage your attempts at CBT, there is an underlying feeling that to go through the process needed to feel better would be worse than feeling bad. For example, suppose you want to overcome social anxiety. You feel lonely and wish you could make some friends. But the prospect of having to talk to others is too overwhelming. You dread the idea of going through exercises that would require you to speak to other people. While you are unhappy in your present life, the process of getting better sounds too difficult.

Make a list of the pros and cons of using the CBT exercises in this book.

For example:

Pros	Cons
CBT is effective.	It takes a lot of time.
I feel better when I change my thoughts to be more positive.	Sometimes it is depressing to think about how negative I am.
I can do this on my own schedule.	I don't always follow through with the exercises.
It is less expensive than going to a therapist.	

Once you complete your pros and cons worksheet, review it to see what stands out as important. Do you notice any patterns? Is one side more filled out than the other? After completing the exercise, are you more apt to stay with the exercises and keep working on changing?

Monitor Your Progress

Recording and monitoring your progress can help you stay motivated. Set up a schedule, such as once a week on Saturday, to review your progress.

Write your problem: Write a short description of your feelings and behaviors that you want to change.

Rate how much this problem interferes with your life. You can use a scale of 1 to 10 or use the words "very much," "somewhat," "a little," or "not at all."

Write down your goal: This is how you want to feel and behave in this situation in the future.

Rate how close you have come to reaching your goal. Again you can use a scale or words.

Fill in ratings every two weeks. When you notice improvements, use this as motivation to continue for another two weeks.

IMAGINE THAT

CBT is sometimes done as a group therapy. You share your experiences with a group of people going through similar struggles. In group therapy, a therapist teaches a specific skill each week and everyone is given a homework assignment. The following week you discuss the outcomes of the assignment together, as a group. This type of therapy is less expensive and can give you a way to further your CBT skills.

Tips for Making CBT Work for You

Are you having a hard time getting started using this book? You are not alone. It is hard to make the decision to change your life, even when it is positive change. The following are some tips to help you:

Just do it. You might be waiting for the right time or for motivation to strike you before beginning the exercises in this book. Instead of waiting, jump in and start. Often, motivation comes after action, not before.

Believe that change is possible. One obstacle to progress is that you believe things will always be the same.

Keep a log. You may tend to have the same inaccurate thoughts in different situations. Keep a log of your thoughts and the evidence against them so you can refer back and remind yourself of the more balanced view you discovered.

Change "always" to "sometimes." Changing the word "always" to "sometimes" gives you a new perspective. For example, you might say, "Bad things always happen to me." Changing it to "Bad things sometimes happen to me" gives you hope that something good might happen.

Keep track of what exercises you find most helpful. These can be used again, in different circumstances.

Break down your goals into smaller pieces. Breaking down your goals makes them more manageable and allows you to focus on each individual step.

CBT techniques are simple. They have often been called common-sense strategies. That doesn't mean they are easy. It takes determination and inner strength to create positive change in your life. You are worth it.

The Least You Need to Know

- When you first start using CBT, you might feel overwhelmed and think it is easier to go back to your old habits. Stick it out and keep trying; as you practice you will begin to notice positive changes in your perspective.

- Not completing exercises and not practicing are some of the common reasons that CBT isn't effective.

- Embarrassment or feelings of shame can stop you from seeking help, but hiding your feelings usually makes things worse.

- Weigh the pros and cons of using CBT in your life to increase your motivation.

CHAPTER 23

Maintaining Gains

Life is filled with ups and downs. After learning CBT strategies, your life isn't going to have only ups. You will still have times you feel down or feel that you are sliding back into old habits. These are called setbacks. In this chapter, you learn techniques to help make sure those setbacks are temporary and are a part of continuing to learn and improve your thinking and behavior.

Move New Beliefs to Your Inner Being

You spent the last several months working diligently on the exercises in this book. You challenged your thinking and changed the way that you think...most of the time. But occasionally you are going to run into old situations that trigger your negative thoughts to come flooding back. Your insecurities flare up. These old situations re-trigger your core belief. For example, suppose you run into an old classmate from high school. During high school, you didn't have many friends and felt you didn't fit in. Seeing your classmate triggers your core belief, "I am not good enough; I am not accepted by others."

In This Chapter

- Watching out for triggers
- The return of negative core beliefs
- Facing negative thoughts promptly
- Developing self-therapy strategies

> **STOP AND THINK**
>
> Core beliefs often hide under other issues. For example, suppose you are overweight. You shy away from making friends or being in an intimate relationship. You blame being overweight for your social problems, thinking, "Other people don't want to be around me because I am overweight." If you dig deeper, below the issue of being overweight, you might find that you think you are "unlikeable" or "not a nice person." You rely on the overweight issue because it is easier than facing the real belief. Ask yourself, "Is this the real issue?"

Core beliefs develop over a long time, often beginning in childhood. They are buried under your problematic thinking patterns and even after you address those, your core beliefs remain intact. When one of these core beliefs is activated, you focus on information that backs up the belief. When you notice negative thoughts cropping back up, don't worry. Setbacks are normal; making changes in your life takes time, patience, and commitment. If you take steps to manage these thoughts right away you have a better chance of this being a short-lived setback.

The first step is to identify situations, events, people, or places that trigger these core beliefs. To do this, start your thought log again, paying close attention to what is happening around you when you notice the negative thoughts taking over. You might write down:

Situation	Negative Thoughts
Saw old classmate	I was such a loser in high school high school.
	People made fun of me all of the time.
	I never had any friends.
	No one liked me.
Co-worker cancelled having lunch together	Here we go again. I am such a loser.
	She probably had a better offer for lunch.
	None of my co-workers like me.

> **CBTIDBIT**
>
> Uncovering your core beliefs sometimes requires you to behave contrary to what makes sense to you. It involves moving out of your comfort zone to test new beliefs. For example, you might think, "I am unlikeable." You can't test whether this is true if you continue shying away from other people and isolating yourself. You need to accept that you have this belief and deal with discomfort to test it. You have to talk to people and make an effort to make friends.

You might notice that when certain situations occur, the same negative thoughts you were sure you had conquered come back. Using the same example, you previously combated thoughts of not having friends, realizing that although you weren't popular in high school, you have friends now and get along with your co-workers. Go back and review the strategies in Chapter 11 to help you reframe your thoughts in a helpful and healthy way. When your co-worker cancels lunch, you might think, "There was probably something she needed to do today. I am sure we will have lunch together tomorrow."

Digging Down to Your Core Belief

Find the underlying core belief the same way you did before. Extend your thoughts to reveal your hidden thoughts. Ask yourself questions, such as:

- What does it mean to me when I feel this way?

- What are the negative consequences of this happening?

- What does that say about me?

As you continue to ask these questions, you should get down to a very basic, core belief about yourself. For example:

When I feel this way, it means:

No one likes me.

What are the negative consequences?

I don't have any close friends.

What does it say about me?

It means something is wrong with me.

What does it mean about my future?

I will always be lonely.

What does it mean about me as a person?

I am unlikeable.

Your core belief is "I am unlikeable."

While you managed to combat a number of negative thoughts using the techniques in this book, you didn't get far enough down to combat your core belief. When this happens the negative thoughts pop back up in stressful situations. It means you still have some work to do, but doesn't mean you are a lost cause.

> **GIVE IT A TRY**
>
> Think about your core belief and come up with a behavior or activity that is completely against this belief. Go ahead and do it. For example, if you think no one wants to talk to you, spend a day making conversation with your co-workers or attend a party and "pretend" you are outgoing. Your subconscious will begin to believe you are good at talking to other people. You will have started the process of breaking down your core belief.

This is where coping thoughts coming in. When you are starting to feel that no one likes you and that you are not likeable, you can resort to your coping statements:

- I am a likeable person.

- No one is liked by everyone.

- I am successful in many areas of my life.

- My happiness does not depend on the acceptance of others.

- I am a great person.

All True or Sometimes True?

Your core belief is usually an overgeneralization; you believe this statement is true all of the time. To combat core beliefs, focus on experiences that prove it is sometimes not true. Using the previous example, you might list the following:

- My co-worker usually wants to join me for lunch.

- I get along with my co-workers.

- No one at work makes fun of me.

- I have a few friends at my church.

Continue to list as many experiences as you can, even if you don't think they are relevant. Come up with a more balanced core belief. You might state:

Not everyone is going to like me, but I am likeable to some people.

If your core belief is not always true, it can't be true "all the time." Write your new belief on an index card and carry it with you. Reread the card when you are in a high-risk or stressful situation. When you find yourself thinking negatively and reinforcing your original core belief, change your thoughts to focus on the experiences that contradict this belief.

Make a list of activities and tasks that reinforce your new belief. Ask yourself, "What would I do if I didn't have this belief?" You might write down the following:

- Attend groups and meetings at church.

- Volunteer for community outreach activities at church.

- Ask someone from church to go out for coffee.

- Smile and say hello to co-workers.

- Ask another co-worker to join me at work.

You might want to write these activities and tasks on the back of your index card where you wrote your new core belief. When you reread your belief, you can turn the card over and reread the tasks to remind yourself of what you need to do.

STOP AND THINK

There are two types of core beliefs: those that remain stable and those that change depending on your mood. For example, when you are experiencing stress or anxiety, you are more apt to believe certain negative core beliefs. The beliefs that change with your mood are sometimes easier to tackle because when you are feeling happy or content, you don't believe or believe it less.

Starting over can be disheartening, but if you find core beliefs returning, it is time to be aggressive at challenging these thoughts. You want your new belief to become part of your thinking. The more persistent you are at combating this thought, the more it becomes integrated into your belief system.

Deal with Problems Immediately

You see negative thoughts resurfacing and want to push them away. You want to avoid it and any situations that bring on these thoughts. But denying the negative thoughts only makes the problem worse. You might…

- Feel like a failure when negative thoughts resurface.

- Believe that setbacks are a catastrophe.

Remember, setbacks are normal. CBT isn't a quick fix, it is a lifestyle change and that means making the techniques part of your everyday life. Think of it as you do an exercise program. While you are focused on the program, you lose weight and stay in shape. As soon as you stop, you start losing your gains. You need to refocus on your program and make permanent changes in your life in order to stay in shape and keep your weight consistent. CBT is like that. When you were focused on keeping thought logs and analyzing and challenging your negative thoughts, it was easier to think in new ways. Once you stop, negative thoughts creep back in. Instead, see CBT as a lifestyle change. Consistently monitoring your thoughts and addressing negative thoughts as soon as they pop up helps you stay on top of your progress and keep moving forward.

Prepare for Triggers

When you completed your thought log, you might have noticed there were certain types of situations that caused you to slide backwards. Some common triggers include the following:

- Physical illness
- Not sleeping
- Relationship problems
- Family illness
- Financial difficulties

When you understand your triggers, you can take steps to prepare. Create a plan of action for when you are in one of your high-risk situations. Chapter 24 covers how to create a crisis intervention plan that can help in these situations. In the meantime, use the following statements to help you prepare for common stress areas in your life. Fill in the blanks to fit your situation.

When I feel _____, I will _____.

If _____, I will _____.

Some examples include the following:

- When I feel angry, I will do deep breathing exercises for 10 minutes.
- When I feel lonely, I will reach out to a friend.
- When I feel sad, I will go to the gym.
- When I have an argument with my partner, I will use the ABCD chart and change to a more positive way of looking at the situation.

Write statements for your common stressors. Keep the statements with you to refer to when faced with a situation or overwhelming emotion.

CBT as Part of a Healthy Lifestyle

Changing your thoughts is only one part of a healthy lifestyle. Adding relaxation, mindfulness, and healthy eating habits increases your overall feelings of well-being and makes you feel more motivated to continue your CBT practice. You are working on getting healthy at the same time as getting rid of the unhealthy habits.

IMAGINE THAT

A positive attitude has been associated with better health, but it can also work the other way. One study showed that living a healthy lifestyle, which includes exercise, good sleep habits, a healthy diet, not smoking, and taking preventative measures to maintain your health resulted in a more optimism, assertiveness, and sociability.

Review what you learned by reading and doing the exercises in this book. Make a list of which techniques work best for you. Spend time each evening to review your day, looking out for unhealthy rigid ways of thinking. Pay attention to when you avoided situations to make you feel better or when you required perfectionism in your thinking or actions. Then, make a plan for each of your unhealthy thinking patterns.

Continue to keep moving forward. When you conquer a negative thought pattern or confront a fear and combat it, start on a new one. As you notice negative thoughts or fears, write them down. Don't spend too much time on trying to correct them if you are still working on other fears or thoughts. Simply note they exist and continue working on your original goal. This list is your "to do" list. Your goal is to continually be moving forward.

Your Turn: Plan Self-Therapy Sessions

It is often helpful to plan a weekly "therapy" session with yourself each week. Block out one hour for you to review your progress and plan for the upcoming week. A typical session might address the following:

- What positive things happened this week?

- What strategies did I use that helped the situation?

- What problems came up through the week?

- How did I resolve these problems?

- Did I overreact?

- What were my common problematic thinking processes?

- Are there other ways I can look at this situation?

- Are there problems I anticipate coming up during the next week?

- What can I do to prepare?

- What skill did I work on this week?

- What skill can I work on during the upcoming week?

As you become more comfortable with your skills and your ability to use them in difficult or stressful situations, increase the time between your sessions.

Your Turn: Create Behavior Markers

In CBT, it's important to monitor yourself and respond immediately to backsliding. One method for doing this is to create *behavior markers*, or benchmarks, which signal you are starting to backslide. When you reach or surpass these particular behaviors, you then need to reactive your CBT methods and put the brake on old habits.

> **DEFINITION**
>
> **Behavior markers** are specific behaviors that signal a return to old habits. For example, if you have depression, behavior markers might include not leaving the house for two days, sleeping during the day, or a loss of appetite. Knowing your behavior markers helps you notice a setback immediately.

Some examples of this include the following:

- Skipping two social events in a row to avoid anxiety

- Consuming dessert two days in a row if you are weight conscious

- Going to the gym five days in a row if you are body conscious

- Sleeping more than 12 hours when you are depressed

- Cursing or yelling if you have a tendency to get angry

Once you see yourself in signaling situations, your job is to return to CBT strategies that worked best for you.

List at least three behavior markers to signal you are starting to backslide. Don't wait until you backslide to create these points. If you do you will end up returning to old bad habits and feel guilty, lose motivation, and start to blame yourself or others.

Tips for Maintaining Your CBT Gains

Keep a lookout for unhealthy thinking patterns that keep cropping up. Develop a plan of action immediately rather than avoiding your thoughts or avoiding certain situations.

Monitor your progress. Compare your previous unhealthy ways of thinking and what you have learned in this book. Noticing the differences helps motivate you to continue.

> **CBTIDBIT**
>
> Always celebrate your accomplishments and successes. Take time each evening to review situations and events where you noticed and challenged negative thoughts. While you need to take responsibility for setbacks, don't get so caught up in your mistakes that you forget to pay attention to the times you used CBT techniques to rethink a situation and react in a more helpful way.

Make a list of the CBT techniques that work best for you. Keep the list handy for you to use when you are in a stressful situation.

Remember that setbacks are normal. Don't catastrophize your setbacks. Accept they will happen and as long as you have a plan to deal with them, you can quickly address a setback.

Look back at your progress. Remember that you have faced this problem before and have learned techniques to solve it. This time it shouldn't be as scary and shouldn't take as long to overcome.

Continue to practice CBT techniques. Without practice you become rusty. Practice and consistency helps keep your skills sharp.

Learn from your setbacks. Take note of what happens when you backslide and come up with prevention strategies for the future.

Put your setback in perspective. How much have you improved? Is the setback a disaster or is it a wrinkle in your progress?

Accept responsibility. Recognize that you are responsible for your setback but don't criticize yourself. Remind yourself that unhealthy thinking may return from time to time. Remember you are overcoming years of thinking in a certain way. It will take time to change these thinking patterns. Think of CBT as a lifetime change, not a one-time therapy.

The Least You Need to Know

- When you run into old situations, old beliefs might return.
- When you find your negative thoughts returning, dig deeper to find the core belief that keeps resurfacing.
- Create a list of possible triggers and write a plan for each one to help you combat negative thoughts before they take control.
- Plan time each week for a "self-therapy" session where you review any problems that came up through the week and how you handled each one.

Preparing to Backslide

You might believe that by the time you finish this book, all your problems should be gone. But this book is just the beginning of your journey to a healthier and happier life. CBT is a lifestyle change, not a "one-and-done" approach to difficulties. Hopefully, you have learned strategies that help you notice negative thoughts and behaviors and address them quickly. The good news is that you can't ever go back to square one. You now know what to do when feeling depressed, anxious, or negative about life. You can't unlearn what you have learned. By the time you complete this chapter you will understand what a relapse is, notice the signs you are backsliding, and know what steps to take to bring yourself back to helpful and healthy ways of thinking and acting.

In This Chapter

- Understanding lapses
- How to identify high-risk situations
- Stopping a lapse in its tracks
- How to make CBT part of your life

The Difference Between a Lapse and a Relapse

A *lapse* is a brief return to your old way of thinking and behaving. It is a setback. A *relapse* is a return to your old way of thinking and behaving. Both lapses and relapses can be triggered by illness, stress, or fatigue.

> **DEFINITION**
>
> A **lapse** is a temporary setback. It is a brief return to your old way of thinking and behaving. A **relapse** is when you return to these old ways for a longer period of time.

Suppose you have a fear of dogs. Using the exercises in this book, you learned to use relaxation techniques and coping statements to help you approach a dog. If you have a lapse, you might see a dog and become scared. You might cross the street to avoid the dog. When you get home, you sit down and try to determine what caused you to avoid the dog. You realize that you haven't been sleeping well over the past few nights because of worry over financial problems. You are tired and stressed about upcoming bills. You think this stress led you to simply cross the street rather than taking some deep breaths and walking toward the dog. You decide you will practice your exposure exercise with dogs so the fear doesn't build up again.

> **STOP AND THINK**
>
> For CBT to be effective in the long term, you must not only reduce your negative thinking but must also learn what to do if the feelings return. In the example of overcoming a fear of dogs, using exposure techniques helps to reduce your anxiety when you see a dog. However, there might be a time when your fear comes back. Incorporating relaxation strategies and other ways to calm yourself ensures that you can deal with the situation, should it arise.

Suppose you cross the street to avoid the dog but when you get home, you think, "I knew this would be a waste of time. I am never going to get over my fear of dogs. I am right back to where I started." You see your setback as a failure. You are ready to give up. This attitude leads to a relapse, where you go back to your original thinking and behavior.

To avoid relapses, accept that lapses might occur. You might suddenly ignore everything you learned and go back to your original thinking and behavior. It is your attitude toward the lapse that makes the difference. Pay attention to your reaction to your lapses.

Your Turn: Preparing for a Setback

When you face a difficult situation and fall back into negative thinking patterns, you might think:

This isn't doing any good.

I am hopeless.

I will never feel better.

CBT doesn't work.

The first step to making sure a lapse doesn't turn into a relapse is to accept this is normal. You are going to have ups, downs, and in-betweens. There are going to be times you feel terrible and times you feel great. There are going to be times you are moving along smoothly.

There are a few ways you can prepare yourself for a setback.

Track your progress. Use a graph to track how you feel. In the beginning, or during stressful times, you might want to track your progress on a daily basis; other times you might find once a week helpful. Give each day or week a rating, such as 0 to 10 or use words such as "very good," "so-so," "not so good," and "very bad." Use words you typically use to describe how you are feeling. Create a graph to help you visually see your patterns. You will probably notice that even though there were times you felt "very bad" there were also times you felt "very good." This helps you see that the bad times are temporary.

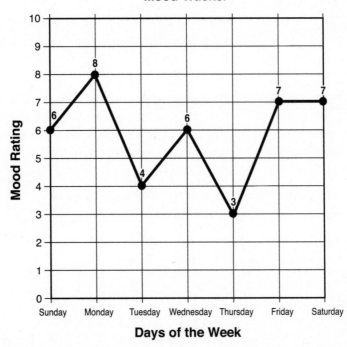

Mood Tracker

Use coping cards. Pay attention to common patterns of thinking and create coping cards with new, positive ways of thinking. Keep these coping cards with you and in places you see them on a daily basis such as your mirror, your refrigerator, and your desk.

Write down what works. Create a list of important points you learned while using this book and the skills you found most helpful. Place reminders in areas you see each day to review this information on a daily basis.

> **CBTIDBIT**
>
> Remember, even if you temporarily lapse or relapse, you can't go back to square one. The techniques and strategies you learned are still there. Although you might need to review and practice, you aren't starting from the beginning.

Accepting that you might have the old urge or old feeling does not mean you have to go full throttle with it. This is where blac-and-white thinking about yourself and your weaknesses can ruin your progress. Suppose you feel angry during an interaction with your partner. You start to yell. Somewhere in the argument you notice you are yelling. You have a choice; you can see it as black and white where you think "It's too late, I already started yelling. I am not apologizing. Why should I always have to apologize?" Or, you can put your reactions into the grey zone. "Okay, I overreacted. I am entitled to not agree with her behavior, but I can stop yelling and apologize for getting worked up." Black-and-white thinking can derail any progress unless you think about your reactions in the grey zone, accept that you won't always be perfect, and take responsibility for your bad behavior.

Knowing you can have a setback and planning for it helps it remain a lapse rather than a relapse. Remember you have a choice. You can continue to think negative thoughts or you can choose to answer and challenge those thoughts.

Warning Signs and Triggers

In Chapter 23, you started a thought log specifically for lapses. You kept track of what was happening around you when you had a lapse. This information can be used to help you determine your own high-risk situations. Some common reasons for a lapse are listed here:

- Negative emotional states such as depression, anxiety, or anger

- Interpersonal problems

- Social pressure

- Feeling overwhelmed with too many tasks

- Trying to please too many people

Lapses also happen when the situation takes you by surprise. Imagine you are walking down the street and a dog runs out of a house and comes running up to you. You don't have time to prepare or to think about how to react. Your fear kicks in.

GIVE IT A TRY

List some of your high-risk situations. Think about whether you should eliminate, reduce the intensity of, or cope with the situation. Then write one or two steps to help manage the problem.

Do this for each trigger or high-risk situation to help you focus on the solution rather than the problem. Be careful you aren't eliminating situations by avoiding them, such as removing social pressures by avoiding parties.

Usually, you have some warning signs before a lapse. These warning signs can be in your thoughts, emotions, behaviors, or physical sensations. Many of these will depend on your individual circumstances. Common warning signs include the following:

Thoughts

- Anxious thoughts

- Negative thoughts about yourself or others

- Blaming others

- Becoming defensive about your behaviors

- Paranoid thoughts

- Ruminations

Emotions

- Feelings of sadness

- Irritability or frustration

- Feelings of being a failure

- Pessimism

- Nervousness

Behaviors

- Rituals

- Over- or under-eating

- Avoiding situations

- Arguing with others and using emotional language

- Not being able to let something unimportant go

Physical Sensations

- Stomachache

- Restlessness

- Fatigue

Based on previous exercises, write down your triggers and warning signs. Continue to monitor your thinking patterns. Take 10 minutes at the end of the day to review your thinking. Choose two or three situations that happened during the day. Write down your thinking process during the situation. Was it healthy thinking or did it fit into one of the problematic thinking processes outlined in Chapter 2? Each time you handle a high-risk situation without falling into a relapse, you gain confidence and add to your belief that you can do this.

Your Turn: Create a Relapse Prevention Plan

Relapse prevention is a process, not a single step. The following is an example but your plan should be specific to your situation.

Step 1: Review the exercises you completed. If you kept a notebook filled with your exercises and go through it, paying careful attention to those geared toward the issues you are experiencing. Highlight those you found most helpful. You can also go through this book and highlight exercises you want to return to and review.

 STOP AND THINK

Preventing lapses involves three steps: learning coping skills; accepting change as a process that includes setbacks; and making lifestyle changes, such as healthy eating, exercising, meditating, and practicing mindfulness. In addition, an effective relapse prevention plan includes continued practice sessions.

Step 2: Review the skills you need to combat your current problem. For example, if you find yourself falling back into depression, your list might include the following:

- Schedule activities, including pleasant activities

- Work on problem solving

- Work on self-esteem

- Be assertive

- Use relaxation techniques

- Practice mindfulness

Decide which of these strategies is most helpful to you. Practice these skills. Overlearning skills helps you to use them in many different situations. Focus on one skill at a time. Once you feel comfortable, you can move on to reviewing and practicing another skill.

IMAGINE THAT

In one study, people with depression who used cognitive behavioral therapy combined with mindfulness decreased rates of relapse by one-half.

Step 3: Complete thought logs. Reexamine your thoughts and work on coming up with more balanced ways of looking at situations.

Step 4: Write coping statements. Some examples include:

- Today was a bad day.

- This will pass.

- I can use the skills I learned.

- This is a temporary setback.

- I know what to do to stop from getting worse.

- Everyone has bad days.

- Using the skills will help tomorrow be a better day.

Write five coping statements you can carry with you and read at least five times each day.

Step 5: List supports you can use to help you from backsliding. This could include the following:

- Calling to talk to a friend or relative

- Finding a support group

- Talking to a medical professional

Tips for Integrating CBT into Daily Life

Sometimes you work on your skills and the exercises in this book and are able to change your thought processes at that time. But when you face a problem, everything you learned goes flying out the window. You don't remember what to do or how to do it; you revert to negative thinking. CBT takes patience and persistence.

GIVE IT A TRY

Keep a blank thought record with you. Use it when you feel overwhelmed or when you anticipate feeling overwhelmed. Remember, you might have started using this book to overcome anger, but thought records can be used for any emotion. Learning to generalize your skills, across different emotions, helps you to employ them in many different situations.

It takes practice and consistency for a new way of thinking to take hold. There are some ways to make this process easier:

Treat any attempt at using a skill or trying a new technique as an experiment. When you do an experiment you can't fail; you just learn from the results. By changing your perception in this way, you remove the word "fail."

Use real-life examples in your practice. Throughout this book there are many different examples. Read through the exercises and then complete them again, based on situations from your life. Think about upcoming problems and use the exercises to gain perspective on the best way to handle the situation. Remember, though, you don't want to focus on solving problems that haven't yet occurred too often as this starts a cycle of worry. Focus on a few "what if" scenarios that have a high probability of occurring to help you look at the situation differently.

Keep a list of what you can do daily, weekly, and monthly to increase your feelings of well-being. Besides CBT techniques, what else can you do to improve your physical and emotional health? You want to focus on your life holistically rather than seeing it in small segments. This helps improve your outlook and keeps your motivation to continue high.

Create a list of questions to ask yourself when you have unhelpful or negative thoughts, feelings, or behaviors. Some examples include the following:

- It this thought consistent with reality?

- Is this thought rigid or flexible?

- Is this thought unhelpful?

- Can I change the wording of this thought to create a more helpful way of looking at the situation?

- Is this thought catastrophizing or overgeneralizing a situation?

Use your common problematic thinking processes to create questions. Write the questions down on an index card and keep them with you. When you are feeling overwhelmed, look at the questions; your answers give you information on how to change the thought.

Think of CBT like learning to play a musical instrument. You practice, alone, until you feel comfortable with your song. Then you go out and play it for other people. CBT is like that. Use the exercises to practice at home, by yourself. As you gain confidence in your abilities to use the techniques, slowly begin integrating them in your everyday life.

The Least You Need to Know

- A lapse is a temporary setback; a relapse is a return to old habits and behaviors.
- Your long-term CBT plan should include steps for identifying and preventing lapses.
- Common reasons for lapses include relationship problems, health issues, social pressures, and the need to please others.
- Relapse prevention is a process, not a single activity. It includes reviewing CBT skills, reexamining your thoughts, and writing coping statements.

CHAPTER 25

Working with a Therapist

Deciding to see a therapist is often a difficult decision. You have to get past the stigma of seeing a "shrink" and you have to come to terms with the fact that you can't handle life by yourself. You aren't alone. Millions of people choose to see a therapist, for many different reasons. Sometimes they have hit a difficult spot in life, other times they have serious mental illness. Luckily, the stigma surrounding therapy is disappearing and reaching out for help is much easier today. In this chapter, we discuss reasons you might want to see a therapist and walk you through the process of looking for the right one. Finally, we go through what you should expect during each session.

In This Chapter

- Deciding if you need therapy
- Talk therapy or CBT?
- Finding the right therapist for you
- What to expect from a CBT therapy session

Should You Seek Professional Help?

The information and exercises in this book can help many people. Working through the sections that most closely relate to the issues in your life might be enough for you to get back on the right track in your life. For others, seeing a therapist makes more sense. You might find doing the exercises in the book make sense but you need extra help—someone to walk through the exercises with you to offer insight and support along the way. You might decide you need a partner in your quest to feel better. Or you might feel your problems are too big to handle alone.

IMAGINE THAT

Therapy was once considered something only "crazy" people needed, but today, more than one-fourth of all adults in the United States have sought help from a therapist. Of those, 80 percent have found it effective, 85 percent were satisfied with their treatment, and over half were very or extremely satisfied. Women choose to see a therapist two times more often than men do.

Some of the reasons you might decide to see a therapist:

- Your current problem is too severe for you to work through on your own. Your symptoms have lasted two months or longer and are interfering with your relationships, job, hygiene, or ability to get chores done. You might have times when you feel better but your symptoms keep returning.

- You have tried self-help programs, such as this book, and have seen some improvement but aren't satisfied with your progress.

- Your problems are interfering with cognitive tasks, such as concentration and memory.

- You are using the exercises but find it hard to apply the concepts to real-life situations. You agree with the principles of CBT and complete the exercises, but you can't make the leap from doing the exercises at home and using them in your daily life.

- You have made progress by using this book but have hit a wall and can't get past where you are now. You want to continue to feel better and don't know how to do that.

- You need someone to keep you on track. You find that you lose motivation while doing the exercises, and working with a therapist can help you stay on course and hold you accountable.

- You find that you are having a hard time uncovering core belief and resolving deeper emotions.

Many CBT therapists use a book like this as a resource and workbook for the sessions. If you have already started using the exercises and want further clarification and assistance, bring this book with you and ask your therapist to use this as a guideline for your therapy.

Conventional Therapy vs. CBT

Although there are many different types of therapy available, the two most popular are psychodynamic, or talk therapy, and CBT. This book and the exercises go along with the CBT model of therapy. When choosing a therapist, it is important to distinguish between the two types of therapy and decide which is best for you. The following gives the general characteristics of each type.

Psychodynamic Therapy

Psychodynamic therapy has been around for a long time and is often effective. This form of therapy, also called talk therapy, is the type of therapy usually portrayed in TV shows and movies. With this approach, the patient describes his or her problems while the therapist listens and asks questions. Your therapist looks for patterns and significant events in your past that contribute to your current difficulties, often delving into childhood experiences to find reasons for your thoughts, feelings, and behaviors.

> **DEFINITION**
>
> **Psychodynamic therapy** is based on the premise that you are a dynamic being and that your formation began in early childhood and has progressed throughout your life. It seeks to find the roots, or causes, for your current problems, often going back to childhood experiences. Mental illness is seen as an unsuccessful progression or a result of unresolved childhood conflicts. By talking about and exploring these unresolved issues, you can accept and resolve them, thereby resolving the difficulties you have in adulthood.

Some of the characteristics of psychodynamic therapy include the following:

- Sessions are unstructured.

- The patient sets the agenda for the session by talking about what is on his or her mind.

- There are no homework assignments.

- Therapy focuses on personal history as well as the present.

- Your relationship with your therapist is considered central to therapy.

- Treatment usually lasts six months or longer.

- You sometimes meet more than one time a week.

Critics of psychodynamic therapy consider it to be time-consuming and expensive. They object to an undefined length of treatment, with some people continuing therapy for years. This type of therapy does have benefits. It provides you with a safe environment where you can talk about your feelings and behaviors without the fear of judgment. It gives you a supportive person to work with when sorting out problems in your life. Many people feel this type of therapy very helpful.

Cognitive Behavioral Therapy

As you have learned throughout this book, CBT focuses on specific problems and the present time. The theory behind CBT is that irrational and faulty perceptions fuel your emotional difficulties. While you might discuss your past, the main goal is to discover problems and make corrections in your thinking processes. Some of the characteristics of CBT include the following:

- Treatment duration is between 12 weeks and 6 months, with the average course of treatment being 16 weeks.

- Sessions are structured or semi-structured with deviation when needed.

- You receive homework assignments to work on skills in between sessions.

- You and the therapist collaborate to set an agenda for each session. In the beginning of therapy, the therapist takes more of an active role; in later sessions, you mostly set the agenda.

- In the beginning, sessions focus on the present. You explore past experiences to determine your patterns of thinking and behaviors that link to core beliefs.

- Your relationship with your therapist is considered important but not central to therapy. The relationship is considered collaborative and active. You are a client, not a patient.

- Treatment relies on goal-oriented and problem-solving approaches.

- You practice new behaviors and work on challenging old thinking patterns.

Many studies have shown that CBT is as effective, if not more so, than medication in treating depression and anxiety disorders. It is a practical approach and provides you with skills for dealing with difficult situations. The goal of CBT is for you to learn skills and techniques and carry them throughout your life, becoming your own therapist once sessions have ended.

STOP AND THINK

Critics of CBT state that this type of therapy focuses on logical thinking and tries to eliminate emotions. They also believe that it ignores or minimizes the history behind issues. They think that changing thoughts may temporarily help the the problems but doesn't resolve them. Both psychodynamic therapy and CBT have positives and negatives. Which therapy form is best for you is a personal decision.

Finding a Therapist

In order for any type of therapy to be effective, you need to trust and feel safe with your therapist. You need to be comfortable so you can talk about your problems, experiences, and feelings. You also need to consider practical matters, such as whether the office location is easily accessible, costs, and scheduling availability. Finding the right therapist often takes time. There are a number of online directories to help in your search for a therapist. Some of these are listed in Appendix B. You can also ask for referrals from your doctor, support groups, or local hospital.

Questions to Ask Before Meeting a Therapist

Your search for the right therapist begins either online or on the phone. Once you have found several therapists in your area, call or email the office and ask for a short telephone consultation. It is reasonable for you to spend 10 minutes on the phone, without charge, to find out more about the therapist. Many therapists these days offer websites that provide the answers to some of the basic questions you should address before you get started. If they don't provide this information on their website, you should ask them directly during the phone consult.

👉 **CBTIDBIT**

> Some people have a preference to working with either a male or female therapist. While there is no "right" or "wrong," it is important that you are comfortable. If you prefer to work with one gender over the other, take that into consideration when choosing your therapist.

Here is a list of the basic information you are likely to find on a website or need to ask prior to arranging an appointment:

- How much do you charge per session?

- Do you accept insurance?

- How long is a typical session?

- Will I have the same time slot each week or does that vary?

- Do you charge a cancellation fee? If so, how much notice do I need to give if unable to come to not be charged this fee?

- What are your qualifications?

- What training have you received in CBT? How often do you participate in continuing education on CBT practices?

- What organizations are you accredited with? What certifications do you hold?

- How much experience do you have using CBT? How much experience do you have treating my problem (depression, anxiety, etc.)?

- Where is your office?

- Is there safe and adequate parking? Is it accessible by public transportation? (Ask based on your individual needs.)

- How soon can I get an appointment?

Some questions you may not find on the website that are important to know are:

- What problems or disorders do you specialize in or have experience treating?

- How much experience and success have you had in the past working with this type of problem?

- Briefly describe how you might approach my problem.

Many therapists participate in online forums or publish blogs. Read some of these before you make an appointment to get a sense of the therapist's style.

If you locate several therapists in your area, contact at least three to compare answers. Be sure to measure how comfortable you feel on the phone talking to the therapist. Narrow your choice based on your needs.

First Session Discussions

You called several therapists, narrowed down your choice and have made an appointment. During your first session, you should discuss the therapist's perspectives and the structure of the sessions. Some topics to cover include…

- What you can expect from your therapist.

- What the therapist expects from you.

- Your reason for coming to therapy at this time.

- Your personal goals.

- The therapist's general recommendations for someone with your problem.

- The average length of treatment for your problem.

- Recommended books and reading materials.

- General explanation of CBT.

- Goals for treatment.

STOP AND THINK

If you are working with other medical professionals, such as a psychiatrist, you might want to discuss whether the therapist is willing to coordinate care and forward reports to your doctor.

Remember, developing a relationship with a therapist takes time. You might not feel an instant rapport or connection; however, if you feel uncomfortable or don't believe this is the right therapist, you can go back to your search and start again.

Characteristics of a Good CBT Therapist

CBT is a highly structured treatment program. There are therapists who might say they use CBT but don't really understand how to implement it.

A good CBT therapist…

Spends time helping you understand CBT. The therapist should explain what CBT is, what the techniques are, and how they are used in enough detail that you can use the strategies on your own after you leave the session. She focuses on the CBT model of identifying thoughts, feelings, and behaviors and defines your problem based on terms of CBT. She is willing to discuss your fears and concerns about therapy.

Is realistic on how CBT can help you. If the therapist doesn't believe CBT is the right treatment or can't help you, he or she should refer you to other medical professionals or make suggestions for other types of therapy.

Collaborates on a treatment strategy with you. Because the therapist is an expert in CBT theories and techniques, the therapist should take the lead in creating a treatment plan with a structured and focused agenda for each session, but you should be an active participant in determining the course of treatment.

Sets clear, measureable goals. Goals should contain language that allows you to say, "I have met this goal," or "We still need to work on this goal." Goals should not be vague. Goals should be set within the first three sessions.

Works to help you understand the relationship between your thoughts, emotions, and behaviors. During therapy sessions, the therapist should ask questions about your thoughts and help you go through the process of evaluating your thoughts. She works with you to challenge thoughts, gives you specific steps to do this on your own, and provides you with thought logs and other handouts to assist you.

Focuses on the present day. Your therapist should delve into your childhood and past experiences only when it pertains to your present style of thinking and behaving.

Monitors your progress throughout the course of your treatment. The therapist tracks and monitors your symptoms. Each session you should answer questions, in writing or orally, on your symptoms over the past week. If you have questions at any time during your treatment, the therapist should answer your questions or refer you to where you can find the answers.

Teaches. Your therapist should teach new skills as well as spend time practicing those you have learned during previous sessions. Your therapist should give you homework assignments at the end of every session to allow you to practice skills outside of therapy. Homework is required in CBT.

CBT is not a quick-fix therapy. It involves learning new ways of looking at situations and changing old thinking patterns. It provides you with skills you can use the rest of your life to overcome all different problems. From the first session on, your therapist should focus on teaching you how to become your own therapist.

Be Prepared to Participate

CBT therapists often provide insight into your problems. They give you their ideas of what might be causing your problem and steps for you to take to overcome it. But that doesn't mean you simply sit there and let the therapist do all the work. CBT is an interactive therapy. In order for it to work, you have to be an active participant. Homework is the key to successful CBT. Those who complete homework assignments have a much better chance of changing their thoughts, behaviors, and feelings.

You will be given a homework assignment each week. This homework has two purposes. The first is to give you a chance to practice the skill your therapist went over during your session. The second is to give you a specific skill to use throughout the coming week. Some of this homework is written, such as completing thought logs and ABCD charts to evaluate your thoughts. At other times, the homework is behavioral, such as talking to three people at a party or being assertive with your boss. In addition to giving you instructions on how to do your homework, your therapist will explain the rationale behind the assignment.

There might be times you don't think you are ready to do the assignment your therapist gives you. It is important to discuss your concerns before the session is over. If you don't think you are ready, let your therapist know. Keep in mind that part of CBT is meant to make you feel some discomfort; this helps reinforce the idea that facing your fears is not going to hurt you. But if you have strong objections to the homework, it is best to discuss them rather than to ignore the assignment.

A Typical Therapy Session

Because CBT sessions are structured, they generally follow a specific pattern. While there might be times when your therapist thinks it is important to deviate from the usual structure or times when you are experiencing a difficult problem and your session is used to discuss possible solutions, in general, your sessions will follow a structured format.

In the beginning of your session, you will be asked to complete a standardized questionnaire or your therapist might elect to ask questions orally. These questions are meant to assess your mood and give an objective view of your symptoms. This information is used to monitor your progress. As the sessions continue, your symptoms should lessen.

Once this is complete, the other parts of the session include:

Review of your week: Your therapist will ask about how you felt during the past week, as compared to other weeks. The therapist will focus on thoughts and feelings. This is another way to check your overall mood. The therapist can adjust the focus of the session based on your mood.

Review of previous session: You and your therapist will discuss the important points from the last session and how that information helped you throughout the week. If you had discussed a specific problem in the previous session, your therapist will ask about the resolution.

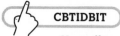 **CBTIDBIT**

You will set initial goals within the first couple of sessions of CBT. However, as therapy continues, those goals might change. Each therapy session, you will review problems and concerns you have. Based on this information, you or the therapist might suggest changes to the original goals.

Review of homework: You will review the previous homework and discuss any concerns or problems you had in completing the assignment.

Discussion of problems that happened during the week: Your therapist will ask if there were any important problems you need help to solve. This information helps determine the content of the session.

Discussion of the agenda: Based on the problems or needs that have arisen, you and your therapist will prioritize areas to be discussed.

Problem solving: At this point in the session, you and your therapist discuss the current problem and work on thought analysis and problem solving.

New skills: If your therapist hasn't introduced any new skills during the problem-solving part of the session, he or she will add a new CBT technique for you to use during the upcoming week or provide an old technique and help you apply it to your present problem.

Practice/exposure: You and the therapist might practice a new skill together; for example, you may role-play or do an imagery exposure in session.

Homework: Your therapist gives you a new assignment for the coming week based on what you have worked on during this session.

> **STOP AND THINK**
>
> CBR sessions attempt not only to teach you new skills, but to help you process information so you can let go of negative emotions and see things in a new light.

During the session, either you or the therapist will write down session notes and summaries of important points. Part of your homework will be to review this information. At the end of the session, your therapist will ask for feedback. You should feel free to share anything that bothered you during the session, ask questions about anything you didn't understand, and list things you would like to see in future sessions. This information helps the therapist customize the sessions to address your specific needs.

The Least You Need to Know

- A therapist can be helpful if you aren't satisfied with your progress, need help to stay motivated, or find it difficult to apply the concepts of this book to your daily life.
- Psychodynamic therapy and CBT have different approaches; psychodynamic works to find the root causes of your current problems while CBT works to change your current thinking processes.
- Before choosing a therapist, do research by looking at his or her website, reading blogs, and asking questions.
- CBT therapy sessions are structured; they usually begin with assessing your mood, then you review your week, evaluate the success of previously learned skills, and move on to learning new skills.

Glossary

ABC model   The theory that core beliefs trigger thoughts, which in turn trigger your feelings and behaviors. In the ABC model, *A* stands for "activating event," *B* stands for "beliefs about the event," and *C* stands for "consequences"—what you feel, think, and do because of your thoughts.

activating event   A stimulus that triggers an automatic thought or belief.

addiction   The physical or psychological dependence on a substance or activity.

affirmation   A positive statement you purposely tell yourself to develop a more positive perception of yourself, to change negative behaviors, or accomplish goals.

anger   A normal human emotion that occurs when you feel stress or when someone infringes on your rights, threatens you, disappoints you, or takes advantage of you. Anger can be healthy or unhealthy.

anorexia nervosa   An eating disorder characterized by an unhealthy effort to maintain a weight far below the normal range for age and height.

anxiety   A perception that you do not have the resources or ability to handle the current situation.

anxiety disorders   A term used to describe a number of different types of disorders characterized by an exaggeration of the fear response.

assertiveness   Expressing your needs, wants, beliefs, and opinions in a direct way that is respectful to you and others.

automatic thoughts   Thoughts that pop into your mind without your consent and are present with or without your awareness.

assumption   Accepting your own ideas are true without proof.

behavioral experiment   Concrete actions that seek to prove your new way of thinking and disprove your old way of thinking. There are three types of behavioral experiments: formal, informal, and observation.

behavior rehearsal   Role-playing skills learned in cognitive behavioral therapy.

binge-eating disorder   An eating disorder characterized by a compulsive need to eat large amounts of food in a short period of time.

black-and-white thinking   A problematic thinking process where you categorize outcomes of events and assume things will either turn out good or bad with no in between.

body image   A term used to describe the way you percieve your body.

bulimia nervosa   An eating disorder characterized by a cycle of overeating and then purging (through self-induced vomiting or by using laxatives) to alleviate feelings of guilt and shame from overeating.

catastrophizing   A problematic thinking process where you magnify every problem and assume every situation is going to end in disaster.

compulsions   A term used to describe behaviors and rituals you feel you must complete to relieve anxiety brought on by obsessions.

cognitive behavioral therapy   A therapy approach based on changing thinking processes in order to change feelings and behavior.

cognitive distortions or **cognitive errors**   See *problematic thinking process*

cognitive restructuring   Process of replacing unhelpful thoughts with helpful thoughts.

cognitive triad   Theory that depressive disorders are characterized by negative views of yourself, your life experiences (the world around you), and your future.

consequences   The events that occur as a result of a behavior.

coping statement   A statement that counters your struggles and gets you to focus on where you have control, who you are committed to, or how you are feeling.

core beliefs   The beliefs you hold strongly that indicate how you see yourself and others and how you view the world.

cost-benefit analysis   A tool for weighing the pros and cons of making a change.

criticism   Pointing out a mistake, fault, or an area to be improved.

depression   A medical condition characterized by a profound feeling of sadness.

dialectical behavior therapy   A type of cognitive behavior therapy that helps patients observe and label emotional reactions.

distortion of reality   The inaccurate thinking processes that cause you to react irrationally or emotionally.

distress   The feeling of being completely overwhelmed because you perceive a situation as too much to handle.

eating disorders   A group of conditions characterized by an abnormal emphasis on body weight.

emotional reasoning   A problematic thinking process where you base conclusions about yourself, others, and the world around you on your feelings.

exposure therapy   The process of gradually exposing yourself to a feared object or situation; it is often used when treating anxiety disorders.

fight-or-flight response   A physiological reaction to stress that results in an increase in heart rate, blood pressure, and glucose levels. Adrenalin levels go up, preparing you to either fight the threat or flee the situation.

flooding   An intense and constant exposure to an object or situation until fear and anxiety lessen.

fortune-telling   Problematic thinking process where you make predictions about the future, often with negative outcomes, and behave based on a reality that hasn't yet happened and may never happen.

generalized anxiety disorder   An anxiety disorder characterized by excessive worry and anxiety without a specific cause.

goals   The endpoint you are trying to achieve. Goals should be specific, measurable, and achievable.

graded exposure   The gradual exposure to your fears starting with imagery exposure, moving to virtual exposure, and then in-person exposure until you can tolerate the experience.

homework   Written or behavioral work to be completed between therapy sessions to reinforce new skills.

hypotheses   A guess based on limited information to be used as a starting point for further investigation. In CBT hypotheses often refers to testing a thought or feeling for accuracy.

ignoring the positive   A problematic thinking process where you only look at the negative aspects of a situation and discredit any positive information.

image rescripting   A way of changing a painful memory by providing a positive and empowering ending.

internal dialogue   See *self-talk*

irrational belief   Unreasonable beliefs about yourself that lead to problematic thinking processes.

***in vivo* desensitization**   The gradual exposure to a feared object or situation in real life.

keynote behavior   A defining behavior that changes your entire perception and experience in one main action.

labeling   A problematic thinking process where you label your behavior or other's behavior in a negative way.

lapse   The brief return to your old way of thinking and behaving.

magical thinking   When you believe that if you do something, or don't do something, it has an effect on your environment or the world.

mantra   A sound, word, or phrase used to create a mental vibration used in meditation.

meditation   The act of consciously clearing your mind from the barrage of constant thoughts.

meridian points   The energy points in the body that are commonly used in acupuncture and acupressure treatments.

metacognition   A term meaning being aware of your thoughts.

mindfulness   The act of directing your attention, thoughts, emotions, and sensations to the present moment.

mind reading   A problematic thinking process of guessing what other people are thinking and assuming it is true.

MUSTerbation   A term that refers to emotional and cognitive demands placed on yourself, others, or a group of people, uses the terms "must," "should," "need," and "have to."

nonverbal communication   The process of communicating with someone through nonverbal means, such as facial expressions, touch, tone of voice, body movements, and eye contact.

obsessions   Intrusive and upsetting thoughts, images, or impulses that occur repeatedly in your mind.

obsessive-compulsive disorder (OCD)   An anxiety disorder characterized by obsessions and compulsions.

overgeneralization   A problematic thinking process that assumes what happened once will always happen and what didn't happen never will.

panic disorder   An anxiety disorder characterized by unexpected and repeated episodes of intense fear accompanied by physical sensations including rapid heartbeat, sweating, and shaking.

passive   Accepting another person's terms without stating your own needs or wants.

passive-aggressive   Agreeing with someone while feeling resentful.

perfectionism   A term describing self-imposed, extremely high standards and constantly working to attain these standards, even when it interferes with your ability to do the task or other areas of your life.

personalization and blame   A problematic thinking process where you take responsibility for events out of your control and blame others for events in their control.

phobias   An anxiety disorder characterized by an intense and irrational fear of an object, situation, or place.

post-traumatic stress disorder (PTSD)   An anxiety disorder characterized by intense feelings of emotional stress and fear as a result of a previous trauma.

problematic thinking pattern   A distorted or irrational way of thinking.

progressive muscle relations   A relaxation exercise where you tense and relax your muscles, group by group.

psychotherapy or **psychodynamic therapy**   A type of therapy focused on discovering the underlying causes and previous experiences for thoughts and feelings.

rational emotive imagery   The process of using imagery to practice new emotional and physical habits.

reality testing   Testing your thoughts using a mini-experiment by looking for facts to challenge negative beliefs and predictions by taking actions that prove your original ideas wrong.

relapse   A term used to denote a return to your old way of thinking and behaving.

relapse prevention plan   A plan to recognize high-risk situations and effectively deal with them in order to prevent returning to old habits.

rituals   The behaviors or thoughts used to help alleviate anxiety caused by obsessions.

rumination   The mental act of reviewing and analyzing thoughts and situations, including why you feel the way you do.

self-acceptance   Recognizing your weaknesses, faults, and limitations and accepting that these do not define who you are or your self-worth. It is liking who you are, faults and all.

self-efficacy   The belief that you have the ability to handle a situation.

self-esteem   Your opinion of your overall value and self-worth.

self-talk   A running commentary in your mind, also known as internal dialogue, that reflects and interprets the world around you. It can be positive or negative.

should and must   A problematic thinking process where you have strong beliefs about how other people should act and become angry when they don't act in that way.

social anxiety disorder   An anxiety disorder characterized by an excessive and unreasonable fear of social situations.

spontaneous imagery   The automatic thoughts that appear as images in your mind.

stress   The emotional or mental strain when you are faced with demanding circumstances.

substance abuse   A milder form of addiction, a psychological dependency rather than a physical dependency.

systematic desensitization   A gradual exposure to a feared object or situation.

talk therapy   See *psychodynamic therapy*

thought log   A written record of your thoughts and feelings.

trigger   A stimulus that causes a thought or behavior.

virtual exposure   Exposure therapy using computer generated images and videos.

visualization   The act of using your imagination to create mental pictures and images.

Resources

National Organizations

The following professional organizations have directories of CBT therapists:

Academy of Cognitive Therapy
260 South Broad St.
18th Floor
Philadelphia, PA 19102

Association for Behavioral and Cognitive Therapies
305 7th Ave.
16th Floor
New York, NY 10001
212-647-1890
abct.org

International Association for Cognitive Psychotherapy
the-iacp.com

National Association of Cognitive-Behavioral Therapists
203 Three Springs Dr., Suite 4
P.O. Box 2195
Weirton, WV 26062
800-853-1135
nacbt.org

Resources for Specific Issues

Anorexia Nervosa and Related Eating Disorders, Inc.
P.O. Box 5102
Eugene, OR 97405
541-344-1144
anred.com

Anxiety and Depression Association of America
8701 George Avenue
Suite 412
Silver Spring, MD 20910
240-485-1001
adaa.org

Depression and Bipolar Support Alliance
730 N. Franklin St.
Suite 501
Chicago, IL 60654
800-826-3632
dbsalliance.org

International OCD Foundation, Inc.
P.O. Box 961029
18 Tremont St.
Suite 903
Boston, MA 02108
617-973-5801
ocfoundation.org

National Alliance on Mental Illness
3803 N. Fairfax Dr.
Suite 100
Arlington, VA 22203
703-524-7600
nami.org

National Anxiety Foundation
3135 Custer Dr.
Lexington, KY 40517
606-272-7166
lexington-on-line.com/naf.html

National Council on Alcoholism and Drug Dependence, Inc.
217 Broadway
Suite 712
New York, NY 10007
ncadd.org

National Eating Disorder Association
165 West 46th St.
Suite 402
New York, NY 10036
212-575-6200
nationaleatingdisorders.org

National Foundation for Depressive Illness, Inc.
P.O. Box 2257
New York, NY 10116
800-248-4344

National Institute of Mental Illness
1201 Prince St.
Alexandria, VA 22314
703-684-7722
nimh.nih.gov

Online Self-Help Programs and Websites

Centre for Clinical Interventions: Self Help Course for Depression
cci.health.wa.gov.au/resources/infopax.cfm?Info_ID=37

Centre for Clinical Interventions: Self Help Course for Panic Attacks
cci.health.wa.gov.au/resources/infopax.cfm?Info_ID=44

Dr. Jayme Albin
CBT-NewYork.com
AsktheCognitiveBehaviorTherapist.com

Judith Beck
beckinstitute.org

Get Self Help
getselfhelp.co.uk/cbtstep1.htm

MoodGYM
moodgym.anu.edu.au

Serenity Programme
serene.me.uk/

Spirit Voyage
spiritvoyage.com

This Way Up Self Help
thiswayup.org.au/self-help/

Apps for Apple Products

Affirmations

CBTReferee

Depression CBT Self-Help Guide

Depressioncheck

eCBT Mood

Fig

Gratitude Journal

Health Through Breath

iCBT

iStress

Mood & Anxiety Diary

MoodKit

Mood Panda

Mood Sentry

Moody Me – Mood Diary and Tracker

MyThoughts+

Panic Aid

SAM – Self-Help App for Anxiety

Stress Doctor

SuperBetter

Thought Box

Thought Diary

Apps for Android

CBTReferee

Cognitive Diary CBT Self-Help

Cognitive Styles CBT Test

Depression

Depression CBT Self-Help Guide

Depression Inventory

Fig

The Habit Factor

Happy Habits

Mood Journal Plus

Mood Panda

Mood Sentry

Positive Thinking

Secret of Happiness

SAM – Self-Help for Anxiety

Self-Esteem Blackboard

Worry Box – Anxiety Self-Help

Further Reading

Anderson, Stephan. *Cognitive Behavior Therapy: A step-by-step guide to understanding and implementing CBT into your life.* Amazon Digital Services, April 9.

Burns, David D., MD. *Feeling Good: The New Mood Therapy.* New York: Harper Publishers, 2000.

Carnegie, Dale. *How to Win Friends and Influence People.* New York: Pocket Books, 1998.

Clark, David A. and Aaron T. Beck, MD. *The Anxiety and Worry Workbook: The Cognitive Behavioral Solution.* New York: Guilford Press, 2011.

Harper, Robert A. *A Guide to Rational Living.* Scottsdale: Wilshire Book Press, 1975.

Knaus, William J., *The Cognitive Behavioral Workbook for Anxiety.* Oakland: New Harbinger Publications, 2008.

Knaus, William J., and Albert Ellis. *The Cognitive Behavioral Workbook for Depression*. Oakland: New Harbinger Publications, 2012.

Pucci, Aldo R., *The Client's Guide to Cognitive-Behavioral Therapy: How to Live a Healthy, Happy Life... No Matter What!* iUniverse, Inc., 2006.

Riggenbach, Jeff. *The CBT Toolbox: A Workbook for Clients and Clinicians*. Premier Publishing & Media, 2012.

Forms

Success with CBT is directly linked with your willingness to complete exercises, or homework, to practice and reinforce skills. Studies have shown that those who go through CBT but don't complete homework take longer to recover. They have a more difficult time putting strategies into practice in their daily lives. While you may feel like you are back in school or think that they are a waste of your time, these exercises help you get the most from CBT.

In this section, we provide many of the forms you need to complete the exercises. When there is a form, it is noted in the exercise. Some of the forms, such as the ABC chart, are used in more than one assignment or are used repeatedly. In those instances, it is noted at the top of the form. You might want to make copies of these forms. Some people might prefer to use a notebook for their exercises. If you do, use the forms in this section as a guideline on how to set up your notebook.

The forms in this section follow one of the "Your Turn" exercises. There are additional exercises, suggestions, and activities in the book that do not require specific forms. These are useful to complete but do not have an associated form in this appendix.

Whether you choose to use the forms in this section or use a notebook, remember to keep your completed exercises to refer to later. This arms you with the information you need should you have a setback.

ABC Chart

This form is an integral part of the CBT process. You will use this chart in many exercises throughout this book. For some exercises, you will only complete some of the columns; for others you will use all six columns. Each exercise lists how to label each column.

F	
E	
D	
C	
B	
A	

Questions to Ask Yourself   **Use with:** Chapter 3

When first starting CBT and learning how to challenge negative emotions, you might find your-self using this form repeatedly. If so, use this form as an example and keep a separate notebook for your responses.

Write down five questions you can ask yourself to challenge your thoughts:

1.

2.

3.

4.

5.

Examples:

- What emotion am I feeling?
- Where do I feel the emotion in my body?
- What was I thinking when this feeling started?
- What am I afraid might happen?
- Can I imagine myself coping with that outcome?
- What self-talk I can use to manage the outcome?

Turning Assumptions Around   **Use with:** Chapter 3

Assumptions are usually quick thoughts and judgments you make without knowing all of the facts. This worksheet follows the four steps for turning your assumptions around. It helps you base your reaction on facts. In the early stages of CBT, you might use this form for practice several times. Use a notebook to record your answers.

Follow the five steps for turning assumptions around. Think about each question and write your answer.

1. What are the facts of the situation?

2. What problematic thinking processes am I using?

3. How can I get more information?

4. Do I have any additional information?

5. Based on the information I have, what is the best response?

Using Emotions to Discover Underlying Attitudes   **Use with:** Chapter 4

By recording and rating your emotional response to events in your life, you can discover your underlying attitudes. Complete the following chart over several days, listing three to four events each day. Rate your emotion with numbers (0 to 10, 10 being the most intense) or words ("little," "somewhat," "very," or "completely").

Event	Emotion	Rating

Ladder Rungs   **Use with:** Chapters 5, 12, and 17

Create a series of steps you need to take to reach your goal. Write each step down, starting with the easiest step at the bottom of the ladder. Each time you set a goal, use this form or write your steps down in a separate notebook.

Most Difficult

Easiest

Cost-Benefit Analysis   **Use with:** Chapters 5, 19, and 22

A cost-benefit analysis is used to weigh the pros and cons of a certain situation. Once you learn this technique, you might find it helpful in many areas of your life and to help in decision making.

Pros (Benefits) of Continuing Behavior	Cons (Disadvantages) of a Behavior
Pros (Benefits) of Discontinuing Behavior	**Cons (Disadvantages) of Discontinuing Behavior**

Creating a Wish List   Use with: Chapter 7

Relaxation is an important part of CBT. When you are troubled about something or have depression or anxiety, it is sometimes hard to get motivated. Having a list of enjoyable activities helps.

Enjoyable Activities (List as many as possible.)	Last Time I Participated in Activity	Most Interesting (Put a star next to two activities.)

Activity Journal   **Use with:** Chapter 7

Exercise improves your physical and emotional health. Write down all of the activities in which you participated.

Date	Activity	Length of Time

Goals for Next Week:

Recording Your Inner Dialogue   Use with: Chapter 9

Your inner dialogue can be positive, negative, or neutral. This narration influences how you see and perceive yourself, others, and the world around you. Complete the following chart over the next one to two days.

Time	Events/Thoughts	Positive, Negative, or Neutral	Emotional Rating 0–100

Which Category?   **Use with:** Chapter 9

Complete this chart when going through a difficult situation. List your thoughts and then decide which category they fall into: the worrier, self-critique, the victim/blamer, or the perfectionist. Determine the thought style (positive, negative, or neutral). For negative thoughts, write a neutral or positive counter thought.

Thoughts/Inner Dialogue	Category	Thought Style	Counter Thought

Testing Your Predictions   **Use with:** Chapter 10

Creating behavior experiments is an important tool in CBT. It encourages you to look at a situation and gather evidence to prove or dispute your beliefs.

Describe the situation:

What negative outcome do I expect?

What assumptions am I making?

What thoughts or facts dispute this thinking?

Which type of reality testing would work best: formal survey, informal survey, or observation?

Results:

New belief:

Self-Assessment   **Use with:** Chapter 11

How do you view yourself? Do you use negative or positive words to describe yourself? In this exercise you explore your feelings about yourself and, when negative, come up with a more balanced and positive statement.

Category	Words or statements I use to describe myself	Problematic thinking processes used for negative self-evaluation	Balanced or positive view	Words or statements I use to describe myself using a balanced and positive view				
Physical appearance								
Inter-personal skills								
Work or School								
Problem solving								
Creativity								
Sexuality								
Personal productiv-ity								
How others see me								

Sharing Preferences   **Use with:** Chapter 13

In your relationship, you have certain expectations; sometimes these expectations become demands and you become angry or irritated if your partner doesn't act the way you think he or she should. Your expectations become "should" or "must" statements.

"Should" and "Must" Statements	Preferences

Problem Solving   **Use with:** Chapter 15

Writing down problems helps you sort out the facts and come up with ideas and solutions.

Problem:

Possible Solutions:

Cross out the unreasonable solution. Circle two or three of the most reasonable solutions. Write down the pros and cons of each.

Solution 1	
Pros	**Cons**

Solution 2	
Pros	**Cons**

Create a Stress Worksheet   Use with: Chapter 15

This exercise helps when you are feeling overwhelmed. By writing down what is going on, how you feel, and evidence to support or disprove your thoughts, you can find the best way to react.

Situation:

Immediate reaction:

Emotion:

Evidence to support any distressing thoughts:

Evidence to disprove my distressing thoughts:

New emotion:

Reduce Your Ruminations   **Use with:** Chapter 16

Ruminations are continuous thought-loops, usually about negative feelings and concerns. They are all-consuming and you feel you can't stop worrying. This exercise helps identify your ruminations and create coping statements. Categorize each problem or worry as relating to yourself, the world, or the future.

Problem or Worry	Category	Coping Statement

Manage Big Problems
Use with: Chapter 17

Feeling overwhelmed often begins when you don't feel you have the resources or ability to handle the situation at hand. Breaking down the problem, identifying problematic thought processes, and restructuring your thoughts can give you a new way of looking at the problem.

My perception of the problem:

My ability to cope with the situation:

My problematic thought processes:

More balanced view:

More balanced attitude:

Create an Anger Log   **Use with:** Chapter 18

Lessening the intensity and frequency of angry outbursts begins with paying attention to your thoughts. By doing so, you begin to identify stressors and situations that trigger your anger.

My Pain or Stressor	What Happened	What I Thought

Criticism, Complaint, or Request?
Use with: Chapter 18

When someone makes a comment about your actions or behaviors, do you automatically feel your anger rising? This exercise helps you sort out whether someone is making a criticism, a complaint, or a request.

Automatic Thoughts	Request and Information Perspective

Identity Blame Statements   **Use with:** Chapter 19

It is easy to blame someone else to avoid taking personal responsibility for your own actions. Pay attention to your thoughts and write down every time you blame someone else, no matter what the reason. Then, write down the same statement, without blame.

Blame	Restructured Statement

The Real Impact   **Use with:** Chapter 21

When you have body image problems, perceived flaws are magnified. You believe your life is limited because of the flaw. In this exercise you look for evidence to support your beliefs.

Step 1: Perceived flaw

Step 2: How this flaw limits my life

Step 3: Evidence to counter my beliefs

Plan Self-Therapy Sessions   Use with: Chapter 23

To help prevent a lapse or relapse, it is helpful to schedule a weekly self-therapy session. Use this worksheet to plan your sessions.

Positive events and situations	
My strategies that helped the situation	
How I resolved the problems	
My problematic thinking process	
Alternative views and perspectives	
Anticipated problems	
Preparation	
Skill I worked on	
Skill for upcoming week	

Preparing for a Setback   **Use with:** Chapter 24

It's normal to have ups and downs. It's normal to have setbacks. During therapy sessions, a therapist monitors your progress by tracking your moods. This helps you see that, while there may be days you are frustrated and feeling down about your progress, on other days when you feel good. Use the graph to monitor your moods.

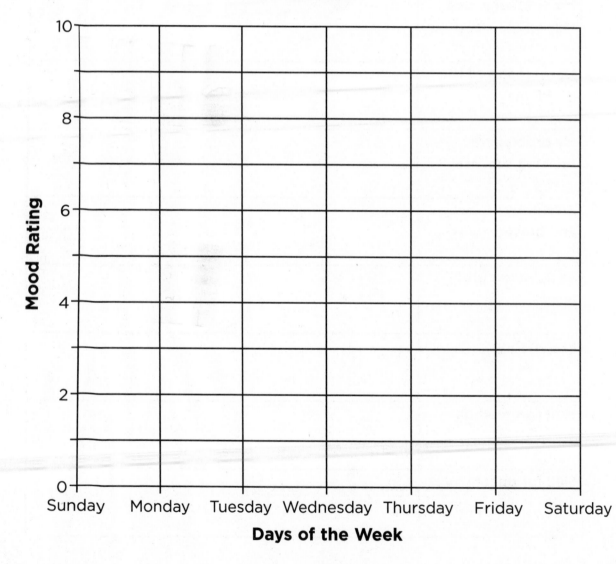

Mood Tracker

References

Allen, David. *Getting Things Done: The Art of Stress-Free Productivity*. New York: Penguin Books, 2002.

Anderson, Stephan. *Cognitive Behavior Therapy: A step-by-step guide to understanding and implementing CBT into your life*. Amazon Digital Services, 2014.

Antony, Martin M. and Peter J. Norton. *The Anti-Anxiety Workbook*. New York: Guilford Press, 2009.

Association for Behavioral and Cognitive Therapies. "What is Cognitive Behavior Therapy (CBT)?" Accessed May 2014. http://www.abct.org/Public/?m=mPublic&fa=WhatIsCBT public.

Baer, Ruth, ed. *Mindfulness Based Treatment Approaches*. Salt Lake City: Academic Press, 2006.

Beck, Aaron T., John A. Rush, Brian F. Shaw, and Gary Emery. *Cognitive Therapy for Depression*. New York: Guilford Press, 1979.

Beck, Judith S. *Cognitive Behavior Therapy: Basics and Beyond*. New York: Guilford Press, 2011.

Becker, R. G. *Cognitive Behavioral Therapy for Social Phobia*. New York: Guilford Press, 2002.

Berna, Chantal. "How a Better Understanding of Spontaneous Mental Imagery Linked to Pain Could Enhance Imagery-Based Therapy in Chronic Pain." *Journal of Experimental Psychopathology* 3 (2012): 258-273.

Borkovec, T.D. and Newman, M.G. "Cognitive-Behavioral Treatment of Generalized Anxiety Disorder." *The Clinical Psychologist* 48 (1995): 5-7.

Brabeck, V. B. *Healthy Expressions of Anger*. Austin: The Clearinghouse for Structured/Thematic Groups & Innovative Programs, 2002.

Braswell, P. C. *Cognitive Behavioral Therapy for Impulsive Children*. New York: Guilford Press, 1993.

Brewin, C. R. *Cognitive Foundations of Clinical Psychology*. Hillside: Lawrence Erlbaum Associates, 2013.

Burns, D. *Positive Psychology*. New York: Plume Publishing, 1999.

Burns, David. *When Panic Attacks*. New York: Morgan Road Books, 2006.

————. *Feeling Good: The New Mood Therapy*. New York: Harper, 2008.

Butler, Andrew C. et al. "The Empirical Status of Cognitive-Behavioral Therapy: A Review of Meta-Analysis." *Clinical Psychology Review* 26 (2005): 17-31.

Centers for Disease Control and Prevention. "How Much Physical Activity Do Adults Need?" Last modified December 1, 2011. http://www.cdc.gov/physicalactivity/everyone/guidelines/adults.html.

Chambers, Richard et al. "The Impact of Intensive Mindfulness Training on Attention Control, Cognitive Style and Affect." *Cognitive Therapy and Research* 32(2008): 303-322.

Connellan, Thomas. *Bringing Out the Best in Others*. Austin: Bard Press, 2003.

Consortium of Social Science Associations. "NIH Conference Highlights Importance of Social and Behavioral Influences on Health." Accessed May 2014. http://www.cossa.org/NIH/nihsocioculturalconference.html.

Cornell, L. S. *Cognitive Behavioral Therapy: A guide to understanding the pros and cons of CBT*. Amazon Digital Services, 2014.

Craske, M. G. *Cognitive-Behavioral Therapy: Theories of Psychotherapy*. Washington, D.C.: American Psychological Association, 2010.

Diagnostic and Statistical Manual of Mental Disorders, Fourth Edition. Washington, D.C.: American Psychiatric Association, 1994.

Dobson, Keith. *Handbook of Cognitive-Behavioral Therapies*. New York: Guilford Press, 2009.

Dryden, Windy. *Be Your Own CBT Therapist*. London: Hodder Education, 2011.

Fairburn, C., ed., and G.T. Wilson, ed. *Binge Eating Nature Assessment and Treatment*. New York: Guilford Press, 1993.

Farhi, D. *Breathing Book*. New York: Owl Books, 1996.

Foa, E. B. "Cognitive Behavioral Therapy of Obsessive-Compulsive Disorder." *Dialogues in Clinical Neuroscience* 12 (2010): 199-207.

Forsyth, John and George H. Eifert. *The Mindfulness & Acceptance Workbook for Anxiety.* Oakland: New Harbinger Publications, Inc., 2007.

Freedman, R. B. "What is CBT?" National Alliance on Mental Illness. Accessed July 2012. http://www.nami.org/Content/NavigationMenu/Inform_Yourself/About_Mental_Illness/About_Treatments_and_Supports/Cognitive_Behavioral_Therapy1.htm

Hebert, S. "The Importance of Proper Breathing in Managing Chronic Pain." Michigan State University Extension. December 4, 2012. Accessed May 2013. http://msue.anr.msu.edu/news/the_importance_of_proper_breathing_in_managing_chronic_pain.

Holmes, Emily A. "Imagery Rescripting in Cognitive Behaviour Therapy: Images, Treatment Techniques and Outcomes." *Journal of Behavior Therapy and Experimental Psychiatry* 38 (2007): 297-305.

Kadden, R. M. *Cognitive-Behavior Therapy for Substance Dependence: Coping Skills Training.* Farmington, CT: University of Connecticut School of Medicine, 2002.

Khalsa, Singh Khala. *Kundalini Yoga, Sadhana Guidelines.* Kundalini Research Institute, 1999.

Leahy, Robert L. *Cognitive Therapy Techniques: A Practitioner's Guide.* New York: Guilford Press, 2003.

Linley, P. Alex, ed., and Stephen Joseph, ed. *Positive Psychology in Practice.* Hoboken: John Wiley and Sons, 2004.

Marlatt, G. A. "Relapse Prevention Therapy: A Cognitive-Behavioral Approach." *The National Psychologist,* September 1, 2000.

Masley, Jerry. "The Role of Exercise, Nutrition, and Sleep in the Battle Against Depression." Family Health Psychiatric & Counseling Center, PC. Accessed May 2013. http://www.fhpcc.com/PDFs/RolesAgainstDepression.pdf.

McHugh, R. Kathryn et al. "Cognitive-Behavioral Therapy for Substance Use Disorders." *Psychiatric Clinics of North America* 33 (2011): 511-525.

Mohan, Amit. "Effect of Meditation on Stress-Induced Changes in Cognitive Functions." *The Journal of Alternative and Complementary Medicine* 17 (2011): 207-212.

Molnar, Danielle. *A Mediated Model of Perfectionism, Affect and Physical Health.* St. Catharines, Ontario: Brock University, 2006

Morone, N.E. et al. "Mindfulness meditation for the treatment of chronic low back pain in older adults: A randomized controlled pilot study." *Pain* 134 (2008): 310-319. 15.

The National Association of Cognitive-Behavioral Therapists. "Cognitive-Behavioral Therapy." Accessed May 2014. http://www.nacbt.org/whatiscbt.htm.

Newman, C. F. "Understanding Client Resistance: Methods to Enhancing Motivation to Change." *Cognitive and Behavioral Practice* 1 (1994): 47-69.

Nordqvist, J. "Lifelong Exercise Significantly Improves Cognitive Functioning In Later Life." *Medical News Today*, March 13, 2013. Accessed May 2014. http://www.medicalnewstoday.com/articles/257562.php.

Pantalon, M. *Instant Influence: How to Get Anyone to Do Anything—Fast*. New York: Little, Brown and Company, 2011.

Schneider, R. H. et al. "Stress Reduction in the Secondary Prevention of Cardiovascular Disease." *Circulation: Cardiovascular Quality and Outcomes* (2012):750-758.

Smucker, Mervin R. et al. "Imagery Rescripting: A New Treatment for Survivors of Childhood Sexual Abuse Suffering from Post Traumatic Stress Disorder." *Journal of Cognitive Psychotherapy* 9 (1995): 3-15.

Stone, D., B. Patton, and Sheila Heen. *Difficult Conversations: How to Discuss What Matters Most*. New York: Penguin Books, 2010.

Teten, J. A. *A Therapist's Guide to Brief Cognitive Behavioral Therapy*. Houston: Department of Veterans Affairs South Central MRECC, 2008.

Tuckington, D. K. "The ABCs of Cognitive-Behavioral Therapy." *Psychiatric Times*, June 20, 2006. Accessed May 2014. http://www.psychiatrictimes.com/schizophrenia/abcs-cognitive-behavioral-therapy-schizophrenia.

Tuschen-Caffier et al. "Body Image Interventions in Cognitive-Behavioural Therapy of Binge-Eating Disorder: A Component Analysis." *Behavior Research and Therapy* (2001): 1325-1339.

Veale, D. "Cognitive-Behavioural Therapy for Body Dysmorphic Disorder." *Advances in Psychiatric Treatment* 7(2001): 125-132.

Walden S., Digiusseppe and R.L. Wessler. *A Practitioner's Guide to Rational Emotive Therapy*. New York: Oxford University, 1980.

Wilson, D. V. *Overcoming Obsessive Compulsive Disorder*. New York: Basic Books, 2008.

Index

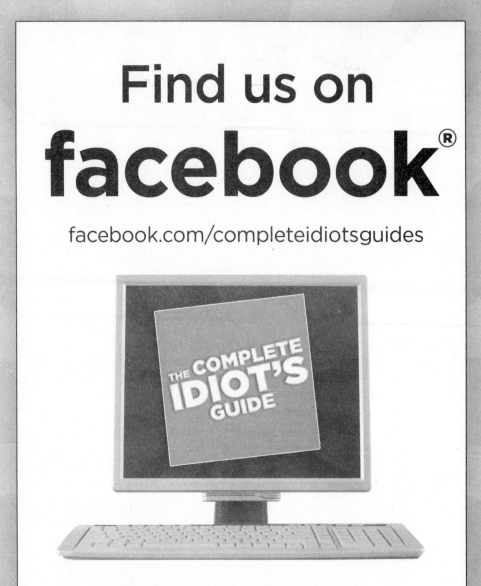